Rev. James Fraser, 1634–1709

Rev. James Fraser, 1634–1709

A New Perspective on the Scottish Highlands before Culloden

David Worthington

EDINBURGH
University Press

Edinburgh University Press is one of the leading university presses in the UK. We publish academic books and journals in our selected subject areas across the humanities and social sciences, combining cutting-edge scholarship with high editorial and production values to produce academic works of lasting importance. For more information visit our website: edinburghuniversitypress.com

Edinburgh University Press Ltd
The Tun – Holyrood Road
12 (2f) Jackson's Entry
Edinburgh EH8 8PJ

Typeset in 10.5/13pt Sabon by
Manila Typesetting Company,
and printed and bound in Great Britain

A CIP record for this book is available from the British Library

ISBN 978 1 3995 0127 9 (hardback)
ISBN 978 1 3995 0129 3 (webready PDF)
ISBN 978 1 3995 0130 9 (epub)

Contents

Illustrations

Acknowledgements

This book has been over a decade in the making. The genesis of it came between 2008 and 2010, when my first boss at the Centre for History, University of the Highlands and Islands, Professor James Hunter, and also my then colleague, Dr Karen Cullen, encouraged my idea to research Fraser. Since 2011, I have had to learn to balance the research and writing required for it with the demands on my time that come with being Head of that Centre. This post has given great joy and satisfaction to me over the last eleven years but has not left a significant amount of time or headspace for monograph preparation. The growing team at the Centre for History have been a source of immense pride, and supportive and tolerant of my focus, at times, on the 'Fraser book' rather than my managerial responsibilities, and I am hugely thankful to them for that. In addition, I was awarded two mini-sabbaticals by the university during the period, one of which was focused on research that went into this project, and I am grateful for that too. Another debt of thanks goes to the many attendees at lectures, talks and seminars (too many to mention) that I have given over the years on the James Fraser theme. The staff at the Highland Archive Centre, the University of Aberdeen's Special Collections and the National Library of Scotland were unfailingly helpful and patient, support that continued through the challenges of the COVID pandemic when my visits to use their materials became more constrained. Thank you to the University of Aberdeen and the NLS for permission to reproduce images from documents in their collection. Meanwhile, Crane Begg of the UHI Archaeology Institute assisted generously with the map of Fraser's travel route. I should not omit to mention that Professor James Hunter and Professor Elizabeth Ewan gave generously of their time to read sections, or all, of the text, and made typically incisive comments about it. In different ways, two Inverness-based writers, Jim Miller and Jennifer Morag Henderson, have offered sage advice and support. I also have a huge debt to repay to other friends and family, especially my parents, who have both, remarkably, tolerated, and even sometimes responded positively to, my rants and ramblings about Fraser over these years. I dedicate this book to you, Mum and Dad, with my love.

Introducing the 'Curious Cleric': James Fraser and the Early Modern Scottish Highlands

B Y SEVENTEENTH-CENTURY STANDARDS, the mid-1660s were stable around the Beauly Firth, according to Rev. James Fraser (1634–1709). He took inspiration from the knowledge that 'historians sometimes entertain themselves with miraculous accidents' and his reflections on that year convey joy, wonder, and even a suggestion of equilibrium being restored following the end of the Wars of the Three Kingdoms (1638–60).[1] Any suggestion of a jubilant tone should not be overstated, however, and a deeper engagement with his work shows how the booming and dissonance of that period of civil war continued to resound and haunt the firthside space where he would live out his years. A modern reader might imagine themselves, alongside Fraser, and below Tomnahurich Hill in his nearest burgh of Inverness, daunted by the chiefs and retinue of MacKenzie and Lochiel who had gathered to settle a dispute, when, he tells us: 'earth, water, aire, Rebounded at the sound of Bagpipes martiall Musick'.[2] Alternatively, they might wonder what it was like to endure that day of 'Cruel Thunder', when there was 'lightning 24 houres' and 'in our hills, the hight of Vrqhart [Urquhart] and Strathglash [Strathglass] fell such pieces of Ice, inch thick and 3 inch broad'.[3] Equally terrifying must have been the sight of the 'dreedfull flame' caused by a barn fire in Culcabock, just to the south-east of the Highland capital, and which put its citizens in a 'consternation'.[4] Fraser also reports the 'signall Instance and dreadfull sight, at 10 houres forenoon' one day when Inverness's populace witnessed the horror of their trusted wooden bridge over the Ness collapsing in a flood with 'about 200 persones, men, women, and Children upon it'.[5] Closer to home, in his parish of Kirkhill, he informs us that the tragedies of 1664 included thirty-nine deaths, some of them children, such as 'Isobel Fraser, Culbokie's daughter died July 13', while thirty-five died in the year that followed, an example being 'Alexander Fraser Ferrier died April 1'.[6]

James Fraser conveys his participation in these enthralling, perplexing or dire local events as an energetic minister, single and in his thirtieth year. By 1665, he had cultivated a world that was, at once, familial and parochial, but also regional, national and transnational, connections that helped him survive such challenges and to interact with a world beyond. Memories of the wider horizons provided by his university years, and of the continental tour which had extricated him from Cromwellian rule, must have been stirred on him bumping into fellow returned traveller, 'Doctor William Forbes', a physician, formerly in the service of the Duke of Florence, and whom he had last seen in Pisa in Italy six years previously.[7] Assisted by such encounters, by his network of fellow scholars in northern Scotland and beyond, via his copious notes and enthusiastic reading of manuscripts, books and newsbooks, Fraser kept up with what was happening across and beyond Europe in the early to mid-1660s: in France, where Fraser informs his readers that Louis XIV was increasing his 'sole government'; in Sweden, where affairs were going 'quite wrong'; in Poland, where the nobility (*szlachta*) were 'discontented'; in Hungary, where the Ottomans had lost the 'flower of their infantry' to the Imperialists; on the Iberian Peninsula, where the Spanish had made 'remarkable' gains against the Portuguese, and, across the Atlantic, where the Dutch-founded colonial settlement of New Amsterdam was being renamed and re-imagined as New York.[8] The place from which this Gaelic-speaking son of the Scottish Highlands viewed the world, in 1664–5 and throughout his life, was rooted in family and parish, but in no sense was it disconnected or unentangled from global events.

PRIMARY SOURCES FOR A BIOGRAPHY OF REV. JAMES FRASER

In the twenty-first century, James Fraser is largely forgotten, even more so than Isobel Gowdie (fl.1662), Martin Martin (d.1718), Iain Lom (c.1624–c.1710) or Robert ('Rob Roy') MacGregor (bap. 1671, d. 1734), other real historical figures who were alive in the seventeenth-century Highlands and who, to some extent, have been memorialised. The legendary and mercurial local prophet, the Brahan Seer (Coinneach Odhar), quite possibly a living, breathing presence in Fraser's lifetime too, continues, similarly, to inspire more commemoration and creative outpourings than the minister from Kirkhill. Who was 'our' James Fraser, then, and how should we balance or juggle those varied elements which compete for our attention from the sources that remain? The first place to turn to here is his written work, that which survives, obviously, but also, less tangibly, those self-penned texts which have been lost. From his manse overlooking the Beauly Firth, Fraser would claim to have compiled and bound a Gaelic dictionary as well as pieces on music, poetry, jokes, folk- and weather-lore, for example, all of which are on the list of fifty-three manuscripts he recorded, late in life, as having been in his possession, but have since vanished.

Six of his own works, along with a smaller number of letters and printed references from church records, remain, however, all from the period of his 1661–1709 ministry. Four of those six manuscripts are relatively short: 'Homilies and exercises theological and moral', completed between 1661 and 1688; *Divina Providentia in Rebus Humanis* ('Divine Providence Plainlie Discerned in Humane Affaires. A Collection of Providential Passages Ancient and Modern, Foreign and Domestick'), in large part a work that is partly anecdotal, on Scottish, 'British' and European history that he had written in the 1670s; a 'Short Chronologie and Genealogie of the Bissets and Frasers of Lovat' (including the appended 'A True Genealogie of the Frasers'), completed after 1698; and, most curiously of all, his 'Bill of Mortality' listing 'all y^t [that] died Natives and Strangers in 48 years' within the parish of Kirkhill, and regarding which the last entry, in 1709, marks his own impending death. All four of these will be referred to occasionally throughout the text, as will the letters and clerical references, although they provide much less information on his social and scholarly world than two other, revelatory sources.

These two other extant, self-written manuscripts of his are vast, sprawling works, each several hundred thousand words in length. They are reflected on and interrogated much more extensively in this book. One of them is Fraser's most famous work, the 'Wardlaw Manuscript', his history of the Frasers to 1674, containing lengthy asides on, for example, regime change at local, national and international level, prophecy and natural history. Compiled over a period of decades in Fraser's adult life, the manuscript's history is complex. Having passed into private hands after his death, it remained poorly known for over a century. The *Inverness Courier* can be credited for bringing it out of obscurity, by publishing extracts from it in 1834, while, nine years on from that, the newspaper's editor, Robert Carruthers, mentioned a public sale at which it had turned up, 'bearing the stains of age', describing its author, albeit 'learned', as someone who 'possessed no small share of the credulity and love of gossip which distinguish chroniclers less favoured by fortune'.[9]

It took till 1905 for the Scottish History Society to publish an edited version of the text, the project led by William Mackay, an Inverness-based solicitor and Gaelic scholar who had been brought up in Glenurquhart just to the south of Kirkhill. Writing the introduction to that volume, Mackay elaborated more effusively on the manuscript than Carruthers had seventy years earlier, asserting that it showed a minister who:

> knew his parishioners and the inhabitants of the surrounding districts by name and headmark; and he went in and out among them, not only as their spiritual guide and temporal adviser, but also as one deeply interested in their manners and customs, and in their Gaelic legends and lore, which he noted mentally as he rested within their turf huts.[10]

Such writing is wonderfully evocative. It also indicates a view, typical of the time, of the Highlands as being essentially 'Celtic', in contrast to an 'Anglo-Saxon' Lowlands.[11] While Mackay's is an impressively detailed presentation of Fraser and his world at Kirkhill, then, in this text I have relied on the original 'Wardlaw Manuscript' instead for all lengthier quotations or reflections, retaining original spellings. Mackay's is an account that is vital and immensely valuable, although overly binary in its view of Kirkhill's place in seventeenth-century Scotland and, at times, not questioning enough as regards its author's reliability.

As shall be seen, Mackay downplays Fraser's linking, or, at times, diametric opposing, of Lowland and Highland worlds. He understates his positioning of himself as a minister who identified with a 'greater' Moray, in ecclesiastical terms (an area of northern Scotland much larger and more of a blend of Scots and Gaelic worlds than the one we know today). Mackay also skates over many of Fraser's, from a modern perspective, less favourable or agreeable actions. Fundamentally, in focusing on creating a reliable and helpful resource for local and family historians, Mackay edits out those sections of the work that concern global politics, empire, travel, languages, theology, meteorology and natural history. He underestimates his subject's polymathic, transnational involvements and entanglements in favour of the familiar and antiquarian.[12]

Not only that, but in relying on the 'Wardlaw Manuscript' alone, Carruthers, Mackay and, by extension, most historians who have covered Fraser since are missing another vital piece in the jigsaw, which emphasises, more than any other text, his international outlook. This is Fraser's extraordinary, autobiographical account of his travels from 1657 to 1660, the text usually abbreviated as the 'Triennial Travels'. This work is a maverick, three-volume memoir, which Fraser wrote up in the decades that followed, and is presented as a record of a three-year journey through Europe. Throughout the text, Fraser conveys a wide-eyed fascination with the world beyond Scotland but seeks also to ensure that what he recorded from abroad might widen the perspective of a broad range of potential readers at home. Scenes witnessed and recorded within the memoir include: a brawl with a 'bastardly fellow' in Alnwick; a rough Mediterranean sea crossing to Genoa discussing classical texts with a vomiting skipper; an English friend's romantic disasters in Regensburg; and the sight of an elephant in a Vienna street. Despite it being marvellously original, detailed and idiosyncratic, Carruthers did not mention the 'Triennial Travels' at all when writing for the *Courier*, while Mackay, on finishing the compiling of his Scottish History Society volume, reported only that it remained in the ownership of a Hilda Paterson (fl. c.1900–42). Indeed, Mackay seems to have seen it only briefly, and few others knew about it at all, it being later that it came – one presumes via Paterson – into the possession of the University of Aberdeen, where it was 'rediscovered in the reserved shelves at the Librarian's Room' in the 1960s.[13] This obscurity means that the insights it provides into the strikingly cosmopolitan worldview of a son of the north Highlands of the period have remained almost entirely concealed from a wider audience.

The case to be made in this book is that this is a vital omission in understanding Fraser's outlook and in the presentation of Highland history from the period, more broadly. The 'Triennial Travels' is the memoir of a middle-aged man recalling a dynamic, worldly three-year period in his twenties. Contrasting with the couthy minister of Mackay's edited version of the 'Wardlaw Manuscript', Fraser presents himself as a polyglot and a polymath, keen to guide his readers on European culture, languages, history and current affairs, and on how family, Highland, Scottish, British and Irish networks functioned in England and on the continent in the mid-seventeenth century. Indeed, in providing a Highland and Gaelic-speaking angle on Christendom, this autobiographical insight into the mental world of an early, non-aristocratic exponent of the 'Grand Tour' can seem completely unique to a modern reader, albeit Fraser did not consider himself to be an oddity, or to represent a 'realm apart'. Thankfully, due to the care and attention the manuscript has received in recent decades at the University of Aberdeen, and the fresh perspective it can provide on an array of historical themes, the memoir is beginning to garner the attention it deserves. Dutch linguist C. D. Van Strien made use of it for a 1993 book.[14] Most strikingly, Jane Stevenson and Peter Davidson considered it, in a 2008 account, to comprise 'one of the most remarkable and substantial texts from early-modern Britain' while, in 2011, Davidson and Carol

Morley described it as 'beyond doubt the most interesting and substantial Scottish non-devotional journal to survive from the whole early-modern period'.[15]

Based on the rich primary source base above, and the two lengthiest manuscripts in particular, this biography considers Fraser in the round: as an engaged observer of, and commentator on, parish, family, local, regional, national and global events. In this way, it examines the self-presentation of an energetic, curious, mobile Highland male and situates him within his locality, his region, Scotland, the three Stuart kingdoms, Europe and its overseas empires. Fraser's accounts are far from being universally dependable, and, where possible, other primary source sets are employed to verify details. But that lack of complete reliability is no reason to dismiss his work. The manner and depth in which Fraser recollects and presents his first-hand experiences is what makes them so unique and so crucial, their degree of trustworthiness being a vital but distinct matter when considering them. This biography of him will thus challenge any possible assumption that Gaelic-speaking Highlanders all lived, worked, played and imagined themselves in a vacuum, sealed off from the rest of Scotland and Christendom prior to the eighteenth century. Instead, it will provide Scottish, British, European and inter-imperial perspectives on the region's early modern (roughly, 1500–1750) history, and highlight an ongoing, outward-looking vitality, one that belied the Stewarts'/Stuarts' attempted imposition of 'civility' upon it. On the threshold of a peripheralisation that would constrain it for the next two centuries and more, there are crucial, neglected elements to Highland society at the time, ones which show that it was reliant upon a distinct engagement with, and enmeshment in, the world outside. This biography thus offers a different view from that to be found in most interpretations of the Highland past during the two and a half centuries between the fall of the Lordship of the Isles in 1493 and the Battle of Culloden in 1746. Rather than assuming gradual decline, disunity or even atrophy, it identifies, in the face of growing external impositions and global entanglements, the retention of considerable individual and collective agency, and the possibility that Highlanders might have pursued or followed alternative trajectories towards modernity than those which many were coerced into, and others chose, in the centuries that followed.

FRASER AND EARLY MODERN HIGHLAND HISTORIOGRAPHY

Fraser's identity was far from simple. It would be most apt to describe it as concentric, in that his actions can be best understood when situated in familial, parochial, Scottish, 'British', pan-archipelagic, European and transnational contexts, the relative emphasis on each depending on which moment or component of his life is being studied. However, in terms of place, as has already been suggested, what makes him most immediately distinct to most of the world is his identification with the northern and western part of the country he was born in and lived out his days in. The modern umbrella term for Fraser's part of Scotland, at its most expansive, is the Highlands and Islands. Many of us take this place for granted today. It denotes most of the north and west, being inclusive of both the mainland Highlands, the Western Isles and the Northern Isles. It thus embraces the Gàidhealtachd, the most strongly Gaelic-speaking part of the country, as well as the predominantly Norse-influenced regions of Caithness, Orkney and Shetland to the north, along with more mixed, multicultural, coastal and, in part, urbanised eastern and south-eastern edges. Regarding historical 'regions', Adrian Green and A. J. Pollard have asserted that, whether supra-national or sub-national in scope, they 'are a necessary feature of scholarly efforts to organise knowledge of society past and present', and, clearly, the Highlands and Islands is, according to this definition, a paramount example. Ewen Cameron's entry in the *Oxford Companion to Scottish History*, published in 2001, argued for it comprising a distinct geographical area of largely 'marginal' land, also linguistically distinctive, and definable additionally, and from a modern perspective, by a 'resistance to authority and central government control'.[16]

Nevertheless, while the term 'Highlands and Islands' was used in the early modern period, being found, for example, in some late seventeenth-century Church of Scotland records, consideration of it as a coherent entity appears to become prominent only with the Crofters Holdings (Scotland) Act 1886 and the associated creation of seven crofting counties, these providing, eventually, the basis for the founding, in 1965, of the Highlands and Islands Development Board (HIDB). The latter was a government agency which evinced a more social (besides an economic) function than one might generally expect from such a body, an objective furthered, during the UK's period of European Union membership, by HIDB'S successor, Highlands and Islands Enterprise (1991). More recently, the geographical scope of HIE has linked closely with, but not paralleled exactly, that of the University of the Highlands and Islands, a multi-campus partnership which has had full university title since 2011.[17] In light of this, one should be cautious of teleology, and Cameron is, indeed, anxious to ascertain the Highlands and Islands as, to some extent, a modern and 'external' construct. Without doubt,

Map I.1 *Extima Scotiae septentrionalis ora, ubi Provinciae sunt Rossia, Sutherlandia, Cathenesia, Strath-Naverniae, cum vicinis regiunculis quae eis subsunt, etiamque Moravia*, National Library of Scotland, EMW.X.015

its expansive geography, its geographical and cultural heterogeneity, its mix of the insular and mainland, from Shetland to Kintyre, from the Butt of Lewis to, in some instances, Moray and Perthshire, and the clustering of organisations concerned with the region since 1886 require one to recognise its modern vitality while simultaneously reflecting on it sceptically when applying it to the epoch in which Fraser lived.

Two other terms already employed, the 'Highlands' and the 'Gàidhealtachd', have apparently simpler, narrower definitions, being, usually, exclusive of the non-Gaelic Northern Isles. But they also prove to be worthy of reflection when connected to Fraser and his world. In the later twentieth century, historian Geoffrey Barrow determined that the concept of a Lowland–Highland divide hardly existed, even in the 1200s. As Barrow asserted, John of Fordun, writing in 1380, comprises the first known writer to have sub-divided Scotland in this way.[18] For Fordun, the 'coastal people' of Scotland were 'docile and civilised, trustworthy, long-suffering and courteous, decent in their dress, polite and peaceable, devout in their worship, but always ready to resist injuries threatened by their enemies'. By this interpretation, the 'island or mountain people' were 'fierce and untameable, uncouth and unpleasant, much given to theft, fond of doing nothing, but their minds are quick to learn, and cunning'. They were 'always hostile and savage not only towards the people and language of England, but also towards their fellow Scots'.[19] A detailed exploration of this Lowland–Highland separation – so often assumed to be intrinsic to Scottish history subsequent to Fordun – can be found in a 2009 volume edited by Dauvit Broun and Martin MacGregor.[20] As the chapters in that book convey, by the end of the fifteenth century, not only had Norse Orkney, Shetland and Caithness been incorporated into the Scottish kingdom, but the Lordship of the Isles, the most formidable Gaelic-speaking polity the Highlands has ever produced, had been annexed out of existence. Isobel Grant and Hugh Cheape wrote, in 1987, of the 'often tangled and lurid' events that marked the two centuries that followed for Gaels, an opinion echoed by Domhnall Uilleam Stiùbhart, who has pointed to 'that confused and violent era of bloodfeud resulting from the final collapse and balkanisation of the Lordship [of the Isles]', the epoch known eventually as the '*Linn Nan Creach*' ('Age of Forays').[21] Certainly, the state's projection of an advanced 'Lowland' and benighted 'Highland' remained in the foreground, affected further by the Protestant Reformation and by the Scottish Stewart dynasty having found themselves, from 1603, rulers of three kingdoms rather than one. Without doubt, James VI's *Basilikon Doron* (1597) and its depiction of the people of the Western Isles as 'utterly barbarians, without any sort or show of civility', and of their mainland fellow Gaelic-speakers as being only slightly more 'civilised', was, at most, marginally more subtle than Fordun's. This antagonistic attitude towards the Highlands is exemplified in the several Scottish governmental impositions leading up to, including and following the Statutes of Iona of 1609, part of a series of punitive measures against Gaelic life.[22] It provides an essential context in which Fraser must be viewed.

Given these, in some ways, relatively shallow roots to the Lowland–Highland divide, however, it is unsurprising that the people of Scotland did not, during Fraser's lifetime, necessarily recognise such a stark binary opposition in their everyday lives. The last few decades of history-writing have brought about a sustained questioning of the notion of the post-Lordship Highlands as 'a realm apart', instigated, firstly, in Allan Macinnes's seminal *Clanship, Commerce, and the House of Stuart, 1603–1788*, published in 1996, and, in 1998, in Bob Dodgshon's *From Chiefs to Landlords: Social and Economic Change in the Western Highlands and Islands, c.1493–1820*. At the time of their publication, this pair of works represented the two weightiest contributions to early modern Highlands and Islands history for decades. While recognising the 'tangled and lurid' elements of the period, they consigned to anachronism the notion of Scottish Gaeldom as 'static socially and undeveloped economically' during the 1600s, and posited commercialisation as already accelerating by then. One can measure their influence when reading the region's most acclaimed and widely read modern historian, James Hunter, in his preface to the 2000 and 2010 editions of his 1976 classic, *The Making of the Crofting Community*, in which he pointed out that 'the beginnings of commercially orientated land management, in a Highland context, are to be found, not in the eighteenth century as I assumed in 1976, but in the seventeenth century'.[23]

Indeed, Macinnes and Dodgshon have influenced not only Hunter, but an entirely new generation of scholars of the region towards a more nuanced understanding of its past in the early modern period. A rich vein of historiography has emerged since the late 1990s, which aspires to a more comprehensive presentation of the social world of the Highlands of the time than that which had been attained previously.[24] It is one which positions the two centuries before Culloden as demanding consideration on their own terms. Alison Cathcart reminds readers not to take Stewart/Stuart propaganda at face value, in her introduction to *Kinship and Clientage: Highland Clanship, 1451–1609*, arguing that the Lowland and Highland divide that had preoccupied Fordun was only 'the most basic of distinctions' by the sixteenth century, and advising historians to consider all sorts of overlaps, grey areas and sub-divisions instead.[25] Among the seventeenth-century-focused writers, such as Allan Kennedy, Thomas Brochard and Aonghas MacCoinnich, there has been a connected response, and, additionally, a reorientation towards more localised studies of the north Highlands and of the Minch, sub-regional approaches which show how local, family and community agency created a patchwork of narratives, which, at various times, anticipated, responded to and reacted to the crown's coercive, aggressive, 'civilising' measures, as well as its more conciliatory approaches. Without doubt, an impressive corpus of historical writing covering the northern and western part of Scotland during the seventeenth century is now growing and is allowing many of the region's range of events and contributions from that time to emerge from the shadows.

BOOK STRUCTURE: RE-PRESENTING JAMES FRASER

This book sharpens the focus further. By placing the sources for James Fraser at the centre, the aim is for family, parish, diocesan, coastal, provincial, national, archipelagic, European and imperial views to reflect, retract and converge so as to form a stronger image of him than has hitherto been achieved, and, from there, provide a different perspective on the Highlands of the time. Using a biographical method, the book follows six themes, broadly chronological, that will both trace the trajectory of his life and emphasise the scholarly and cultural contribution that he made from and to the region. These six themes are mapped to two phases: 1634–60 and 1660–1709. Each of the six chapters seeks to engage, as much as is possible, with Highland, Scottish and broader historiographical trends as regards their respective thematic areas, albeit the biographical approach means that this coverage is, by no means, always exhaustive. The first phase ('The Student', 'The Traveller' and 'The Linguist') encompasses Fraser's elementary education and secondary schooling, then his university years in Aberdeen (1651–5), followed by a brief, intense return to the Cromwellian garrison town of Inverness (1655–7), and also his time abroad (1657–60). His three-year tour will be shown to have been disproportionately influential on his personal and scholarly development, and also linked to the later part of his life, when he wrote up and communicated his experiences of it. In this way it provides a bridge to Part Two of the book. This part (covered by the chapters titled 'The Scientist', 'The Minister' and 'The Historian') comprises Fraser's return, settlement and latter years at Kirkhill.

The three respective chapters in it focus thematically rather than chrono-logically, evidencing slightly narrower, Scottish and 'British' horizons than in the first part, and yet covering a hugely productive period of writing in strikingly settled times (1660–88), this book-ended by the lesser-known final twenty-one years of his life (1688–1709). The sources that remain for Fraser's last two decades suggest a reappearance of the turbulence of his early years, although coverage of these times will show that, in adversity, Fraser retained, to an extent, a 'telescopic' focus on the world both beyond and within his parish.[26]

No primary sources are objective, as the case of Fraser makes abun-dantly clear. It is our task as historians to interrogate, critique and inter-pret them for a broader audience, and, where the evidence from them supports it, to convey their meaning and significance. In this case, the evidence is overwhelmingly autobiographical – thus, of course, fallible and yet simultaneously original and informative – and so the approach taken is to deal with both historical facts and memory. It is for these reasons that the biographical method has been chosen as the best and most accessible one, the objective being to provide a new pathway into the world of the Highlands as it was before Culloden. It is not a route that is presumed to supersede all others, but the measure of the success or otherwise of the book will be, one assumes, whether it provoked and generated new discussion and debate, and thereby opened up new approaches.

NOTES

1. James Fraser, '*Polichronicon seu Policratica Temporum*' or 'The True Genealogy of the Frasers, 916–1674' [hereafter 'Wardlaw Manuscript'], National Library of Scotland [hereafter NLS], MS 3658, pp. 304–11; William Mackay, ed., *Chronicles of the Frasers: The Wardlaw Manuscript Entitled 'Polichronicon seu Policratica Temporum' or 'The True Genealogy of the Frasers', 916–1674* (Edinburgh, 1905), pp. 453–5.
2. 'Wardlaw Manuscript', p. 312; Mackay, ed., *Chronicles*, p. 454.
3. Ibid.
4. Ibid., pp. 453–5.
5. Ibid.
6. 'Bill of Mortality – Containing All y[t] Died Natives and Strangers in 48 Years', Highland Archive Centre, Inverness, Old Parish Register, 52.
7. 'Wardlaw Manuscript', p. 312.
8. This follows earlier interjections on continental and Scandinavian events of the 1630s and 1640s, suggesting his sources for the international aspects must have been copies of historical works in his own possession, given

Fraser was born only in 1634. For Fraser's pan-European panoramas, which extend to Muscovy and the Ottoman Empire, and which span a period from well before his own lifetime down to the 1670s, see 'Wardlaw Manuscript', pp. 72–4, 169–71, 183, 188–92, 257–9, 304–11, 328–30, 345–6. Readers gain an overview of a similarly international, even global, arena from his more anecdotal '*Divina Providentia*' from 1678. See *Divina Providentia* ('A Collection of Providential Passages Ancient and Modern, Foreign and Domestick'), NLS, Adv.MS.32.4.7.

9. Robert Carruthers, *The Highland Note-Book* (Edinburgh, 1843), p. 88; 20 April 1855, *The John O'Groat Journal*. This comprises a reference to a 'John Fraser of Phopachy' and his talent for eating large quantities or 'indulging freely in gastronomic performances', and purports to involve comments from the manuscript of 'his brother, Mr James Fraser, the curate of Wardlaw or Kirkhill'. Thank you to Malcolm Bangor-Jones for the reference.

10. Mackay, ed., *Chronicles*, pp. viii–ix, xxvii.

11. For more on Mackay, see Graeme M. MacKenzie, 'The life and work as a historian of Dr William Mackay – a founder of the Gaelic Society of Inverness', available at: <https://soundcloud.com/user806452300/graeme-m-mackenzie-2013-09-27> (last accessed 2 March 2021); Melanie Manwaring-McKay, 'Charles Fraser-Mackintosh (1828–1901) and his books: book collecting, bibliomania and antiquarianism in the Victorian Scottish Highlands', Masters dissertation, University of the Highlands and Islands (2019); Ewan A. Cameron, *The Life and Times of Fraser-Mackintosh Crofter MP* (Aberdeen, 2000).

12. The National Library of Scotland has digitised a version of the 1905 *Chronicles*, annotated by Mackay, and presented to a 'Mr A. MacDonald' in 1925. Further analysis of that might reveal more as regards his editorial decisions. Available at: <https://digital.nls.uk/histories-of-scottish-families/archive/95123974#?c=0&m=0&s=0&cv=0&xywh=-1461%2C-224%2C5420%2C4462> (last accessed 25 May 2022).

13. Peter Davidson and Carol Morley, 'James Fraser's Triennial Travels', in Iain Beavan, Peter Davidson and Jane Stevenson, eds, *The Library and Archive Collections of the University of Aberdeen: An Introduction and Description* (Manchester, 2011), p. 206; Mackay, ed., *Chronicles*, p. ix.

14. C. D. Van Strien, *British Travellers in Holland During the Stuart Period: Edward Browne and John Locke as Tourists in the United Provinces* (Leiden, 1993).

15. Jane Stevenson and Peter Davidson, *The Lost City: Old Aberdeen* (Edinburgh, 2008), p. 111; Davidson and Morley, 'James Fraser's Triennial Travels', pp. 206, 208.

16. Adrian Green and A. J. Pollard, 'Introduction', in Adrian Green and A. J. Pollard, eds, *Regional Identities in North-East England, 1300–2000* (London, 2007), p. 4.

17. Subsequent to that, the achieving of Objective 1 status within the European Union, a means of promoting regions in line with the EU's 'Cohesion Policy', and also the influence of the University of the Highlands and Islands, awarded university title in 2011, has been powerful in seeking to position this area not only as an economic driver but one that concerns itself with the social, cultural and community transformation of what has become a largely depopulated and, in part, denuded northern and western Scotland.

18. Geoffrey W. S. Barrow, *The Kingdom of the Scots: Government, Church and Society from the Eleventh to the Fourteenth Century*, 2nd edn (Edinburgh, 2003).

19. Martin MacGregor, 'Gaelic barbarity and Scottish identity in the later Middle Ages', in Dauvit Broun and Martin MacGregor, eds, *Mìorun mòr nan Gall, 'The great ill-will of the Lowlander'? Lowland Perceptions of the Highlands, Medieval and Modern* (Glasgow, 2009), 2007 e-version available at: <http://eprints.gla.ac.uk/40251/> (last accessed 8 November 2021).

20. Broun and MacGregor, eds, *Mìorun mòr nan Gall*, p. 7.

21. I. F. Grant and Hugh Cheape, *Periods in Highland History* (London, 1987), p. 105; Domhnall Uilleam Stiùbhart, 'Women and gender in the early modern western Gàidhealtachd', in Elizabeth Ewan and Maureen Meikle, eds, *Women in Scotland c.1100–c.1750* (East Linton, 1999), p. 233; Donald Gregory, *The History of the Western Highlands and Isles of Scotland, 1493–1625* (Edinburgh, 1836).

22. Charles Butler, ed., *Basilikon Doron; or, His Majestys Instructions to his Dearest Sonne, Henry the Prince* (London, 1887), pp. 42, 43, 50.

23. Allan Macinnes, *Clanship, Commerce, and the House of Stuart, 1603–1788* (East Linton, 1996); Robert A. Dodgshon, *From Chiefs to Landlords: Social and Economic Change in the Western Highlands and Islands, c.1493–1820* (Edinburgh, 1998); James Hunter, 'Preface to the 2000 Edition', *The Making of the Crofting Community* (Edinburgh, 2010), p. 24.

24. Thomas Brochard, 'The integration of the elite and wider communities of the northern Highlands, 1500–1700: evidence from visual culture', *Northern Scotland*, 6(1) (2015), pp. 1–23; Thomas Brochard, 'The socio-economic relations between Scotland's northern territories and Scandinavia and the Baltic in the sixteenth and seventeenth centuries', *International Journal of Maritime History*, 26(2) (2014), pp. 210–34; Aonghas MacCoinnich, *Plantation and Civility in the North Atlantic World: The Case of the Northern Hebrides, 1570–1639* (Leiden, 2015); Alison Cathcart, *Kinship and Clientage: Highland Clanship, 1451–1609* (Leiden, 2006); Barry Robertson, *Lordship and Power in the North of Scotland, 1603–1690* (Edinburgh, 2011); Allan Kennedy, *Governing Gaeldom: The Scottish Highlands and the Restoration State, 1660–1688* (Leiden, 2014); Allan Kennedy, 'Reducing that barbarous country: centre, periphery and Highland policy in Restoration Britain', *Journal of British Studies*, 52(3) (2013), pp. 597–614; Allan Kennedy,

'"A heavy yock uppon their necks": Covenanting government in the northern Highlands, 1638–1651', *Journal of Scottish Historical Studies*, 30(2) (2010), pp. 93–122; Allan Kennedy, 'The urban community in Restoration Scotland: government, society and economy in Inverness, 1660–c.1688', *Northern Scotland*, 5 (2014), pp. 26–49; David Worthington, 'The settlements of the Beauly-Wick coast and the historiography of the Moray Firth', *The Scottish Historical Review*, 95(2) (2016), pp. 139–63.

25. Cathcart, *Kinship and Clientage*, p. 6.
26. Other biographies of early modern figures that have been influential on this include, but are not limited to: Natalie Zemon Davis, *Trickster Travels: A Sixteenth-Century Muslim Between Worlds* (New York, 2006); Claire Tomalin, *Samuel Pepys: The Unequalled Self* (London, 2002). Contributions focusing on other periods but nonetheless helpful include: Linda Colley, *The Ordeal of Elizabeth Marsh: A Woman in World History* (London, 2008).

PART ONE (1634–60)

Acquiring Knowledge:
Fraser's Training as an Early Modern Scottish
Highland Scholar

1

The Student:
The Curious Mind of James Fraser

'living then by the shoare at Phopachy'

INTRODUCTION

IN THE YEARS AROUND 1620, Sir Robert Gordon (1580–1656), tutor to the Earl of Sutherland, advocated a brutal approach to education in his part of the Highlands. He instructed his nephew, a future heir to the earldom, to 'take away the reliques of the Irishe barbaritie which as yet remains in your countery, to wit, the Irishe langage, and the habit' by establishing 'schooles in ewerie corner' that would 'instruct the youth to speak Inglishe'.[1] By 'Irishe', Gordon meant 'Scots Gaelic', and, indeed, during James Fraser's lifetime, a Highland educational world revolving around hereditary bards, historians, medics and other scholars was put under threat from such attitudes and actions: Gordon's proposed 'seminary of wertue [virtue]' in Dornoch can be viewed as an aggressive local expression of anti-Gaelic educational measures fostered by the Scottish government, and outlined most clearly via national-level statutes created or ratified in 1609, 1616, 1633 and 1646.

Yet, most seventeenth-century contemporaries concerned with everyday schooling in the region – a mix of, often, bilingual Gaelic- and Scots-speaking representatives of the Protestant churches – did not have access to the kind of capital or influence enjoyed by the likes of the Gordons of Sutherland. Rather than any attempt to root out their prospective ministers' and parishioners' native language, voices from the kirk reported and acted on a more basic concern: how to build new schools and recruit the necessary schoolmasters required for them at parish level. Put another way, a more visible preoccupation than how to limit the use of Gaelic

by the kirk's local representatives was finding the required funding from
heritors (landholders) that would pay for, and meet demand for, parochial educational provision, within what became, from 1638, a civil war
situation. As for James Fraser, one sees an engagement with schooling
that began and ended with Gaelic, in that the initial provision at parish
level that he received as a child, and later arranged and supported as
a minister, was delivered, in part, in his first language, in opposition
to crown-level instructions. Without doubt, nonetheless, national-level
constraints of policy, finance and war would combine to disrupt his elementary education, and, to some extent, affect his experience even of
Inverness Grammar School, which he attended in the 1640s, and King's
College, Aberdeen, where he studied from 1651 to 1655. A pull towards
the North Sea was a feature of Fraser life, in the world of scholarship as
in many other areas. Thus, as Thomas Brochard has argued, 'intellectual
and practical education' was far from lacking in the north Highlands
during the century following the Reformation, with influences coming
from Orkney, Aberdeen and beyond, in the decades leading up to Anglo-
Scottish political union. In this way, Fraser backed the use of Gaelic language and methods, but looked to his immediate north and east too, and
then used this experience of secondary and tertiary education in order to
transform schooling in Kirkhill during his period as minister.[2]

This chapter will consider the fundamental part of school and university in forming Fraser's identity and influencing his behaviour and
attitudes, both during childhood and in his adult years, when he proved
to be committed to increasing educational facilities and infrastructure
at home. In so doing it will back the argument of Brochard, also Jamie
Kelly and, before him, the late Donald Withrington, in highlighting that
the degree of parochial education provided by the kirk in the Highlands
vastly exceeded that which used to be assumed.[3] As Rab Houston
and, more recently, Kelly have shown, in seventeenth-century Scottish
life, parish church and school were intertwined in a system led by the
state, one that aimed to provide a national system of parochial schooling paid for by landowners at a local level. Highland parishes were not
always stymied by anti-Gaelic government policy and posturing in this
regard, but sought, actively, to encourage both construction of, and provision for, schools run and funded by local figures familiar with, and
committed to, the language of their communities, all of this many decades
prior to the founding of the Society in Scotland for the Propagation of
Christian Knowledge (SSPCK), in 1709. Fraser was part of those kirk-
and community-led efforts, and despite the abovementioned challenges
in relation to parish schooling, he fought for, attained and supported

thereafter strikingly high scholarly standards within his locale through a large part of his adult lifetime.

It is vital to consider why and how this was possible. As a young child, Fraser learned, via Gaelic, from local tradition-bearers and hereditary scholars, making use of locally available books and manuscripts. Although these early years in Kirkhill did not give him a thorough grounding in what was needed to prepare for higher education, the Scottish grammar school system did, via his nearest burgh of Inverness.[4] Furthermore, in terms of his subsequent life as a university student, the chapter will follow Goeing, Parry and Feingold in seeing seventeenth-century academia not as an 'ivory tower' world, but one that could be both influential on and informed by broader policy and networks. While one can only imagine how much Fraser might have contributed, had there been a higher education institution in the Highlands, university life in Aberdeen provided a vital bridge, for him, towards becoming 'embedded in complex scholarly and scientific developments', an engagement to be covered in Chapter Four, and one which helped guide him, eventually, on how to implement schooling in an effective manner at home.[5] Fraser's early experience of Gaelic learning ultimately blended with an urban secondary and tertiary education that, formally, eschewed his first language but, practically, relied on it. The evidence suggests that he combined both local and transnational perspectives in his views and merged elements of both worlds. Under his leadership, teaching in his parish retained the Gaelic element that had characterised his learning in his early years. Put simply, a mainstream Scottish grammar school and university education in the Lowlands did not lead Highland scholars inexorably towards internalising the anti-Gaelic attitudes of a Robert Gordon. The example of James Fraser suggests different conclusions.

A SCHOLAR ON THE SHORE: FRASER AND COASTAL HISTORY

Phopachy and Early Modern Scottish History

Phopachy House lies less than 5 miles west of Inverness, alongside the A862 road as it snakes to the west of the shore-side settlement of Bunchrew. In the seventeenth century, this spot by the Beauly Firth fizzed with scholarly activity. It was where James Fraser was born, if we believe his claim, on New Year's Day 1634, one of twenty-four children of Reverend William Fraser (d.1659), a local church minister, and Alison Fraser, daughter of a James Fraser of Tain. Rev. William's father, the grandfather of the subject of this biography, had been chief household servant to Simon Fraser, 6th Lord Lovat, and so connected this scion with the Fraser clan elite (*fine*). He had obtained a wadset or mortgage in Phopachy, then in the parish of Fernua, in 1599, a spot which would provide a manse and home for William and Alison. This allowed the couple a base from which William would take up three successive ministerial positions between 1630 and 1659, in locations to the immediate west, north and east, respectively: Kilmorack, Killearnan (Redcastle) and the second 'charge' (parish) of Inverness.[6] All were a short journey from Phopachy, and, evidently, the young James Fraser grew up there with a sense of it being central, not just for his father, but for his more distant forebears. He picked up a detailed knowledge of local land and firth, and of lore relating to its ancient and more recent historical environment. For example, he acquired, and contributed to, the latest thinking on the crannogs that lay just offshore, 'three great heaps of stones in this lake [Beauly Firth] . . . at considerable distance from one another', one of them of 'huge bigness' when revealed by a low tide, and which Fraser asserted to be a 'burial place from the urns that are sometimes discovered'.[7] Local tradition-bearers and, he claimed, manuscripts in Lovat Fraser possession also encouraged in him the belief that there had once been a cell of scholarly hermits at Bunchrew.[8]

Fraser's identification with his shoreside home commenced well before any household schooling had begun at the clan's nearby Beaufort Castle, prior to him assuming the status of Lovat Fraser *seanchaidh* or genealogist, perhaps even before the life-changing potential of history had first gripped him. His accounts of everyday incidents at Phopachy confirm his involvement in all manner of domestic happenings there as a child.[9] He has left reports of a 1640s murder on the shore committed by Rory Mackenzie from Dochmaluag and six horsemen of 'John Mckgeorge, tennant in Phoppachy and Thomas Mckthomas, an old man, Miller to his own Father in law Hugh Fraser of Belladrum', after which, Fraser recalled, the guilty escaped across the firth northwards at low tide.[10] Elsewhere, he informs his readers of the capture of so many herrings just offshore that '40, 50, boats and more were every day fishing'.[11] Also from his adulthood, we learn of the 1670 capsizing of the boat of Londoner Captain Phineas Pett (Pot, Potts), near the Phopachy landing point, upon which Fraser 'happened to be there and some friends with me, and hearing the cry we run out and rescued the boat'.[12] That capsizing brought him not only a welcome donation of a work of history by the English historian William Camden, and other books, but also an unexpected supply of mace, nutmeg, cinnamon, cloves and ginger, highlighting the entangling influence of empire.[13] Becoming head of the

Figure 1.1 Wardlaw mausoleum and churchyard, Kirkhill

household on returning from his travels (his father having passed away in 1659) Fraser would maintain the Phopachy property and, upon his own death, pass it on to his son, Alexander, who would, in turn, leave it to a grandson, Robert, until it fell out of the family's hands in 1740.[14] For James Fraser, Phopachy was a firthside home, one which allowed him to move easily between two other local seats of learning, which acted as magnets, in a religious and educational sense.

Wardlaw and Kirkhill before Culloden

Just under 5 miles further west along the shore and slightly inland from Phopachy lies the settlement of Kirkhill. It was a township that would mature into a place of learning following it being created a parish by means of the uniting of Wardlaw, to the west, and Fernua (to which Phopachy belonged) to the east, in 1614 or 1618.[15] The bringing together of the two former congregations allowed for the growth of a relatively dense, and majority Gaelic-speaking, community that sat in the Inverness presbytery and on the western edge of the sprawling diocese of Moray. Kirkhill parish's scholarly remit and reach would increase considerably during Fraser's lifetime, although it must be granted that this process began even before his birth. He could make no claim to instigating what would become a series of architectural renovations to the church and churchyard, additions there having begun in 1633 by means of a new stair and gallery leading to the loft. The latter was a construction topped ostentatiously, from 1635, by a 'large, shaply bell' with 'hansell, tolling chaimes', parts having been taken from the former Valliscaulian priory in Beauly and modified in the Netherlands.[16] By 1636, builders had constructed the Lovat Fraser mausoleum in a position adjacent to that. In this way, a cluster of church and associated buildings began to emerge on this hilltop spot, 'the watch hill' to which 'Wardlaw' refers. It is not clear whether Fraser kept both his manse and lodgings at Kirkhill as an adult, since he refers, on different occasions, to having a study both there and in Phopachy. Yet, until elderly, he must have made the easy walk or pony trek between them on a regular basis. Kirkhill provided not only for an impressive soundscape, but for a geographically elevated centre of faith and learning, giving him horizons to the north-west, north and north-east: to the lower reaches of the River Beauly, the firth and, on a good day, to the Black Isle and the mass of Ben Wyvis beyond.[17]

As Chapter Five will show, it seems to have taken until 1672 for Fraser and his Kirkhill parishioners to implement the Education Act ratified by the Scottish government in 1633, this calling for the establishment of a school for each parish under church auspices.[18] Nevertheless, the Lovat Frasers had already created a broader base for scholarship nearby that Fraser claimed, with some exaggeration, impressed Lowland visitors, finding their home to be a 'cultivat Canaan' ('Canaan' being a Hebrew term referring to that part of the Middle East known more frequently as the Levant) in terms of its learning. According to Fraser, the educational element in this reputation was based on the clan chief, MacShimi (Lord Lovat), his patronage of scholars, and his maintaining of a library and a 'charter chest' or 'kist' at the family's Beaufort Castle, a collection which the young Fraser made full use of for his own research.[19] Fosterage was another possibility, in terms of scholarly advancement within the clan, although not one which Fraser's parents opened up for their children, according to the sources available.[20]

Certainly, Kirkhill parish did not provide an idyllic place for study after 1638, it being no less devoid of dramatic incident than Phopachy in his childhood.[21] Terrible problems impinged on Fraser's pre-teen years when Montrose's army passed through in 1646, with the horrific result that 'betuixt the bridge end of Inverness and Gusachan, 26 miles, there was not left in my countrie a sheep to bleet, or a Cock to crow day, nor a house unruffled'.[22] The available narrative indicates that quieter times returned in the 1670s, though, when, under Fraser's lead, the parish school was built and its first schoolmaster, Thomas Fraser, appointed.[23] Fraser authorised several additions to the church subsequent to that: he claimed, in 1682, to have hosted one John Fraser, 'a great mason, a sharp schollar, and exact historian' who oversaw 'the building of the wester gavell of our church'. Indeed, the Kirkhill school and church survived the upheavals of the 'Glorious Revolution', the latter being retained as the parish's major place of worship until 1790, while the mausoleum stands and attracts visitors to this day.[24] In this way, scholarly activity in the northern and eastern parts of Kirkhill parish changed noticeably, if sporadically, during Fraser's childhood and lifetime. It, and nearby Beaufort Castle, provided a locus for Fraser's educational and social world from his earliest life on and give an indication of how he could look immediately west and south for his intellectual training, as well as north and east.

Fraser and the Firthlands

'Arms of the sea' are vital to Scotland's geography. In the north-eastern part of the mainland, the foremost of these 'limbs' is the Moray Firth, which can, somewhat contentiously, be defined to comprise the widest of the country's saltwater inlets, linking Fraserburgh in the south-east,

Figure 1.2 The parish of Kirkhill, viewed from Redcastle

Beauly in its south-west, Wick to its north and, it might be argued, all points in between. This makes for a roughly indented triangle of sea and coast, one that provides a vital backdrop to the history of the far north in many instances and periods.[25] In its inner part, geology, the tide and human engineering have interacted to bequeath a topographically unique section of channels and peninsulas linking east Sutherland to coastal Moray. Specifically, this 'firthlands' space involves one tidal inlet, Loch Fleet, and three other bodies of seawater – the Dornoch Firth, the Cromarty Firth and the Inner Moray Firth (incorporating the Inverness, Kessock and Beauly Firths) – each compressed and crinkled almost together.[26] This has created winding, looping shores, 'like arrows in a gigantic herringbone pattern' in the words of Isaac Land, coastal settlements and communities encouraged, until very recently, and in all but the worst weather, towards trans-firth activity.[27]

In the days before modern roads and bridges, Inverness was not quite as dominant in uniting this 'amphibious' or 'ruro-maritime' environment as it is today.[28] Seals, salmon and stranded whales were all prized, if contested, commodities in the locale, with ferries interconnecting communities, for social and economic reasons, until the early 1800s. This could be dangerous. Fraser records the capsizing of an overloaded ferry off Dingwall in February 1668, following which, although 'those uppon the shoare could not reach to recover them', by 'casting out their plaids, others long poles' they pulled some of the passengers on to dry land. Fraser's own brother-in-law, William Monro, had been 'uppon the Bank, and rescued 6 persones by casting out roapes and plaids wʰ they laid hold on and were draggd ashoare'.[29] Phopachy and Kirkhill were in no sense outposts in the area, being pivotal to an ecological, social and commercial space spanning the 'firthlands', and for which a coastal history approach proves to be most revealing.[30]

This had a scholarly aspect too. The Lovat Frasers inhabited a spot – this including but not limited to Kirkhill parish – known as The Aird, from where, on the other side of steadily inclining hillsides south and inland, lay a steep drop to the freshwater highway provided by Loch Ness. However, their family friendships and rivalries caused them to look very much in the other direction, to the saltwater of the firthlands and the North Sea beyond.[31] Indeed, James Fraser regarded Hugh Fraser, 8th Lord Lovat, as being at the centre of a veritable network, which, by his definition, extended beyond family and kin to a wider orbit of 'friends and neighbours' stretching out northwards and eastwards, evidenced by way of the 'progresses' that Lovat made around the firthlands space.[32] Scholarly interaction was important here, not the least of

Figure 1.3 Loch Ness and the Moray Firth, looking north-east from Meall Fuar-mhonaidh

Figure 1.4 Kirkhill and the Beauly Firth, from The Aird

Figure 1.5 The Beauly Firth and the Black Isle, from Abriachan

it history-writing, as will be shown in Chapter Six. Certainly, the Lovat Frasers participated in a firth-facing exchange of arguments, ideas, manuscripts and books along with other intellectually prominent local families such as the Urquharts, MacKenzies and Gordon earls of Sutherland.

Inverness Grammar School: Secondary Education in the Seventeenth-century Highlands

Phopachy and Kirkhill provided Fraser with the perspectives he needed to glimpse wider educational and intellectual horizons. But he did not have to take a ferry to get to grammar school or find cosmopolitan figures to meet and learn from. His overland pathways to the east from Phopachy soon led him to a nearby urban centre too: Inverness. While the burgh had a majority Gaelic-speaking population, tax contributions, hearth and poll tax records indicate it to be markedly Lowland in flavour in terms of its seventeenth-century governance. In his later years, it was one of the top ten urban centres in the country, with an estimated population of 2,500–3,000.[33] But Inverness shared, with other Scottish burghs, the horrors of the mid-century, when the Frasers' loyalties became divided. When considering Fraser's education in that context, it is vital to remind ourselves that his comments that survive are not contemporary, immediate reflections but the writings of a man of the 1660s and 1670s establishment. He informs us that his parents followed Lord Lovat, who had a town house there, in backing the challenge to Charles I's attempted political and religious impositions that was the National Covenant of 1638. The next twenty-two years comprised a period of civil war and discord, which began by pitting covenanters against royalists and grew more complex from there. Writing from the more settled atmosphere of the 1660s, Fraser's assessment of the pro-covenanting element to the burgh in the first part of the wars is strikingly mild.[34] He does not seek to denounce the early subscribers of the covenant, and, indeed, his depiction of the Lovat Frasers resisting the 'yellow banner of Colkitto [Coll Ciotach]' of Clan Donald, so proudly and 'stoutly' that 'eighty-seven widows were left', shows his partisan willingness, from a Restoration perspective, to proclaim his and their early support for that cause, and to criticise the 1644–5 royalist campaign led by the Marquis of Montrose and Alasdair MacColla.[35] However, Fraser's recollections show him keen also to convey that he experienced remorse as regards the aggression meted out by all sides in those years, referring elsewhere to that 'dissloyall, rebellious covenent which we fought for', and decrying the 'great trouble and cost' that was involved in the covenanting regime's construction of the burgh's defences, including a wall, trench, ramparts and four 'ports' or gateways.

As regards the later 1640s, and the Cromwellian period that would ensue from the early 1650s until 1660, his, and the burgh's, political allegiances became even more complicated, and this affected his Inverness schooling considerably.[36] Although no evidence has been uncovered of how he or his family financed grammar school, as a child he boarded in the burgh, at times, with schoolmaster John Robertson, who he compared to a 'pope', presumably with irony and due to his assumed authority and standing. Little architectural detail of the 'grammar scule of Innernes' at this point survives, although one assumes it, like the 'auld scule' which predated the Reformation, stood at the north end of Church Street ('Kirkget') until 1668, when Dunbar's Hospital was built further up the road, it becoming the location for the school soon after.[37] As early as 1650, nonetheless, Fraser recalled a 'slavish calm' to have descended upon the burgh, unsurprising in the wake of the regicide of Charles I of 1649, and revealing perhaps of a longer-term change in fortunes for him and family that affected his final days at school.

Fraser would leave Inverness, and the region, for university study from 1651. Thus, we might expect him to recall his engagement with the Highland capital's occupiers in the ensuing years as having been reluctant and cursory, as is, indeed, suggested by him mentioning only one fatal incident caused by the presence of Cromwell's garrison.[38] Yet, as with the garrisons in Leith, Perth and Ayr, the Inverness citadel, once fully functioning, had a 'profound effect on the surrounding communities'.[39] Shunning conformity and at some risk, Fraser goes out of his way in his writings to highlight his familiarity with, and even admiration for, the Cromwellian governor of the burgh, Colonel Thomas Fitch's, 1,000-strong 'regiment' and their learning. He recalls vividly his presence at the 'first draught cut in that ground' of their enclave on the 'Schipland', what is now the Longman industrial estate. He highlights to his readers how the garrison's hospital, drawbridge (the 'blew Bridge'), granary, ale houses and taverns, its 'appothecary shop with drugs', its 'chyrurgion [surgeon]' and 'phisitian', and the cheap English cloth and claret wine the garrison members brought to the market impressed him. As he expresses it, the Cromwellians 'not onely civilised but enriched this place'.[40] They did eventually leave, of course, although, for Fraser, with that departure passed the 'glory of the world'. As he expressed it, it was:

> sad to see and heare sighs and teares, pale faces and embraces, at their parting farewell from that town. And no wonder; they had peace and plenty for

10 yeares in it. They made that place happy, and it made them so . . . I saw it founded, I saw it flourish, I saw it in its glory, grandeur and renoun, and now in its ruins. *Sic transit gloria mundi.*[41]

Although the Cromwellian 'yoke' was unfastened in the 1660s and Inverness fully engaged with crown-level educational policy once more, the burgh remained far from idyllic for a scholar, if we believe Fraser's account. He recorded local clans preparing to 'sally out, sorn uppon, and pillage their nighboures, for the Highlanders are now brakeing out to prey uppon the Low Countries [Lowlands] in Robberies and Depredations everywhere'.[42] There were incidents such as the 'battle of the Cheeses' or 'Cabog day', in 1668, when a Finlay Dow handled a cheese at the Castle Hill mercat, only for it to slip out of his hands and then roll down the slope into the River Ness. The seller objected and a fracas escalated, leading to at least two MacDonnells being shot dead, two other fatalities, and severe damage to the burgh.[43] The implication from Fraser's account of these events is that Inverness's governance barely recovered at all with the expiry of the garrison.

In numerous other instances, however, he expresses horror about the Cromwellian period and seeks to promote the time that followed as a great improvement. Conforming to a more typical episcopalian viewpoint, Fraser vents his spleen elsewhere on the English garrison having been 'a sacrilegious structure', its stone foundations having been gathered from the leading medieval religious houses of the locality.[44] At another point he reports himself delighted to have seen the English soldiers leave, contradicting many of his other statements on it entirely.[45] A key figure for this posture of loathing was Colonel Fitch, who Fraser had known in 'grandure and State' in Inverness but who, by the final months of the interregnum in early 1660, could be found in the darker recesses of London, where Fraser saw him 'in a Privat lane, most dejected; all alone', the prospect of the Restoration having 'brought such snakes to Skulc up and down the City obscurely and in disguise'.[46] Suggestive again of royalist nostalgia, Fraser also recorded, in later years, the joy he felt at the return of horseracing to the route around Inverness's Tomnahurich Hill two years later, in 1662, after a twenty-four-year gap.[47] This was an event which he reported to have suffered under military and Cromwellian rule but which had the potential to match similar ones in Lowland towns, according to Fraser. Clearly, horse breeding was taking place locally in the seventeenth century, the Lovat Frasers involved in it, and this led not just to local entertainment, but to new overseas engagements and colonial entanglements.[48] Dutch

Figure 1.6 The port of Inverness today

ships stopped off on at least two occasions in Inverness en route to their colony of Suriname in the 1680s to take horses on board: they picked up fifty-six horses in the Highland capital on a Rotterdam-registered ship in August 1683 and a further thirty-nine on a Flushing-registered vessel in March 1684.[49] At this stage, it is impossible to confirm whether these Highland horses arrived as a direct exchange for Surinamese sugar or other products, but they do suggest the cultural and economic value of the equine to local families both before and after the civil wars, and also how locally sourced commodities could link them with colonial markets and the enslavement of African and indigenous American populations. We do not learn much from the equine about Restoration-period education in Inverness, but we do see a leading, if rarely acknowledged, example of the inter-imperial nature of life for James Fraser and his fellow scholars in Inverness, an aspect that was apparent from his days at the grammar school.[50]

King's College, Aberdeen: Fraser and the Early Modern Scottish University

One wonders if his schooling and young adulthood in the 1640s and early 1650s led to Fraser growing up with a perception of being a Highlander? Today, Inverness is often viewed as linking a 'Highland' hinterland to the west, north and south, with a 'Lowland' world largely to the east, and the Lovat Frasers would surely have recognised this notion of being a 'bridge' between two societies. Without doubt, there are senses in which the young and adolescent James Fraser looked upland within the Highlands for his scholarly references, not just to The Aird, but well beyond. Later in life, as a Gaelic native speaker, ministering over a congregation speaking 'our Irish language' (as he referred to Scots Gaelic when writing about it for a Scots and English-speaking audience) Fraser engaged strongly, socially and intellectually, with the Gàidhealtachd. He talked, ministered and, we assume, prayed, in Gaelic for much of his life. Not only that, but he wrote of the Frasers as a 'clan', recorded, with approval, customs like the 'Doch an Dorris' (*Deoch-an-Doris*), the 'door drink on leaving', was fundamental to the establishing of the reputation of Highland bagpipe music, thus to the growth of piobaireachd ('pibroch'), and appraised much else that came from the cultural, linguistic, military and medical life of Gaeldom in positive terms.[51] As will be shown in Chapter Three, he also peppered his surviving English-language writing with Gaelic words.[52] Indeed, in backing the Gaelic language, and choosing to reject the 'official antipathy' to it that was encapsulated in the Statutes of Iona, and the educational acts referred to, his approach, throughout his life, stands in contrast to that of his firthland neighbour Robert Gordon, as was suggested at the outset of the chapter.[53]

However, once again there are paradoxes. As regards certain other elements of Highland life, Fraser's opinions, at least as filtered through his English-language manuscripts, could be highly critical, even scathing. While it is worth recalling that these texts were intended for a non-Gaelic-speaking audience, they are much less positive towards aspects of the culture of his region than his self-presentation as a scholar of the language might lead us to expect. He gives an indication of this tension as a formative influence on his scholarly development when discussing his own, and his family's, historical tie to the area. Fraser is at pains to indicate how the family, after first arriving from France, 'where we had our first origin', tried to maintain their separateness, while also attempting to 'polish and reform' the local population in The Aird.[54] Not only that, but Fraser presumably built on his educational experience at grammar school in Inverness in being dismissive and even insulting about some features of Highland life. Scattered through his surviving works in English, one finds references to the stereotypical 'robber', 'sorner', 'thief', 'villain', 'vagabound', 'ruffian', 'bruit', 'varlet', even the 'vile, flagitious, proflagat' or 'vile Scithian outlaw' that Lowland literature propagated as typifying the 'wild Highland Irish'. Despite his integration in local life, then, at numerous points in his surviving texts Fraser fashions himself as being different, defining some of his close neighbours to his immediate west and south as 'rude Highlanders', 'unquiet and turbulent men', even, on one occasion when referring to historical issues, as having been, potentially, 'cannibals', reinforcing clichés usually associated with Lowland governance which modern readers will, quite reasonably, find highly offensive. It may have been that Fraser sought to exaggerate consciously, for effect, by using such words. Would he have been so caustic when writing in Gaelic? Whatever the answer to that question, and despite being a Gaelic speaker who prided himself on being part of that society, in many ways, it is extraordinary for a modern reader to see him claim an especial potential for 'barbarity and inhumanity' in Gaeldom, and position this as a threat to the Lovat Frasers' own liminal, 'plain and champion countries'.[55]

In this tense interplay between two worlds, we get a sense not only of the non-Highland nature of Fraser's readership for his English-language works, the only ones of his that survive, but of the expression of a hybrid, even conflicted, identity that his urban grammar schooling probably encouraged. It gives further strength to the argument already indicated, that Fraser grew up with a North Sea orientation, learning to travel and communicate almost as much within the Lowlands as within the Highlands, and experiencing a mix of both worlds via the multi-lingual synod of Moray. The firthlands setting nudged him towards looking eastwards and, eventually, outwith the Gaelic world. Beyond Inverness in that direction lay the bulk of his Moray diocese where Fraser, in 1669, would find a wife: Margaret Symmer, a minister's daughter from Duffus, towards the coast from Elgin.[56] Furth of that were his Fraser cousins at Philorth (founders of the settlement of Fraserburgh). Ever more distant, geographically, but a more immediate influence on his teenage years was what became, in 1651, his university of study: King's College, Aberdeen.[57]

Along with St Andrews, King's College was the Lovat Frasers' favoured seat of higher education.[58] James Fraser arrived there for the start of his first session, aged sixteen, in October 1651, a decade after King's had been united, temporarily, with its younger Aberdeen neighbour, Marischal College. Never fully supported by the King's staff, this merger failed to extinguish fires of dissent among Aberdeen's academic community. Flames were kindled further with the purging of 'malignants' (that is, royalists) and through additional coercion (including removal of the offices of chancellor and rector) by the republican regime. A most obvious expression of this enforced conformity at King's occurred in 1652, when a new principal was appointed: John Row, a covenanter with a developing 'Independent' affiliation, this meaning he was broadly accepting of Cromwellian rule and wished for toleration for non-conformists but with little compromise towards the then-exiled Stuart court. Row's appointment marked a major change, given that he replaced the more conservative, episcopalian, former 'Aberdeen doctor' William Guild, who had managed to stay in place as principal since 1640.

This turbulence aside, in the course of his four years of studies in Old Aberdeen, James Fraser experienced a degree of continuity in terms of the syllabus, studying Greek, logic, rhetoric, arithmetic, ethics, physics, geometry, astronomy and geography, from a rather traditional and, to modern readers, astonishingly strict approach. The 'hebdomadar', the staff member who was responsible for enforcing discipline, prohibited the speaking of Gaelic, Scots or English among his teenage students, thus forcing Fraser to rely on Latin or Greek; it was a demanding stipulation, perhaps especially debilitating for a Highland student, given the need, fought for hard by sections of the kirk under the Covenanting regime, to train a ministry that was conversant in the languages of their parishes.[59] Row also banned quarrelling and the carrying of weapons, and curtailed anything more than limited time away from the buildings to play sport on the links or visit the town. Time would have rarely allowed Fraser such leisure, in any case, since studies at King's began at 5am and ended at 9pm.[60] Nevertheless, even this strict regime did not prevent Fraser from occasionally looking up from his books to the skies above the lower Don, witnessing events such as a 'dreedfull eclipse' one March day, what would become known as 'Black Moonday' when 'the Starrs being visible, Birds frighted and fluttering, so astonishing that such as were surprised with it on the rode or by sea thought that it was the day of Judgement'.[61] Furthermore, he remained acutely aware of the equally apocalyptic atmosphere around the ongoing disagreement between the two universities in the city, noting Robert Ferguson ('Ferguson the Plotter') leading twelve disaffected students to Marischal College with him. Fraser described this same Ferguson, on seeing him later in London, as 'a pregmattick head, who kendled [kindled] a fire in our University at Aberdeen anno 1654'.[62] To conclude, while Fraser's route through the disturbances of the early 1650s is not always easy to trace, he gives the appearance, distorted or not, of being strengthened, if anything, by the adversities. Whatever the personal trauma experienced, he survived the tumult and tension. As 'Mr Jacobus Fraserius, Moraviensis' (Moray being 'Moravia' in Latin) he graduated as master of arts from Aberdeen in 1655, an occasion that led to him returning westwards as far as Inverness for what, it seems, would be two rather obscure years back in the firthlands, years in which Cromwell's control of the burgh was at its firmest.[63]

FRASER'S NORTH SEA HORIZONS: SCOTLAND, BRITAIN AND EUROPE

As Fraser had grown up, he had, as has been shown, established educational connections extending ever outwards from Kirkhill, to some degree, further west and south into the Highlands, but much more so northwards across the firthlands and, to an even greater extent than that, eastwards as far as Aberdeen. Beyond all of this lay the less familiar expanses of the rest of Scotland, the 'British Isles' and a wider North Sea world, all places which contributed extra concentric layers to his identity. In terms of Scotland, as a whole, the pages of his later history-writing abound with references to national figures like Aidan, MacBeth, Margaret, Wallace, Bruce and Mary, Queen of Scots, who he had clearly learned about, enjoyed and taken courage from, when still of a young age. Yet the divisions of the civil war years would lead him later to mourn 'O Scotland wert thou mad' and implore his fellow Scots to 'spare thy own bloud, thy brothers, thy bone and flesh, with pain born, with expense nurtured, must fall in a moment, and by whom? One son of Adam by another, one Scots man by another!'[64] While Scottishness was something to exclaim a mix of pride and vexation about, then, 'Britain' and 'Britishness' were more abstract. Undoubtedly, the Stuart multiple kingdom could take on significance for him in a geo-political sense, as shown when reflecting as an adult on the royalist campaigns of his childhood, regarding which he remarked that 'all Brittain' was 'now in a confusion' due to 'intestin, civil, uncivil broiles', it being, moreover, 'not a condition but sanction of nature' to 'spare the bloud of citizens, connatural, colateral, conational with our selves', suggesting that there should have been an obligation, in the wars, to seek peaceful solutions to the carnage evident across the islands. The 'British Dominions'[65] was the entity he described as subject to the Act of Oblivion of 1660, while, in 1670, 'Britain' was 'at peace with all the world; our sea safe for navigation, free of pirates'.[66] But this nascent, Protestant 'British' perspective does not account for his equally striking engagement with Ireland, as will be shown, and provides only the beginning in seeking to comprehend Fraser's supranational, transnational focus on the world that lay beyond the north of Scotland.[67] Fundamentally, and according to his own reflections, from 1657, Fraser had come to the conclusion that Great Britain comprised 'an Island . . . divided from parts of the world' and so, as islanders, its people were 'lost and oft in need of forrein travels'. According to his own later words, this was the impulse, in part a scholarly one, which, that year, prompted him, aged twenty-three, to seek both a passport and a testimonial from the Inverness magistrates and the acting colonel and secretary of the town's garrison, so he could set out 'to view this universe'. It was granted without any apparent obstacle and enabled the first move in a journey that would take this young Highlander, a European from its north-western edge, to the 'very naval [navel] centre' of Christendom, and beyond, to the frontier with the Ottoman Empire.[68]

Across two firths to the north, Robert Gordon had asked his nephew to 'civilise' the Gaels of Sutherland, and to ensure, in doing so, that his 'chief scooles for learning be at Dornoch'. His aim had been to encourage local students, on one hand, to read books but, on the other, prevent them from receiving education in their first language.[69] Fraser's experience of, and philosophical approach to, developing the intellect was different, and never led to him abandoning Gaelic, it being essential to his everyday, at times multilingual communication. He did not need to traverse the North Sea to become engaged in European intellectual life and entangled in empire: scholarly routes had nudged the elite of his clan eastwards to Inverness, Aberdeen and beyond, even to retrace their continental origins, for many generations before him. His own intellectual openness thus predated the pivotal year of 1657. Fraser's three-year journey through Europe would, nevertheless, have a galvanising influence on his subsequent scholarship and help shape his identity as a scholar. That identity was one which, at times, was brutally critical of aspects of Gaelic culture. But it was also rooted in his parish and took for granted that the language spoken by him and its majority as their first tongue was an intrinsic part of Highland, Scottish, 'Three Kingdoms' and European culture.

NOTES

1. William Fraser, ed., *The Sutherland Book*, 3 vols (Edinburgh, 1892), II, p. 359.
2. Thomas Brochard, 'Intellectual and practical education and its patronage in the northern Highlands in the century after the Reformation', *Northern Scotland*, 12(2) (2021), pp. 174–195.
3. Donald Withrington, 'Education in the seventeenth century Highlands', in Loraine MacLean, ed., *The Seventeenth Century in the Highlands* (Inverness, 1986), pp. 60–9; Jamie Kelly, 'The Society in Scotland for Propagating Christian Knowledge: education, language & governance in the British state and empire, c.1690–c.1735', PhD thesis, University of Glasgow (2020); Frank D. Bardgett, 'The Reformation in Moray and Mr Robert Pont', *Journal of Scottish Historical Studies*, 39(1) (2019), pp. 1–39; Macinnes, *Clanship*, p. 176; Rab A. Houston, *Scottish Literacy and the Scottish Identity: Illiteracy and Society in Scotland and Northern England, 1600–1800* (Cambridge, 2002), p. 5.
4. Richard Saville, 'Intellectual capital in pre-1707 Scotland', in S. J. Brown and Christopher Whatley, eds, *The Union of 1707: New Dimensions (Scottish Historical Review Supplementary Issue)* (Edinburgh, 2008), pp. 45–60; Janay Nugent and Elizabeth Ewan, eds, *Children and Youth in Premodern Scotland* (Woodbridge, 2015).
5. A. Goeing, G. Parry and M. Feingold, eds, *Early Modern Universities* (Leiden, 2020).
6. These parishes, especially Killearnan, may have been more connected with Kirkhill's than first appears, due to ferry links. See Worthington, 'Ferries in the firthlands: communications, society and culture along a northern Scottish rural coast (c.1600–1809)', *Rural History*, 27(2) (2016), pp. 129–48. A perhaps unexpected comparison for a firth-based approach

to local religious history comes from nineteenth-century New York's sail-ortown, where a decommissioned ferry was used as a 'floating church'. See Johnathan Thayer, 'Merchant seamen, sailortowns, and the philanthropic encounter in New York, 1843–1945', in David Worthington, ed., *The New Coastal History: Cultural and Environmental Perspectives from Scotland and Beyond* (London, 2017), p. 73.

7. Alex Hale, 'Phopachy (Kirkhill parish): intertidal crannog', in Colleen E. Batey and Muriel King, eds, *Discovery and Excavation in Scotland* (Edinburgh, 1994), pp. 35–6; 'Phopachy (Kirkhill parish), intertidal cran-nog', in Colleen E. Batey, ed., *Discovery and Excavation in Scotland* (Edinburgh, 1995), p. 40; 'Part of a Letter Wrote by Mr. James Fraser, Minister of Kirkhil, near Invernes, to Ja. Wallace at Edinburgh, Concerning the Lake Ness, etc.', *Philosophical Transactions of the Royal Society*, 21 (1699), pp. 230–2; Mackay, ed., *Chronicles*, p. 3.

8. Mackay, ed., *Chronicles*, p. 110.

9. James Fraser, *Triennial Travels, containing a succinct and briefe narra-tion of the journay and voyage of Master James Fraser through Scotland, England, all France, part of Spain, and over the Savoyan Alps to Italy [also in the Tyrol, Bavaria, Austria, Bohemia, Germany, Holland, Picardy etc. and back to France, England and Scotland]*, 3 vols, University of Aberdeen, Special Libraries and Archives, MS 2538, II, 'Preface'.

10. 'Wardlaw Manuscript', p. 217.

11. 'Wardlaw Manuscript', p. 344.

12. 'Wardlaw Manuscript', p. 325.

13. Ibid.

14. Ibid., pp. vii–viii, xviii.

15. Hew Scott, ed., *Fasti Ecclesiæ Scoticanæ: The Succession of Ministers in the Church of Scotland from the Reformation* (Edinburgh, 1926), VI, pp. 472–4.

16. Mackay, ed., *Chronicles*, pp. 259, 267, 271; Scott, *Fasti Ecclesiæ Scoticanæ*, VI, pp. 472–4.

17. Mackay, ed., *Chronicles*, p. 259.

18. Kelly, 'The Society in Scotland', pp. 29–30; Withrington, 'Education in the seventeenth century Highlands', p. 65.

19. Mackay, ed., *Chronicles*, p. 125.

20. Brochard, 'Intellectual and practical education'.

21. Kelly, 'The Society in Scotland', pp. 29–33, 119–20; William Mackay, ed., *Records of the Presbyteries of Inverness and Dingwall, 1643–1688* (Edinburgh, 1896).

22. Mackay, ed., *Chronicles*, p. 315.

23. Kelly, 'The Society in Scotland', p. 31.

24. Mackay, ed., *Records of the Presbyteries of Inverness and Dingwall*, p. 80.

25. Its geographical range is usually assumed to include all of a roughly indented triangle of sea and coastal fringe between the mouth of the River

Beauly in the west, a northernmost point of Duncansby Head north of Wick in Caithness and, to the east, Kinnaird Head next to Fraserburgh. For a 'Moray Firth' historiography, see James Miller, *The Gathering Stream: The Story of the Moray Firth* (Edinburgh, 2012); Worthington, 'The settlements of the Beauly-Wick coast and the historiography of the Moray Firth', pp. 139–63; Worthington, 'Ferries in the firthlands'.

26. John R. Baldwin, ed., *Firthlands of Ross and Sutherland* (Edinburgh, 1991); Ian R. M. Mowat, *Easter Ross, 1750–1850* (Edinburgh, 2006); David Alston, *My Little Town of Cromarty* (Edinburgh, 2006); Marinell Ash, *This Noble Harbour: A History of the Cromarty Firth* (Bristol, 1991).

27. For the 'herringbone' interpretation of this geography by Isaac Land, via his excellent 'Coastal History' blog, see: <http://porttowns.port.ac.uk/the-coastal-history-blog-no-50/> (last accessed 21 July 2021).

28. For 'pluriactivity' in relation to coastal Brittany, see Christophe Cérino, Aliette Geistdoerfer, Gérard Le Bouëdec and François Ploux, eds, *Entre terre et mer: sociétés littorales et pluriactivités (XVe–XXe siècle)* (Rennes, 2004); Gérard Le Bouëdec, 'Small ports from the sixteenth to the early twentieth century and the local economy of the French Atlantic coast', *International Journal of Maritime History*, 21(2) (2009), pp. 104, 106. See: <http://porttowns.port.ac.uk/the-coastal-history-blog13/> (accessed 28 February 2021).

29. 'Wardlaw Manuscript', p. 320.

30. Michael Pearson, 'Littoral society: the concept and the problems', *Journal of World History*, 17(4) (2006), pp. 353–73; Isaac Land, 'Tidal waves: the new coastal history', *Journal of Social History*, 40(3) (2007), pp. 731–43; John Gillis, *The Human Shore: Seacoasts in History* (Chicago, 2012). For recent monographs, see David Gange, *The Frayed Atlantic Edge: A Historian's Journey from Shetland to the Channel* (London, 2019); Bathsheba Demuth, *Floating Coast: An Environmental History of the Bering Strait* (New York, 2019); Kara Schlichting, *New York Recentered: Building the Metropolis from the Shore* (Chicago, 2019); Elsa Devienne, *La Ruée vers le sable: une histoire environnementale des plages de Los Angeles au XXe siècle* (Paris, 2020).

31. Richard D. Oram et al., *Historic Tain: Archaeology and Development* (York, 2009), p. 43. The Frasers and their kin around the Beauly Firth tended towards episcopalian practice at this point and continued to seek connections across the firthlands.

32. Mackay, ed., *Chronicles*, pp. 264, 470–2, 481, 490, 492.

33. Kennedy, 'The urban community', pp. 27–9, 31.

34. *Triennial Travels*, I, f. 297; James Miller, *Inverness: A History* (Edinburgh, 2004), p. 74.

35. For the Covenanting sympathies of the Lovat Frasers, see Edward M. Furgol, *A Regimental History of the Covenanting Armies* (Edinburgh,

1990), pp. 60–3, 138–41, 227, 251, 276; Laura A. M. Stewart, *Rethinking the Scottish Revolution: Covenanted Scotland 1637–1651* (Oxford, 2016).

36. *Report by Thomas Tucker upon the Settlement of the Revenues of Excise and Customs in Scotland [1655–56]* (Edinburgh, 1824), p. 36; Allan Kennedy, 'Civility, order and the highlands in Cromwellian Britain', *The Innes Review*, 69(1) (2018), pp. 49–69; Allan Kennedy, 'Cromwell's Highland stronghold: the Sconce of Inverness', *Scottish Local History*, 106 (2020), pp. 3–7; Allan Kennedy, 'Military rule, protectoral government and the Scottish Highlands, c.1654–1660', *Scottish Archives*, 23 (2017–19), pp. 80–102; Miller, *Inverness*, pp. 75–6.

37. Kelly, 'The Society in Scotland', pp. 29–33, 119–20; William Mackay and Herbert Cameron Boyd, eds, *Records of Inverness*, 2 vols (Aberdeen, 1911), I, pp. 112–14.

38. Mackay, ed., *Chronicles*, p. 406; Miller, *Inverness*, p. 85.

39. Kennedy, 'Cromwell's Highland stronghold', p. 3.

40. 'Wardlaw Manuscript', p. 263; Mackay, ed., *Chronicles*, pp. 401, 413–16, 441–2.

41. 'Wardlaw Manuscript', p. 298; Kennedy, 'Urban community', p. 36.

42. 'Wardlaw Manuscript', p. 314.

43. Ibid., p. 322; Miller, *Inverness*, pp. 92–3.

44. Fraser stated that 'Most of their best hewn stone was taken from Chanory [Chanonry], the great Cathedrall and Steeple, the Bishops Castle, to the foundation, rased, the church and Abby of Kinloss and Beuly, the Gray Friars and St. Maries chappell at Inverness, and many more . . .' See Mackay, ed., *Chronicles*, pp. 414–15.

45. Ibid.

46. 'Wardlaw Manuscript', p. 281.

47. Mackay, ed., *Chronicles*, pp. 165, 447–8; Eila Williamson 'Horse-racing in Scotland in the sixteenth and early seventeenth centuries', *Review of Scottish Culture*, 14 (2001–2), pp. 31–42; John Burnett, 'The sites and landscapes of horse racing in Scotland before 1860', *The Sports Historian*, 17(2) (1998), pp. 55–75; Miller, *Inverness*, p. 89. My thanks also to Dave Selkirk for his insights on horse stock in the region.

48. Borland brought forty-one horses from New England to Suriname in 1685. See 7 May 1685, Surinam, Francis Borland to Mr Andrew Russell, RH15/106/567, National Records of Scotland [hereafter NRS]; 31 July 1687, Surinam, Henry Mackintosh 'for Mr Andrew Russell, Marchant at Rotterdame', RH15/106/631; 20 January 1689, Surinam, 'Henry McIntoshe from Surinam to Mr Andrew Russell merchant in Rotterdam', RH15/106/683, f. 1; 25 April 1689, Surinam, The same to the same, f. 2; T. C. Smout, *Scottish Trade on the Eve of Union, 1660–1707* (Edinburgh, 1963), p. 114; John Spreull, *An Accompt Current Betwixt Scotland and England* (Glasgow, 1705), pp. 18–19. For current writing on early modern Scottish horse breeding and its connections with empire, see Charlotte

Carrington-Farmer, 'Trading horses in the eighteenth century: Rhode Island and the Atlantic world', in Kristen Guest and Monica Mattfeld, eds, *Equestrian Cultures: Horses, Human Society, and the Discourse of Modernity* (Chicago, 2019); Miriam Bibby, 'How northern was Pistol? The Galloway nag as self-identity and satire in an age of supra-national horse trading', in Kristen Guest and Monica Mattfeld, eds, *Horse Breeds and Human Society: Purity, Identity and the Making of the Modern Horse* (London, 2019).

49. NRS, Exchequer Records: Customs Books, Second Series, E72/11/7, Exportations (Inverness), 1 Nov. 1682 to 1 Nov. 1683; E72/11/9, Exportations (Inverness), 21 Aug. 1684; David Worthington, 'Sugar, slave-owning, Suriname and the Dutch imperial entanglement of the Scottish Highlands before 1707', *Dutch Crossing: Journal of Low Countries Studies*, 44(1) (2019), pp. 3–20.

50. Kirsten Sandrock, *Scottish Colonial Literature: Writing the Atlantic, 1603–1707* (Edinburgh, 2021).

51. Mackay, ed., *Chronicles*, pp. 36, 38, 84, 124.

52. Roderick D. Cannon, 'Who got a kiss of the King's hand? The growth of a tradition', in James Porter, ed., *Defining Strains: The Musical Life of Scots in the Seventeenth Century* (Bern, 2007), pp. 197–226.

53. Macinnes, *Clanship*, pp. 76–7.

54. Mackay, ed., *Chronicles*, p. 29.

55. Ibid., pp. 13–14, 84, 88, 99–100, 230, 457, 486–7.

56. Mackay, ed., *Chronicles*, p. 484.

57. David Worthington, 'A northern Scottish maritime region: the Moray Firth in the seventeenth century', *International Journal of Maritime History*, 23(2) (2011), p. 206.

58. Mackay, ed., *Chronicles*, pp. 192, 242, 260, 350.

59. Salvatore Cipriano, '"Students who have the Irish tongue": the Gaidhealtachd, education, and state formation in Covenanted Scotland, 1638–1651', *Journal of British Studies*, 60(1) (2021), pp. 66–87; David Ditchburn, 'Educating the elite: Aberdeen and its universities', in E. Patricia Dennison, David Ditchburn and Michael Lynch, eds, *Aberdeen Before 1800: A New History* (East Linton, 2002), pp. 327–46; Jennifer J. Carter and Colin A. MacLaren, *Crown and Gown – 1495–1995: An Illustrated History of the University of Aberdeen* (Aberdeen, 1994); Cosmo Innes, ed., *Fasti Aberdonenses: Selections from the Records of the University and King's College of Aberdeen, 1494–1854* (Aberdeen, 1854); P. J. Anderson, ed., *Roll of Alumni in Arts of the University and King's College of Aberdeen 1596–1860* (Aberdeen, 1900).

60. Carter and MacLaren, *Crown and Gown*, pp. 33, 37.

61. 'Wardlaw Manuscript', p. 254.

62. Ibid., p. 428.

63. P. J. Anderson, ed., *Officers and Graduates of University and King's College, Aberdeen, 1495–1860* (Aberdeen, 1926), p. 193.

64. Mackay, ed., *Chronicles*, p. 306.

65. Ibid., p. 306.

66. Ibid., p. 485. During his travels too, Fraser had expressed an 'aversion to the present state of Britain under a rebellious usurpation' and remarked more generally on 'the whole island of Britain' being 'divided into several Clans and Nations'. See *Triennial Travels*, I, ff. 1–3.

67. For Ireland, see 'Wardlaw Manuscript', pp. 183, 223, 236, 256. Fraser's 'Providential Passages' also indicates how his range of interests straddled both 'foreign and domestick'. See *Divina Providentia*.

68. *Triennial Travels*, II, ff. 48–52.

69. Robert Gordon to 'his nephew and heir to the earldom of Sutherland', c.1620, in Fraser, ed., *The Sutherland Book*, II, p. 359.

2

The Traveller:
Fraser's 'Grand Tour' in Early Modern Europe

'at length I stept out to view the universe'

INTRODUCTION

IN JUNE 1657, JAMES FRASER set off on an adventure of a unique type for a Highlander in the early modern period. According to his own account, his travels between then and early 1660 took him, by horseback, boat and mostly foot, across swathes of southern, central and western Europe. Fraser's initial route would introduce him to London, carry him across the English Channel to Dieppe, and on to Marseille. Diverted by pirates to north-east Spain, he would venture east via Corsica and then Genoa, choosing to extend his stay in Italy by spending nearly a year in Rome, besides taking in many of the peninsula's other major cities. From Venice, Fraser would venture through Alpine passes, heading eastwards through Bavaria, Austria and north-western Hungary, then making an abrupt westward turn into Bohemia, Germany and the Low Countries, on to northern France, London and, eventually, back home to the Highlands of Scotland.

This maverick journey changed his life and is captured in fulsome detail in Fraser's own writing, most especially the 'Triennial Travels', the several hundred thousand-word, three-volume memoir he wrote up in the years that followed. Despite it being barely touched on in Mackay's 1905 volume, this rich source is now achieving recognition from modern scholars, within Highland, Scottish, British and European contexts.[1] While exhaustive coverage of it as travel writing is a project which is beyond the aims of this book, there are recurring features in it which this chapter and the next will show to be vital in affording a reappraisal of aspects of pre-Culloden Highland society. The first section will consider the account against the background of the family, regional, national and transnational networks in which Fraser took part, revealing new angles on the Scottish, British and northern European, Protestant approach to tourism in the period. However, since his journey is uncorroborated in any other known contemporary records besides those he authored himself, it is vital to reflect on the possibility of conscious concealment of emotional experience, even fraudulence, within it, and to seek to shine a light on both his deeper motivations and intended audience. The second part of the chapter will thus commence with a consideration of references to one specific theme, sport and recreation, in the account, as a way of assessing the degree to which it relies on first-hand evidence or constitutes what we would understand as a rather blatant form of plagiarism. Subsequently, the main chapter body will rely on three case studies of different cities that he wrote about – Dieppe, Prague and Utrecht – this allowing for an examination of Fraser's broader objectives, not in travelling per se, but in writing up and communicating his experiences of the journey in the form of a memoir. This latter section of the chapter will compare the themes he focuses on in those three cities with how he covers them at other points in the account and elsewhere. Indeed, if we are to understand Fraser's autobiographical perspective, as this book claims to, the major themes of the 'Triennial Travels' must be scrutinised as 'life-writing'. Rather than as a stand-alone travel account, the case to be made is that it is best interpreted as a crucial element in Fraser's presentation of his time on this earth, that it fits it into a jigsaw which begins in his early childhood and ends with his passing. In so doing, the chapter follows the model of Alan Stewart in relation to England, and also of scholars like Rosemary Sweet, Mark Williams and Eva Holmberg. Their approach has sought to consider early modern travel memoirs as having 'afterlives', deeper impressions which impacted on the subsequent mental world and memory of their authors.[2] One might add that these impressions did not come out of the blue for Fraser and that his early life had already prepared him for its more cosmopolitan, multicultural elements. The chapter will not isolate or exceptionalise this rich source, then, but integrate it within Fraser's surviving body of written work, leaving a comprehensive scholarly edition of the text as a crucial follow-up project.

THE FRASERS AND TRAVEL IN EARLY MODERN EUROPE

Fraser's other extant manuscripts all have relevance here since each of them mixes the local with the international and draws, to varying degrees, on his travels. For example, the quotation below comes from

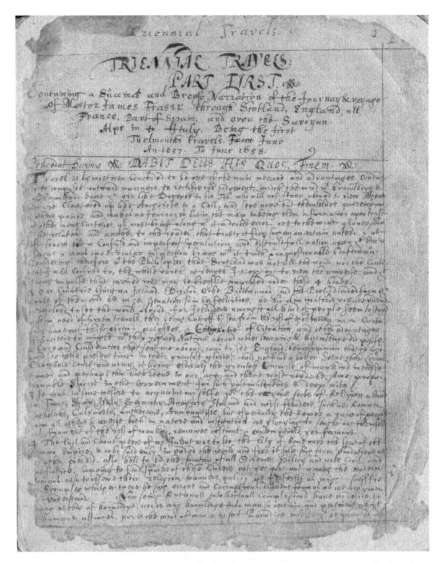

Figure 2.1 Title page of the *Triennial Travels*, first volume, University of Aberdeen, Special Libraries and Archives, MS 2538

the 'Wardlaw Manuscript', and refers to the long evenings of January and February of 1672, when:

> I read over to him my own Trienniall traveles abroad, in 3 tombes [tomes]; and often would he passionaely expresse himselfe, I wish God I had travelled w^t yow, Jacob [James], O, that I had been your fellow traveller . . .[3]

Figure 2.2 Extract from the *Triennial Travels*, third volume

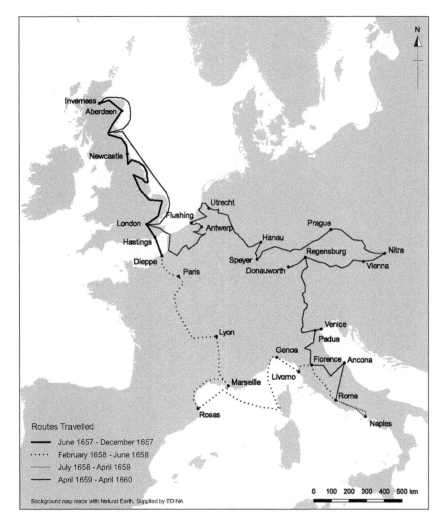

Map 2.1 Fraser's route through Europe

The enthusiastic listener referred to was the well-travelled, if ailing clan chief or MacShimi, Hugh Fraser, 8th Lord Lovat. Fraser's recital of the 'Triennial Travels' to him that winter signals both that the bulk of it was written up within a decade of his return to the Highlands (before the 'Wardlaw Manuscript') and that one element of the intended audience for it was his own kith and kin. Indeed, Fraser tells us that Lovat took courage, while on his deathbed, in recounting how 'travels abroad had polisht me [Lovat], prevented my numerous inconveniencies, yet had made me a man, a wholsom man, a long lived man'. In reading to him from his newly drafted memoir, Fraser hoped to augment that sense of pride and test out his own writing on a sympathetic and informed local and familial expert.[4]

Travelling in continental Europe was not unusual among the Lovat Fraser elite. It was something James Fraser had seen other relatives besides his chief do, often for the purpose of either military service, trade or scholarship. One of them was Colonel Hugh Fraser (d.1649), a veteran of Swedish service in the central European theatre during the Thirty Years' War, who, when James was in his mid-teens, returned home to continue his military career, firstly, as a covenanter, then, from 1648, as a supporter of the 'Engagement'.[5] There was also William Fraser of Phopachy, who 'went abroad with Captain James Fraser, my Lord Lovat sonne, anno 1656, in the quality of an ensign in the Lord Cranston's regiment, for the service of Carolus Gustavus, King of Sweden'.[6] Other early to mid-seventeenth-century Frasers who James claims went overseas included 'Andrew Frasers 2. sone Andrew, his 3. sone Doncan, his 4. sone William, all went abroad', an Alexander Fraser from Phopachy who 'traveled over to France, and died abroad', and Hugh Fraser, 'a sea captain in France, never married, never returnd home'. Perhaps most remarkable, he tells his readers that 'James Fraser of Phopachies 6. sone, John, was a Dutch captain, and died in Arlena in East Indies', Fraser claiming to be in possession of a 1644 letter sent home by him from there.[7] A more distant relative, Kincardineshire-born Alexander Fraizer (1607?–81), studied medicine at Montpellier in the 1630s before returning as far as England, although he was on the continent once more by 1657. In 1651, a 'Iakub Fresser' (James Fraser) paid, in the city of Lviv (today in Ukraine), a subsidy imposed on the Scots and English merchants in Poland–Lithuania.[8] In short, there were numerous Fraser clan members living elsewhere in Europe and beyond in the 1650s, for various reasons and with varying degrees of permanence, of whom James was aware before leaving home. Indeed, there turned out to be even more numerous kinfolk whose hospitality and guidance, while he was en route, would influence and, in most cases, ease his itinerary.

CONTEXTS, MOTIVATIONS AND INTENDED AUDIENCES FOR FRASER'S TRAVEL MEMOIRS AND LIFE-WRITING

This regional–transnational network of Frasers was not unique in mid-seventeenth-century Scotland. One could highlight similar examples from other families, which would illustrate how ordinary it was to connect with dispersed kin groups, and, for some, even engage in an early form of 'roots tourism', in order to experience the lands their relatives had earlier fought, traded, studied or settled in, and bring the rewards of that back home.[9] In terms of other Scottish, 'British Isles' and European contexts that must be considered, these can position Fraser even more fully in terms of the society whence he came. Fraser's wide-ranging linguistic coverage is an element that is more unusual, even at an international level, and is explored in the next chapter. Moreover, his social background, as a relatively poor 'ancestral tourist' – not a soldier, diplomat, political exile, merchant, student or aristocrat – is another aspect that makes his account stand out to any historian of the period.[10] Not only that but, as regards regional, Scottish or English parallels, it is a memoir that is far more detailed than the cursory sketches of tours abroad left by contemporaries from the region like Sir Robert Gordon or Martin Martin. The account compares slightly more easily with the exceptional Lowland Scottish narratives of William Lithgow and Patrick Gordon, in their geographical and thematic range, albeit Lithgow had his printed while Gordon's intended readership was probably smaller than Fraser's. There are also some synergies with the contemporary records of travel left by, for example, John Lauder of Fountainhall, or those of Gilbert Burnet or the Clerks of Penicuik, which cover the arts and intellectual life.[11] But it is not until into the eighteenth century that one sees other Scottish accounts of European travel that are of similar scope and style to Fraser's. Might we find analogous works emanating from England, Wales or Ireland, then? To consider contemporary English accounts first, Fraser's presentation of his travels sits somewhere between John Taylor's 'penniless pilgrimage' and John Evelyn's writings as a connoisseur, although neither followed his specific route. A closer and, in many ways, unwelcome parallel is the work of the antisemitic Welsh royalist, clergyman's son and linguist, James Howell (1594?–1666). As Daniel Jütte has argued, while there was an 'overall increase in travel and mobility during the early modern period', this did not lead to travel being 'necessarily connected to tolerance or even openness' and, in Fraser's case, while he was not averse to different Christian denominations, he was hardly a peacemaker. Like Howell, he was strikingly narrow-minded at times. Perhaps under the Welshman's influence – a significant one on him in terms of the text, as shall be shown – Fraser reserved a great deal of his religious 'othering' while en route to the Jewish people, a streak of xenophobia of this sort being evident at several points in the 'Triennial Travels'.[12]

There are other contexts, those of the Protestant traveller – whether travelling as himself or in disguise as a Catholic – and, going further, the possibility that Fraser might have had a very specific intended readership, even that he might have ventured as spy, which all have to be considered and contended with too. While he did not know while travelling that he would, after returning home, become minister at Kirkhill, consciously or not, religion and theology are also powerful undertones in Fraser's presentation of his three-year journey. Put another way, his memoirs comprise the reminiscences of a Protestant-educated youth and future minister recalling, and using notes from, a time when he was not a man of the cloth, and he probably chose to give them more of a religious emphasis when writing them up because of that. Due to his extended itinerary east of the Rhine, in particular, his memoir benefits from greater comparison with the work of other contemporary, footloose British and Irish Protestants, as well as travel accounts written by travellers from elsewhere in Calvinist and Lutheran northern Europe. There are numerous, fascinating cases in which their itineraries were not limited to Protestant locations but involved movement into Catholic regions and, in some cases, beyond, to Orthodox Europe or the Ottoman Empire. Thus, while there is debate among historians of, for example, the United Provinces, France, northern Germany and Scandinavia, regarding the degree of significance of Rome in the itineraries of travellers from those places of the time, Sweet, Verhoeven and Goldsmith make a key point about it not being the ultimate destination in all such itineraries.[13] This is certainly emphasised in the case of Frenchman Jean Gailhard (fl.1659–1708). While his work was not directed specifically at those training for the clergy, in 1678, Gailhard published the first two volumes of a four-part work, *The Compleat Gentleman, or, Directions for the Education of Youth as to Their Breeding at Home and Travelling Abroad*, in which he asserted that visits to central European cities like Vienna or Prague comprised a valuable part of any young Protestant gentleman's sojourn abroad.[14] Fraser was one of a rather smaller group of British and Irish travellers who stole a march on this, offering us an adventure that involved long periods spent beyond Italy, not just in France and Spain, but also in confessionally diverse Germany, Hungary, Bohemia and the United Provinces.[15] All roads did not lead to Rome for Fraser, who was, evidently, as excited by what he saw in Europe's west, north and east as he was by Roman antiquities.

However, he did spend longer in the 'Eternal City' than anywhere else on his journey, and, while there, and in most other Catholic locations, he depended on a remarkable ability to 'dissimulate' so as to convince others that he was a follower of the 'Old Faith'.[16] John Gallagher has considered that 'disguise was a key practice of early modern travel' and there are cases of other Protestants such as Robert Dallington and William Slingsby resorting to this in order to reach accommodation with their Catholic hosts.[17] Thus, Fraser's decision to adopt Catholic guise can appear to have been calculated, devised as a way of ensuring hospitality, or even as a political act. Another conclusion would be that he made this choice, due to his lack of the social, economic or religious capital required to get by in any other way.[18] Fraser also ventured into the Catholic world, to some extent, out of curiosity, and an assumed universal respect for *Cuid-Oidhche*, a Gaelic cultural feature based on the obligation of a host to provide a night's entertainment for a guest, as a political strategy.

Authorial intentions are always complex. Although the 'Triennial Travels' would give Fraser cultural capital within his family, it was written in a Scots-influenced English and not the Gaelic that was their, and his, first tongue; it was not a text designed solely for them. Similarly, it has been shown that he did not write it only for his Restoration-period clerical networks, due to its strongly secular aspects, and since, where his gaze is on religion, it moves between Catholic, Orthodox and Jewish Europe too. Who was it for, then? Evidently, the 'Triennial Travels' aimed to serve some form of broader readership, to act as a guide for a tranche of readers who were comfortable with English script and spelling. Given that, one would have to ask if it succeeded: no other contemporary is known to have referred to it and it sank into obscurity for over a century after his death. One possibility is that this lack of a wide readership across the Stuart kingdoms was of no great concern to Fraser, even when writing it up in the 1660s and 1670s, due to it serving more personal goals in terms of his career or even his psychological profile. Is it also feasible that he was commissioned by the Cromwellian regime to undertake the journey and record his observations? Expressed another way, a notion that can emerge from even an initial consideration of the account is that the memoir involved not just partial dissimulation, but was a wholesale, elaborate fabrication, based on Fraser's considerable imagination, reading and ambition rather than any actual tourism. It is striking to note how parts of the memoir, especially the introductory section outlining motivations, 'borrow' entirely from Howell's 1642 work, *Instructions for Forreine Travel*.[19] Assuming Fraser's motivation to have been to write up a series of remarkable first-hand experiences on the road as a 'rough guide' for curious budget travellers, the question remains of why he follows Howell so closely and, indeed, how we explain his tarrying in London in the autumn of 1657. Elsewhere in his work he makes abundantly clear his complex, ambivalent feelings towards the Cromwellian regime. Furthermore, he does not ever indicate in his memoirs, as might have been simpler, that he was a royalist agent of any sort.

Therefore, it is important to consider another general feature that might account for the memoir: whether Fraser might have left London as a Cromwellian spy, only to have had to reassess this situation during his travels or on his return homewards. On arrival back in the English capital, in December 1659, he reported that 'few knew us being disguised with wiggs after our Travels abroad', also pointing out, from the relative safety of the 1670s, how it seemed to him in 1660 that 'Great and many have the alterations been which happened here upon the British Stage in these two bygon years.'[20] One wonders if the dynamic final years of the Cromwellian period forced a reappraisal of what Fraser had hoped to achieve by his travels, and persuaded him to fabricate a revised version of his experiences, rather than the one he had envisaged originally. Even if that dramatic conclusion should not be entertained, the narrative presented in the account is one which he edited significantly after 1660. At some stage, Fraser decided his journey required to be presented as written evidence in the form of a memoir, and so it is possible that, eventually, it turned into a more orthodox, clerical interpretation of events, one which he 'spun' ever further in the direction of his Restoration audience as he wrote it up.

'OCULAR INSPECTION': SPORT AND RECREATION IN FRASER'S TRAVEL MEMOIRS

The theme of sport and recreation provides one lens through which Fraser claimed to glimpse most locations he visited, and which can be highlighted as a microcosm of the range, depth and 'authenticity' of his observations. In this way, it is a useful sample of evidence for the historian of the twenty-first century to use in assessing just how politically motivated his journey was, and what the degree of 'dissimulation' was within it. In 2009, Wolfgang Behringer proclaimed the early modern period 'not merely as an independent era in the history of sport, but as the formative period of modern sport'.[21] For every sport that received an encouragement another received a criticism, while, for travellers, not only did they notice differences in local attitudes and approaches to physical recreations, but they often commented, approvingly or disparagingly, on these.[22]

As regards Fraser, it is an area which shows how he could diverge from and exceed otherwise influential accounts such as Howell's in terms of the granularity of his observations. Commencing with England, he announces to his readers that 'no nation excels the English for variety of Divertisements [amusements]' before going on to list upwards of thirty such activities.[23] France was similar. Paris was a city in which he found the citizens to travel 'up and down in their pleasure boats'[24] while the French, more broadly, supported 'varieties of divertisements and recreations and must be still in Exercise, fencing Schooles, Jumping and wrestling schools, an Accademy in every corner, a Dancing School in every house'. Indeed, 'a Frenchman thinks his legs are given him for that use', this focus on the French predilection for dancing finding agreement with numerous other accounts from the period.[25] Elsewhere, he adds: 'The French have their stages continually set up, Balls, Mascarades and Stage Playes is his delight and Bowling greens in every garden' while the 'more serious frequent the Tennis' to the extent that 'the meanest village in France must have the tennis court and it is the common report that Paris hath 400 which I never question this being an exercise fit for French bodies and to which they are infinitly wedded'.[26] Fraser moves on from Paris to note student recreations in Aix-en-Provence, where young scholars 'have the best fields to divert themselves', while, in Marseille, the inhabitants were 'much given to swimming, fencing, dancing, jumping and arching and the *jeu de la palm* / tennis play of which severall Courts are found here, which appear after the restraint of quarantine or the 40 days of Lent'.[27] Northern Italy brought further sporting insights. Regarding the Duke of Florence and his entourage, they were 'ordinarily exercised' in 'rideing', 'vaulting', 'dancing' and 'tilting', with the Duke employing 'the best and most expert horsemen in Italy'.[28] Not only that, but they 'have several schools here of Dancing, Jousting, Wrestling, whither all the Gentry resort.' Venice again gave him considerable impressions of recreation, especially its 'Sea Triumph', a celebration of the Adriatic, which he witnessed on 25 April 1659, it involving 'gondolas and pleasure boats' as well as 'watermen in silk liverie, musicians and trumpeters', albeit, during this particularly bad winter, the gondolas had been 'laid up' since 'all the streets of Venice are frozen upon Ice'.[29] Travelling onwards, he considered the Germans too fond of alcohol and to 'sing and chatter every evening', although noting that, in Nuremberg, 'university persons of all sorts divert themselves either walking or tilting'.[30] In Franconia, 'the free gentlemen have their forests stored with Deer and Roes, foul and Pheasant', while Hungarians, although 'Naturally sloathfull, very like our highland Irish', had the freedom to 'kill foul and venison at pleasure'.[31] There is little on Bohemian sport from the account. Towards completing his circuit, however, in Leiden, he notices 'artificial groves and avenues without for the recreation of the students', while, at Douai, in the Spanish Netherlands, 'the English plantain [?] and walks are the best where the students and citizens divert themselves in the shade with grate pleasure'.[32]

Based on this richness and partiality of evidence, it seems reasonable to conclude that this is neither the account of an armchair observer who has read a brief chorographical or historical survey alone, nor, it would appear, that of a spy or wholly that of a political or religious polemicist. While far from unquestionable in terms of reliability, and awash with subjectivity, Fraser's account of sport and recreation gives an impression of someone who has, at some stage, been an eyewitness, or who is, at least, reciting the testimony of a first-hand, fascinated observer. Moreover, there was a relative scarcity of books in the northern Highlands, no printing press and no public libraries there until 1706, and Fraser lacked the finances to buy the texts he would have needed to write up these sorts of reflections as a synthesis of existing research. Thus, Fraser's accounts of these themes, as with his travels more generally, suggest strongly that what he reported was based on memory, albeit fallible, of what he himself called 'ocular inspection'. They also confirm a degree of consistency in his focus across his 'Triennial Travels' and beyond, in that his other writings show that he was interested in sport and recreation at home too, both in his childhood and as an adult.[33] Fraser chose to be a close observer of cultural life, wherever he was, and his curiosity with such themes is not only apparent throughout the 'Triennial Travels', but essential to his life-writing in the widest sense. It leads to the premise that Fraser did, indeed, travel extensively, and used this as a basis for his memoir, even if there are exaggerations and inaccuracies in it that need to be considered too.

DIEPPE, PRAGUE AND UTRECHT: TRACING THE MAJOR THEMES OF FRASER'S TRAVEL ACCOUNT

If we turn to Fraser's commentary on the major thematic areas covered in his travels, a consideration of his accounts of the cities of Dieppe, Prague and Utrecht, as case studies, can evidence clearly his concentric family, regional, national, transnational and religious networks and tell us something more about his personal motivations.[34] It is possible to separate out seven recurring themes via what he says on these three places, these providing a route towards understanding broader features in how he presents the seventy-plus locations he overnighted in on his route. These seven themes are: modes of transport; travel companions;

arrivals; hosts and accommodation; food and drink; sites and sights; history and local character.

Transport

Fraser was used to travelling by horse, foot and boat, in varying combinations, throughout his life, and must have been fully aware of the pros and cons of each of these means of getting about prior to setting forth on his European adventure. In terms of equine travel, it proved normal and functional for movement through his parish, presbytery or synod.[35] However, as regards his journey abroad, from the moment he saddled up in Inverness on 8 June 1657, he faced challenges. From the everyday issue of finding oats or other feed while on the road, to replacing the 'dead old beast' who, sadly, survived for only nine weeks after he rode out of Newcastle, to the delays and alarm caused by highwaymen between York and Tadcaster, Fraser exploited the ease and speed, but also experienced the discomforts and perils, of travelling this way. Indeed, horseback travel proved to be such a mixed blessing for Fraser while away from the Highlands, that, once he was on the continent, he gave up on it. From there, he tells his readers, he preferred to move onwards on foot instead.

It was in his first residence on the continent, Dieppe, that Fraser made the fateful decision to travel as an assumed Catholic pilgrim. Walking was thereafter necessary, required him to drop all but the most minimal baggage, and was slow and arduous at times, perhaps especially in southern and central Europe, where his routes often became more alpine. There were, nevertheless, advantages. Fraser became accustomed, on an everyday basis, to lingering for longer in places of interest. Moreover, in terms of the locations where he stayed overnight or for several days or more, as a pedestrian, he saw them in detail and at a leisurely pace, taking time to observe them gradually while walking to and in them. In Dieppe, in the winter of 1657–8, he noted how '3 or 4 men may walk in a row' along the city wall, albeit learning first-hand from his wanders that 'when you goe through the street you find a vile fashion of throwing out watter or chamber potts' accompanied by a verbal warning to those below them. In this we have a precursor to the infamous accounts of eighteenth-century Edinburgh residents emptying their waste water from upper storeys and crying 'Gardyloo' (a version of the French 'Prenez garde à l'eau!').[36] As for his summertime period in Prague, in 1659, from his 'ascent pretty steep' to the city via the 'Coach way by road' onwards he was similarly accustomed to navigating the streets by foot, and became familiar with the cityscape through these means. The flatness of Utrecht, early that autumn, was a contrast, where 'the artificial canals run almost through or by every street in this City carrying boats', providing him with inland echoes of Venice.[37]

Longer, more arduous forms of boat travel, similarly, were a requirement at home, in order to get around the firthlands effectively, this once more preparing him well for his European travels. Fraser wrote in detail on six European sea journeys he made, with his coverage of some additional Mediterranean crossings being sketchier. There were no organised shipping companies catering for seaborne travel in the period, with passengers experiencing often long delays at ports, mariners still often relying on celestial, meteorological, topographic and other visual landmarks ('kennings'), and piracy an ever-present risk. All of this led to some unpredictable and often difficult and perilous hours and days at sea. The first of these that Fraser accounted for was what he claimed to have been a forty-hour sail, in December 1657, from Rye in Sussex to the 'brave harbour' of Dieppe in Normandy. This Channel crossing brought together an international gathering of supporters of the Stuarts, there being 'about ten pasingers of us aboard of the ship called *The Roe of Rye*'. The skipper 'drank the Kings good health *vive lay Roy D'Angliter:* Happy may the King of England live . . . and we were all Kings men aboard of the Roe'.[38] But a 'pretty faire' wind became a 'hard gale' as the first day progressed. Fraser had to distract himself with cards and drink, averting seasickness only until evening and what turned into a terrible night. Indeed, the storm was so horrific that he and his fellow passengers feared for their lives until with 'cleare day light we are upon the French Normandy Coast', luckily, 'in a calm'. While Fraser had good meteorological reasons to complain about this tempestuous journey to Dieppe, it was perhaps less frightening than his next major journey across sea, when, in April 1658, he left from Marseille, ostensibly bound for Genoa. On this occasion, 'about 3 o clock in the morning our ship was assaulted by a nimble Pirat' and the passengers began to conclude, again, that they would be 'sent all to feed fishes'.[39] But instead their ship harboured in Roses (Rosas), in the northern part of the Costa Brava, Catalonia, where Fraser was delayed for around a week. The next major sea crossing accounted for by Fraser is his staggered journey, once back on course, across the Ligurian Sea, in the northern Mediterranean, to Savona in Italy. One leg in this network of crossings proved to be equally alarming as the earlier sailings, involving discussing classical texts with a 'noble skipper', and for whom 'the little interval respite that he had betwixt his sick vomiting fits was spent in historie repeating perils of Virgil's navigation'.[40] Unsurprisingly, then, by the time he reached Livorno, Fraser had decided he was 'weari of water voyages', and 'seeing as I was a Pilgrime I would now travel onely by land and see the Countrie'. It is not until his return journey, when sailing from Calais to Hythe, that we receive another major account of a sea crossing, Fraser and his fellow passengers' relief on arrival being so profound that they 'kissed the very earth in gratitude to our good God'. This was followed by a final maritime voyage, his embarkation in the midst of a 'prosperous gale' from Gravesend to Inverness aboard the *Mary* of Dundee. Fraser listed Highland apothecaries and merchants amongst his fellow passengers for what appears to have been a relatively painless journey, at least the second leg from Burntisland.[41]

Travel Companions

Another notable feature of Fraser's Scottish, English and continental adventure is that he almost never travelled alone. As well as this being based on a desire to fend off loneliness, one wonders if it may have been strategic in the sense of helping him smooth administration and obtain passes and permissions. From the outset of his journey, the company he kept influenced his travel choices, even if the degree to which these were planned and not accidental can be overestimated. On his first day's ride, 'Doctor Monro Phisitian to the Regiment and one Ralph Miller Chyrurgion' travelled with him from Inverness to Elgin while 'Henry McKie Chamberlan to My Lord Rothes' picked up the baton from there onwards to Keith. Several days on, a Joseph Hampton accompanied him across the Scottish border into England, while Alexander 'Sandy' Maxwell went with him southwards from Durham towards London. As regards the continental co-travellers, there were three of them, each of whom accompanied him for longer periods, and on foot, as fellow pilgrims. Indeed, there is a section of his account relating to his second sojourn in England, when about to embark on his final sea journey homewards, where he records a fortuitous and remarkable rendezvous with this trio: Henry Jordan, William Wait (Waite) and Godfrey Hartley. All three were Englishmen, and yet of such diverse backgrounds that the account of the reunion stretches credulity. According to Fraser, the serendipitous gathering involved Jordan and Hartley travelling with him by boat from London to Gravesend. There, they met with Wait, with whom he proceeded, or perhaps stumbled, to the 'Checker [Chequers]' and

Crown taverns to drink prior to boarding for his voyage to Scotland. Fraser claims:

> I am now at Gravesend, the dearest hole in England; and I record this Passage for the rarity of it, that my three Cammarads and fellow travelers abroad should, by a happy Providence, run counter and trist together in one place, and no design in it. Henry Jordan, my first fellow traveler through France; Will Wait my Second through Italy to Rome; my 3d and last, the best off all the three, Godfrey Hartlay, w^t whom I travelled a tedious but pleasant Pilgremage from Rome to London, where now I must leave him, and much of my heart with him . . .[42]

Prior to this, these four travellers had never met as a group. Nevertheless, Fraser's account is consistent in terms of the respective legs of the earlier, continental journey that he asks us to believe the three of them had each joined him on individually. Considering Jordan first, Fraser had 'contracted an intimat friendship' with him while he was a 'Prisoner in the Common Gaole' in Dieppe. Concocting a plan for his escape, which centred first on Jordan disguising himself as a woman, it had eventually involved Fraser, who was on familiar terms with the prison guard, smuggling in a rope to the Englishman's cell. From there, it was with Jordan that Fraser had travelled in 'pilgrimage all over France and part of Spain from Normandy to Savoy in three months time'.[43] Fraser had met Wait, in turn, in either Genoa or Lucca and, still in pilgrim's clothing, travelled with him from there to Rome. Whether reflecting Wait's personality or a sense of *la dolce vita*, this is presented as the most hedonistic section of the tour, with Fraser recording the two men sampling the sites, music, dancing, food and drink of each city on their complex route south.[44] Hartley, in turn, 'the best of all three' companions, had accompanied Fraser from Rome through central Europe and westwards back to London. Fraser recounts the most diverse detail about him, including, for example, his short-lived romance with a woman in Regensburg, their mutual encounter with hosts who had 'sinistrous designes upon poor travellers' in rural Moravia, and their first-hand view of Charles II ('Prince Charles' still in English terms) in the Low Countries.[45]

Arrivals

Fraser seems to have had in common with all three of his continental travel companions a wish to venture as freely and spontaneously as possible. However, in order for him to enter new cities or countries and fulfil his complex itinerary, there was administration to see to. The most immediate of these obstacles in Fraser's way was the securing of a pass or testimonial, actually a range of document types, written in Latin, which contemporary Europeans required to enter most states and some specific cities.[46] Fraser leaves records of obtaining passes in Inverness, Aberdeen, Berwick, Rye, 'Albara' [?], Florence and Regensburg, thus not just when crossing national borders but, at times, simply to enter urban environments, due to health, military or other, civic restrictions. In terms of the three cities to be highlighted here, Dieppe was the only one that required him to prepare such a document, a French-issued '*passe-port*' that supplemented, or replaced, the pass to enter France that he had obtained in Rye. A fellow Scot in Dieppe, Strathbogie-born Father James Duncan, confessor in a city convent, intervened to provide the testimonial for Fraser, a document which he transcribes, as with several others, in his account. Both Prague and Utrecht were more straightforward in this respect, the only point Fraser makes being that, in the latter, 'All travellers are permitted to entere this city without strict examination only we laid up our leathers as badges of our pilgrimage and entered with our long coats and staffe.'

Subject to crossing this administrative hurdle, Fraser, a man with few or no savings, occasionally needed coins in his pocket in order to experience the full range of delights or horrors of a new location. Once found or exchanged, money could be precious and thus dangerous for travellers to carry with them in large amounts. In the same period as Fraser, James Howell recounted how:

> I have heard of a French Painter who having got a considerable som of mony changed all into small pistolets of gold, which he swallowed down, The Gards having notice before hand that he carried a quantity of mony about him, and searching narrowly every place, his mouth and his tayle not excepted they threw him twixt fower walls, and administred unto him som pills, and a glister, so that the Gards found all the mony by this means.[47]

Fraser did not have to resort to such drastic measures, most obviously since he did not ever acquire such riches, but also due to his decision to don the outfit of a pilgrim. Indeed, the reason for this was, in part, one assumes, to try to avoid relying on cash. Nevertheless, his dramatic decision in Dieppe did not prevent him requiring it thereafter from time to time, and conceals his fascination for the novel sight of mints and coinage, which he made drawings and rubbings of while in London.[48] A striking account of his occasional fiscal needs and shortcomings occurs towards the end of his peregrination, in the Spanish Netherlands, when a pitying fellow Highlander, John McKenzie of 'Littlefindons

[Little Findon]', gave him some cash to buy a new pair of breeches. One can trace his lack of money in both Dieppe and Utrecht too. In the former, he sold his 'clock, boots, and all that I could not carry with me and got a good rate for them'. In Prague, Fraser had enough money to go to the market, where he bought some 'big mellow peares for two farthings'. In Utrecht, once more he had to ask for the intervention of his host, a suitably named English cobbler, Mr Price. Through Price he obtained 'a contribution for us here among Scotch and English', which one assumes was again material. This consideration of economic capital shows how Fraser sometimes had to turn to his compatriots or 'country-men' for financial assistance, and, indeed, could meet with some success in this, a point which moves this text on to a reflection on more symbolic expressions of status: his choice of hosts.[49]

Hosts and Accommodation

For Fraser, pretending to be a Catholic or having 'brass in pocket' was not always a precondition to a comfortable and free overnight stay. Indeed, his expectations of being provided with lodging and food were influenced profoundly by his Highland background. Fraser paints a picture of having received hospitality from nearly all his continental hosts, no matter where they came from. This even leads to the suggestion of a shared multiculturalism at many points, linking back to earlier encounters with non-Scots in the Lovat Fraser household, in Inverness, and at university. For example, in Padua, Fraser's host was a Mr George Rater, a Dutchman who 'spoke good English and swore he loved an English or Scot better than 20 dutches' and regarding whom 'after two or three long hours good fellowship, he conducted us to his owne house where we fared well'.[50] But Fraser's chosen support network extended beyond his British and Irish 'countrymen' elsewhere too. In Vienna, he found 'strangers from all parts of Europe at the court'.[51] Dieppe was 'crowded with strangers very many Dutchmen', Prague had a mixed 'Sclavonic', German and Jewish population, while, in Utrecht, 'strangers come from far to learn', with Divinity, Philosophy, Humanity, Law 'all taught here in their vigour'.[52] An incident in Livorno is worthy of reflection here too, his social interactions with a local woman there leading her to look 'most wistfully upon me'. Thinking he was English due to 'my complexion for my beard now was right reverend reed [red], a colour which the Italians love' and 'after a long parlie with mee of my condition and countrie', Fraser records that she invited him to her parlour, where 'she gave me a good shirt' and some wine.[53]

Sometimes Fraser could fail to secure, or turned down, local hospitality or cash, and had to rely on institutional support and charity instead. On the rough roads and tracks that led to Moravia, he and Godfrey Hartley slept out in the open air one night, having been troubled by an encounter in which 'an aged woman sitting on a set by her door gave us a dish of good milk and brown bread and offerd an outer lodging full of hay to sleep in'. Fraser and Hartley thanked her, presumably in the German language, but declined the offer of lodgings since 'we spied no good in the grim faces of the fellowes about the place'.[54] More often, when he could not rely on friendly locals, Fraser stayed in a variety of urban 'hospitals'. This was the case in Prague, for example, the 'hospital' there being a place accommodating poor travellers, as well as the sick, destitute and elderly.[55] As John McCallum has put it in a recent work, 'it is misleading to focus too closely on medical treatment when examining the early modern hospital'.[56] Certainly, in Utrecht, the institution where he found shelter was again vital, initially, providing 'a diet for meat and drink, bed and all necessaries, singularly fine'.[57]

More widely, though, it is striking that Fraser only rarely found hosts who were not from Scotland or one of the two other Stuart kingdoms. Wherever possible, he records staying with fellow Frasers, other Highlanders, Scots, English or Irish émigrés. This might seem to have been surprising. But the sixteenth and seventeenth centuries witnessed extraordinary levels of Scottish, Irish and, to a lesser extent proportionately, English and Welsh dispersal eastwards to the continent and Scandinavia. The numbers, in the case of Scotland and Ireland, vastly exceed those recorded with reference to English or Scottish imperial locations in the same period. Detailed research has led to the assertion that somewhere between 60,000 and 80,000 Scots left for European destinations (excluding those who went to England, Wales and Ireland) between 1600 and 1650, with a further 10,000–20,000 doing the same between 1650 and 1700.[58] Scholars of Irish emigration, meanwhile, tend to agree that Ireland lost around 30,000 people to parts of Europe beyond the archipelago in the first half of that century, besides more than 50,000 between 1650 and 1700.[59] Thus, in the period covered by Fraser's account, even the most cautious of guesses suggests that the dispersal around the European continent and Scandinavia of Scottish and Irish émigrés was of profound significance. Meanwhile, a tradition of contacts linking Wales and England with continental Europe or Scandinavia is harder to detect, partly due to it having been researched less. The Welsh could be difficult to differentiate when on the continent in early modern times, at least if evidence from the military and intellectual spheres is of value when making more general assertions.[60] As regards England, though, a quotation from William Harrison, who said of his compatriots in 1577 'the wise and better-minded doo either forsake the realme altogether, and seek to live in other countries, as France, Germanie, Barbarie, India, Muscovia and verie Calecute', is suggestive of the geographical range of English emigration and exile as, at least in continental Europe, it peaked in the seventeenth century.[61]

Fraser usually reported staying with his 'countrymen', a term by which he meant any male from the three Stuart kingdoms. He made the most of them as hosts in inns, hostels and private households. Dieppe provides an excellent initial illustration of this since, on arrival, his skipper:

> guided us to our quarter in the town of Diepe close at the Porta Marin neare the shore a Scots mans house Thomas Lithgow his wife also a Scot Beatrix Narden: at the sign of the King of Britains armes, we had indeed a hard voyage of it, but a happy harbour makes amends for all. Our host and hostess kindly welcomed us, and we sang – *Post motum dulcior inde Quies . . .*'[62]

Fraser soon learned that Thomas Lithgow knew an uncle of his and had been a servant of another of his relatives, the aforementioned Alexander Fraizer, physician at the exiled court of Charles II. Revealing the impact of some further cultural connections linking the Stuart kingdoms, Lithgow and Beatrice Narden's other boarders were not Scots but named as 'a Finch and a Mr Hotchkins', both from, one assumes, an English background. On other occasions (Durham and Padua), Fraser's main host was a fellow Fraser, although, more frequently, it was another Highlander or Lowland Scot. Indeed, he became involved in a vexatious debate regarding the Scottish or Irish origins of the 'Scotic' religious foundations while in Germany, which encouraged him towards Scottish or English networks only for a time.[63] However, when his reliance on Catholic networks of hosting and hospitality was tested again in Prague, Fraser expressed delight at being hosted by, in his estimation, upwards of fifty Irish fathers then present in the city's Irish Franciscan College. In particular, the:

> prior of the Convent invited us every day to dine where we got great entertainment . . . These fathers were so communicative that there could be nothing fit for a traveler to know but they informed us of by word and write and had complaisure in being asked of all manner of questions concerning city, country, government and temper of the people, nay more, they would take occasion to walk with us through and about the City and give us a particular description and account of everything worthy of observation.[64]

On departing westwards from Prague, Fraser recorded that the Irish Franciscans gave them a convivial send-off. Fraser's effusive description of his communication with the Irish friars is certainly in marked contrast to his comments on the state of relations between those Scottish, English and Irish Catholics referred to in some earlier sections of the account and shows once again the episodically strong, if fluctuating and inconsistent, levels of hospitality he expected from 'countrymen' from throughout the Stuart kingdoms. In Utrecht, finally, the intervention of an Englishman, 'Miles Clerk, a cobbler', and his wife, led to two nights of lodging in his house, 'which for neatness and handsome rooms might accomodat a Peer in England'.[65]

Food and Drink

Food and drink offered another way of bestowing and receiving hospitality. The sight of lavish meals was not an unusual one for Fraser, having grown up around the Lovat Fraser household. In terms of drinking habits, he records supping ale, claret and 'aquavity' when travelling through Scotland, while London's 'coffee, chocolat, brandy' provided new and exciting tastes on his first visit there.[66] Drink was a social lubricant in his previously mentioned exchange in the back streets of Livorno, too. Moreover, one reads of him combining white wine with milk and vinegar to combat the 'giddy head' of travel sickness on his final leg home from Burntisland.[67]

In terms of the three case-study cities, as regards Dieppe, after reaching harbour: 'Our first drink was good Claret wine, brunt and spiced, and this setled our stomacks a bit.' Thereafter, Fraser recalled the 'whit & claret' wine, and 'especiall good beer for drink', with 'their brown breead very dark but savorie', and an 'abundance of Cidar [cider] and perry fresh & stale for drink, butter and cheese', which the locals let 'stink by lying in horsedung a while'. Fish was also a feature, with 'reed herring or salt salmon oft called for in taverns'.[68] While Dieppe's salmon was imported from Scotland, and very probably from rivers which Fraser knew first-hand, Prague's salmon was all the more astonishing to him for having been caught in the Elbe, it being a 'wonder that salmon should be found in a river 300 miles from salt sea'. He considered the Prague locals, more broadly, 'voracious eaters and profound drinkers, the liquor here is ale beer', while 'Perri', 'Cidar' and 'Mede' were also popular, the latter leading him further towards mentioning their 'frequent eating of hony'.[69] Moreover, the Irish Franciscans by whom they were entertained:

> invited us every day to dine where we got great entertainment. It is incredible what good faere and plenty of provision is spent in these walls, and how cheerful they treat strangers. They have their vast Garden which furnish them all manner of root, fruits, their fish ponds for carp, tench and trout in abundance and salmon from the Elbe.[70]

Utrecht, meanwhile, was notable, like Dieppe, for its bread, Fraser recording an encounter in which 'we see a woman taking bread out of an oven and the bakeing shovel in her hand, the loaves in a heap before here', upon which Fraser 'made adrese to her for a peece of bread being hungry after our slender commons the forgoing night'. The Dutch baker at first 'frightened me w^t her Stern frown', haranguing Fraser in Dutch. She then shouted at him to leave, 'which we readily obeyed'.[71] Thankfully for Fraser, the baker's daughter then came with a basket of bread upon her head and 'we heartily thanked the good girle', wishing her 'a better husband than she had a mother'.[72]

Sites and Sights

Once the basics of sustenance had been met, Fraser's days and evenings usually gave him copious time to observe and sightsee, and it is in this context that the account appears most tourist-like and distinct from his wider life-writing. Italy's antiquities, galleries and monuments were inspirational. But architecture was often a source of fascination elsewhere, too, and inspired him occasionally to draw. In London, Fraser was excited by the Royal Exchange, Banqueting House and Westminster Abbey, while Joad Raymond has commented on Fraser's curiosity, while there, as regards, for example, street lighting, waste disposal, piped water and fire engines, as well as his sightings of the 'gums of Arabia, the silks of Asia, the spices of Africa, the riches and rareties of America & the gold of Both the Indies'.[73] In Dieppe, he commented on the 'nastiness of their houses' but also admitted the effectiveness of the chimney sweeps and the prevalence of windmills. Prague's brick and wooden framed houses also impressed him, as did the well-built burghers' houses of Utrecht, their cleanliness and the locals' predilection for street washing. It was a feature which appears to have influenced his subsequent attitudes as a minister, with architecture becoming an area in which he would be noted later for his expertise.[74]

Local History and Character

Houses of worship were another source of fascination for Fraser while travelling and led him often towards wider conjectures about the past. Indeed, regarding all locations he stayed in for several days or more, he pauses to comment on local religious history, this causing him often to go further from there and fulminate to his reader, imagined or otherwise, on the citizens' character. As Fraser states at the outset of the 'Triennial Travels': 'It was in some mesure to acquaint myself with the various sorts of religion abroad in France, Spain, Italy, Germany, Hungary, Holland and west Flanders such as Roman Catholics, Calvinists, Lutherans, Anabapptists, but especially the Jewes'. Therefore, Dieppe's recent history of relative Catholic–Protestant acceptance intrigued him, and he even considered the locals got on better than Scottish presbyterians and episcopalians, a notion that might have been challenged by 1685 when the French revoked the Edict of Nantes and French Protestants (Huguenots) began to go into exile in ever greater numbers. Prague, similarly, had a recent history deeply coloured by its religious mix, dominated by Habsburg-sponsored Catholicism, on one hand, but with still important Hussite, Lutheran, Calvinist and much longer-standing Jewish legacies, on the other, a co-existence which fascinated Fraser and which he researched in some detail. He also learned that Utrecht, in turn, had emerged from under Burgundian and Habsburg rule to occupy a central position in the newly created, Protestant-ruled United Provinces.[75]

On social and cultural characteristics, his combination of first-hand 'fieldwork' and local, documentary research led him, similarly, to make sweeping assessments at a wider level before honing in on more specific attributes. Towards the end of his account he regales his readers with a survey of national stereotypes, on the basis that there was 'No country without her nick!'[76] He had much to comment on in this respect as regards the English, French, Spanish, Italian, German, Hungarians, Bohemians and Dutch, as a future study of the account must look to show. Regarding the latter people and their nature, for example, a recent writer has claimed Fraser may have been responsible for the first transcription, possibly even the coinage, of what would later become a well-known phrase in national memory: 'God created the earth, but the Dutch made their own country.'[77] For Fraser, the Basques and Hungarians had particular characteristics and bore similarities, both positive and negative, with Highlanders. To move to an even smaller scale and consider the three city case studies for a final time, Fraser found the citizens of Dieppe rather like English and Scottish people, save for language, noting their fondness for wearing white plaids from his home country. On Prague, he admired the 'robustness' of the locals, but also the many freedoms that the city's residents, especially those who followed Judaism, experienced, albeit visually the Bohemians appeared to him similar to Germans, and the Jewish citizens impossible to distinguish, physically. Utrecht was less of a stand-out in this regard, with its populace sharing the broader Dutch characteristic of being great 'aquaticks', if also being 'boorish'.[78]

A scepticism towards the 'Triennial Travels' is not only reasonable but essential. However, Fraser showed the capacity in it, and his other surviving works, to write substantially for what he may always have predicted to be a small, if enthusiastic, readership. He was far from alone among early modern travellers in making mistakes, exaggerating or seeking to impress as well as inform by way of his account. This chapter has, it must be hoped, made the case that the memoir is best viewed as an original, if by no means always accurate, first-hand overview. Following some reflection and consideration of the content, the research has concluded that, as far as can be seen, he did visit most, probably all, of the places covered before constructing his own narrative about them.

Fraser's version of Europe as presented in the 'Triennial Travels' not only is based on travel, but reflects broader themes in his life-writing. Fundamentally, it is a version of Lovat Fraser history that depicts the family as the Highland, yet cosmopolitan representatives of a dynasty that had dispersed from their original homeland in France. The medieval Frasers had become a northern Scottish-based clan who, in James's lifetime, continued to be diasporic, keen to celebrate their continental origins, and also those of their members who had ventured abroad thereafter and brought their experiences back to their 'second homeland' of the Highlands of Scotland. Via several mobile, contemporary clan members, Fraser had gained some knowledge of continental Europe even prior to his 'triennial' journey, a wisdom he sought to show was strengthened by his time away. To add to that, in terms of religion, his is an account which, although Protestant in emphasis, is not strongly missionary in nature, engaging with Catholic, Orthodox and Jewish, as well as Islamic communities, all of the continent's major religious groups.[79] Moreover, while Rome was, indeed, the place where he lingered longest, there is no evidence of it being paramount in terms of the impact it had on his later life. Fraser was keen to present himself as having an open and pragmatic approach to travel, and as having written up an informative, panoramic guide intended for an unspecified, wider readership across later seventeenth-century Scotland and the Stuart kingdoms. While any modern reader engaging with the account needs to be alive to the possibility of fraudulence and what we would now consider plagiarism within it, when read with caution, it makes for a remarkable contribution to early modern travel and life-writing, one that is unparalleled in its detail and range from the perspective of a traveller from the Scottish Highlands. The case studies explored – Dieppe, Prague and Utrecht – show how recurrent themes emerge in the account, and in his work more broadly, and signal its maverick nature and the need for a full transcription and assessment of the contents. Travel was a bridge. It opened Fraser up to new experiences and areas of knowledge and was deeply educational. But in all the areas examined, it tended also to encourage interests he already had, leading to reflections and ideas that would busy his mind for the rest of his years. Nowhere is this more than the case than with language, the focus of the book's next chapter.

NOTES

1. Stevenson and Davidson, *The Lost City*, p. 111; Davidson and Morley, 'James Fraser's Triennial Travels', pp. 206, 208.
2. Rosemary Sweet, Gerrit Verhoeven and Sarah Goldsmith, eds, *Beyond the Grand Tour: Northern Metropolises and Early Modern Travel Behaviour* (London, 2017); Alan Stewart, *The Oxford History of Life-Writing, Volume 2: Early Modern* (Oxford, 2018), pp. 1–20; Mark R. F. Williams, 'The inner lives of early modern travel', *The Historical Journal*, 62(2) (2019), pp. 349–73; Eva Johanna Holmberg, 'Writing the travelling self: travel and life-writing in Peter Mundy's (1597–1667) *Itinerarium Mundii*', *Renaissance Studies*, 31(4) (2017), pp. 608–25.
3. 'Wardlaw Manuscript', p. 349.
4. Ibid. For more detail on Fraser's account of this Lord Lovat's travels in continental Europe in 1671, see 'Wardlaw Manuscript', pp. 333–43.
5. Ibid., p. 347. In 1649, he became a lead figure in the local 'Pluscarden Rising'. See Dave Selkirk's entry in the 'Scotland, Scandinavia and Northern Europe' database, available at: <https://www.st-andrews.ac.uk/history/ssne/item.php?id=3472> (last accessed 16 November 2021).
6. Mackay, ed., *Chronicles*, p. 424.
7. Ibid., p. 118.
8. Peter Paul Bajer, *Scots in the Polish-Lithuanian Commonwealth, XVIth to XVIIIth Centuries: The Formation and Disappearance of an Ethnic Group* (Leiden, 2012), p. 361.
9. Steve Murdoch, 'Children of the diaspora: the "homecoming" of the second-generation Scot in the seventeenth century', in Marjory Harper, ed., *Emigrant Homecomings: The Return Movement of Emigrants, 1600–2000* (Manchester, 2005), pp. 55–76.

10. Most Scottish travel accounts of the period come from students or political exiles at Charles II's court. See Matthew Glozier, 'Scottish travellers abroad 1660–1688', *Journal of the Sydney Society for Scottish History*, 8 (2000), pp. 25–39.

11. David Stevenson, 'Gordon, Sir Robert, of Gordonstoun, first baronet (1580–1656), historian and courtier', *Oxford Dictionary of National Biography* (Oxford, 2004), available at: <https://www.oxforddnb.com/view/10.1093/ref:odnb/9780198614128.001.0001/odnb-9780198614128-e-11075> (last accessed 16 November 2021); Rosalind Mitchison, 'Clerk, Sir John, of Penicuik, second baronet (1676–1755), politician and antiquary', *Oxford Dictionary of National Biography* (Oxford, 2004) , available at: <https://www.oxforddnb.com/view/10.1093/ref:odnb/9780198614128.001.0001/odnb-9780198614128-e-5617> (last accessed 16 November 2021); William Lithgow, *The Totall Discourse, of the Rare Aduentures, and Painefull Peregrinations of Long Nineteene Yeares Trauayles, from Scotland, to the Most Famous Kingdomes in Europe* (London, 1632); James Robert Burns, 'William Lithgow's Totall Discourse (1632) and his science of the world', PhD thesis, University of Oxford (1997); Clifford Edmund Bosworth, *An Intrepid Scot: William Lithgow of Lanark's Travels in the Ottoman Lands, North Africa, and Central Europe, 1609–21* (London, 2006); Dmitry Fedosov, ed., *Diary of Patrick Gordon of Auchleuchries*, 6 vols (Aberdeen, 2009–16); Donald Crawford, ed., *Journals of Sir John Lauder* (Edinburgh, 1900); Bishop Burnet's Travels Through France, Italy, Germany and Switzerland (London, 1750); Gilbert Burnet, *Some Letters Containing an Account of What Seemed Most Remarkable in Switzerland, Italy etc.* (Rotterdam, 1686).

12. Bernard Glassman, *Anti-Semitic Stereotypes Without Jews: Images of the Jews in England 1290–1700* (Detroit, 1975); Daniel Jütte, 'Interfaith encounters between Jews and Christians in the early modern period and beyond: toward a framework', *The American Historical Review*, 118(2) (2013), pp. 388–9; Jeremy Fradkin, 'Protestant unity and anti-Catholicism: the irenicism and philo-semitism of John Dury in context', *Journal of British Studies*, 56(2) (2017), pp. 273–94.

13. Sweet, Verhoeven and Goldsmith, eds, *Beyond the Grand Tour*, pp. 1–24.

14. Jean Gailhard, *The Compleat Gentleman, or, Directions for the Education of Youth as to Their Breeding at Home and Travelling Abroad in Two Treatises* (London, 1678).

15. David Worthington, *British and Irish Experiences and Impressions of Central Europe* (Aldershot, 2012).

16. Perez Zagorin, *Ways of Lying: Dissimulation, Persecution and Conformity in Early Modern Europe* (Cambridge, MA, 1990); Jon R. Snyder, *Dissimulation and the Culture of Secrecy in Early Modern Europe* (Berkeley, 2009); Miriam Eliav-Feldon and Tamar Herzig, eds, *Dissimulation and Deceit in Early Modern Europe* (London, 2015).

17. John Gallagher, *Learning Languages in Early Modern England* (Oxford, 2019), pp. 3–5, 115–25, 190, 200.

18. Paris O'Donnell, 'Pilgrimage or "anti-pilgrimage"? Uses of mementoes and relics in English and Scottish narratives of travel to Jerusalem, 1596–1632', *Studies in Travel Writing*, 13(2) (2009), pp. 125–39.

19. James Howell, *Epistolae Ho-elianae Familiar Letters Domestic and Forren Divided into Sundry Sections, Partly Historicall, Politicall, Philosophicall, vpon Emergent Occasions* (London, 1650). Howell's work has itself been subject to some scrutiny on account of his heavy borrowing from other texts. See Michael Nutkiewicz, 'A rapporteur of the English civil war: the courtly politics of James Howell (1594?–1666)', *Canadian Journal of History*, 25 (1990), pp. 21–40.

20. *Triennial Travels*, III, f. 153r.; Allan Kennedy, 'Highlanders and the city: migration, segmentation, and the image of the Highlander in early modern London, 1603–c.1750', *Northern Scotland*, 12(2) (2021), pp. 111–31.

21. Alessandro Arcangeli, *Recreation in the Renaissance: Attitudes Towards Leisure and Pastimes in European Culture, 1350–1700* (Basingstoke, 2003); Wolfgang Behringer, 'Arena and pall mall: sport in the early modern period', *German History*, 27(3) (2009) p. 331. Wider surveys of early modern sport history tend to situate themselves within the context of related debates around, for example, 'civility' and the 'civilising process', 'confessionalisation', social discipline or even the military and scientific 'revolutions'.

22. Jeffrey Hill, *Sport in History: An Introduction* (Basingstoke, 2010), p. 34.

23. *Triennial Travels*, I, f. 44r.

24. Ibid., f. 81r.

25. Ibid., f. 84v.

26. For more on tennis in France, see Behringer, 'Arena and pall mall', p. 341.

27. *Triennial Travels*, I, ff. 128r, 131r; Behringer, 'Arena and pall mall', p. 333.

28. *Triennial Travels*, II, ff. 32–3.

29. Ibid., p. 211r.

30. *Triennial Travels*, III, f. 56r.

31. Ibid., ff. 39, 41.

32. Ibid., ff. 96r, 113r, 119r, 137v.; Behringer, 'Arena and pall mall', p. 341.

33. For instance, Edward Lhuyd's correspondence with Fraser in 1699 involved a request for an account of 'The peculiar Games & customes observed on set days throughout the year' in the Highlands. See Michael Hunter, *The Occult Laboratory: Magic, Science and Second-Sight in Late Seventeenth-Century Scotland* (Woodbridge, 2001), pp. 205–6; John Burnett, *Riot, Revelry and Rout: Sport in Lowland Scotland Before 1860* (East Linton, 2000); Wade Cormack, 'Playing by the rules? Early modern sport and control in the northern mainland royal burghs of Scotland', *Sport in History*, 36(3), pp. 305–27.

34. For Dieppe, see *Triennial Travels*, I, ff. 47r–61v; for Prague and Utrecht, see ibid., III, ff. 46r–53r, 87v–91r.

35. For an account of everyday reliance on horses in the 'Three Kingdoms' at the time, see Peter Edwards, *Horse and Man in Early Modern England* (London, 2007).

36. *Triennial Travels*, I, f. 48r. The scotticisation of the term is first recorded in 1662. See 'Gardyloo *interj.*, *Dictionary of the Scots Language* (2004), available at: <https://www.dsl.ac.uk/entry/snd/gardyloo> (last accessed 21 November 2021).

37. *Triennial Travels*, III, f. 88r.

38. Ibid., I, f. 46r.

39. Ibid., I, ff. 129r–131v.

40. Ibid., II, f. 12r.

41. Ibid, III, f. 176v; Mackay, ed., *Chronicles*, pp. 429–30.

42. 'Wardlaw Manuscript', p. 281.

43. *Triennial Travels*, I, ff. 50v, 60r.

44. Ibid., II, ff. 21–54.

45. Ibid., III, f. 45.

46. Valentin Groebner, *Who Are You? Identification, Deception, and Surveillance in Early Modern Europe* (New York, 2007), p. 1.

47. James Howell, *A New English Grammar Prescribing as Certain Rules as the Languages Will Bear, for Forreners to Learn English: Ther Is also Another Grammar of the Spanish or Castilian Toung, with Some Special Remarks upon the Portugues Dialect, &c.* (London, 1662), p. 49.

48. The mints of London were a source of great interest to him, to the extent that he made drawings and rubbings of Cromwellian coinage. See *Triennial Travels*, I, f. 2r; Helen Pierce, '"The bold adventure of all": reconstructing the place of portraits in Interregnum England', British Art Studies, 16 (2020), available at: <https://doi.org/10.17658/issn.2058–5462/issue-16/hpierce> (last accessed 1 June 2022).

49. *Triennial Travels*, I, f. 59r; III, ff. 51r, 88v, 133r.

50. Ibid., I, f. 213r.

51. Ibid., II, ff. 33–4.

52. Ibid., I, f. 50; ibid., III, f. 87v.

53. Ibid., II, ff. 20–1.

54. Ibid., III, f. 45.

55. Presumably this was the central St Francis's Hospital (Hospital Na Františku), on the banks of the Vltava.

56. John McCallum, '"Nurseries of the poore": hospitals and almshouses in early modern Scotland', *Journal of Social History*, 48(2) (2014), pp. 427–49.

57. *Triennial Travels*, III, f. 88v.

58. Steve Murdoch, 'Introduction', in Steve Murdoch, ed., *Scotland and the Thirty Years' War* (Leiden, 2001), pp. 19–20; Alexia Grosjean and Steve Murdoch, eds, *Scottish Communities Abroad in the Early Modern Period* (Leiden, 2005); Steve Murdoch, *Network North: Scottish Kin, Commercial*

and Covert Associations in Northern Europe 1603–1746 (Leiden, 2006); Steve Murdoch and Esther Mijers, 'Migrant destinations, 1500–1700', in T. M. Devine and J. Wormald, eds, *Oxford Handbook of Scottish History* (Oxford, 2012), pp. 320–7; Kathrin Zickermann, *Across the German Sea: Early Modern Scottish Connections with the Wider Elbe-Weser Region* (Leiden, 2013).

59. Louis M. Cullen, 'The Irish diaspora of the seventeenth and eighteenth centuries', in Nicholas Canny, ed., *Europeans on the Move: Studies in European Migration, 1500–1800* (Oxford, 1994); Thomas O'Connor, 'Ireland and Europe, 1580–1815: some historiographical remarks', in Thomas O'Connor, ed., *The Irish in Europe, 1580–1815* (Dublin, 2001); Thomas O'Connor and Mary Ann Lyons, eds, *Irish Communities in Early Modern Europe* (Dublin, 2006); William O'Reilly, 'Ireland in the Atlantic world: migration and cultural transfer', in Jane Ohlmeyer, ed., *The Cambridge History of Ireland, Volume II: 1550–1730* (Cambridge, 2018).

60. Gwyn A. Williams, *The Search for Beulah Land: The Welsh and the Atlantic Revolution* (London, 1980).

61. David Worthington, ed., *British and Irish Emigrants and Exiles in Europe, 1603–88* (Leiden, 2010); Alison Games, *Migration and the Origins of the English Atlantic World* (Cambridge, 1999), pp. 38–40; Lothrop Withington, ed., *Elizabethan England: from 'A Description of England,' by William Harrison* (London, 1876), p. 125.

62. *Triennial Travels*, I, f. 46v.

63. Ibid., I, ff. 204r, 213r; III, ff. 8–10, 13. Their original, Gaelic-speaking occupants had lost possession of these entirely. However, Scottish Catholics had more recently succeeded, following numerous representations and publications, in being 'restored' to three of the monasteries: in Würzburg, Erfurt and, crucially, the 'mother-house' in Regensburg. See, for one perspective, Mark Dilworth, O.S.B., *The Scots in Franconia: A Century of Monastic Life* (Edinburgh, 1974).

64. *Triennial Travels*, III, ff. 49v, 50r; Jan Pařez and Hedvika Kuchařová, *Hyberni v Praze – Éireannaigh i Prág: Dějiny františkánské Koleje Neposkvrněného Početí Panny Marie v Praze (1629–1786)* (Prague, 2001); Worthington, *British and Irish Experiences and Impressions*, pp. 173–4.

65. Ibid., I, f. 50v; III, ff. 50–1, 88v.

66. Ibid., I, ff. 4, 7, 29v.

67. Ibid., III, f.176v.

68. Ibid., I, ff. 46v–48r.

69. Ibid., III, ff. 49v, 51r.

70. Ibid., III, f. 50.

71. Ibid., III, f. 87r.

72. Ibid., III, 87v–89v.

73. Joad Raymond, 'A Scotsman in Cromwellian London: the diary of James Fraser of Phopachy', *History Today*, 47(7) (1997), p. 36; Davidson and Morley, 'James Fraser's Triennial Travels', pp. 208–11.
74. *Triennial Travels*, I, f. 49v; III, f. 46r, 86v.
75. *Triennial Travels*, I, 47v, 51r, III, 47r–49v, 88r.
76. Ibid., III, f. 115r.
77. Frits Niemeijer, 'God created the Earth, but the Dutch made their own country', published on the Internet and available at: <http://vakbladvitruvius.nl/images/essay/TheDutchMade_F.Niemeijer_May2021_DEF-dd27mei.pdf> (last accessed 21 November 2021). The author considers Fraser to have been the first to write down the phrase.
78. *Triennial Travels*, I, 49v, III, ff. 48–52; 105–8, 113r.
79. In so doing, Fraser's account raises questions of Europe as an 'unmarked category'. See Maria Todorova, 'Spacing Europe: what is a historical region?', *East Central Europe*, 32(1–2) (2005), pp. 59–78; Manuela Boatcă, 'Thinking Europe otherwise: lessons from the Caribbean', *Current Sociology*, 69(3) (2021), pp. 389–414.

3

The Linguist:
Fraser and a Multilingual Scottish Highlands

'a language which none of them could understand'

INTRODUCTION

IN 1898, ENGLISH SCHOLAR and critic Charles Whibley claimed James Fraser's north Highland contemporary, Sir Thomas Urquhart of Cromarty (1611–60), to have been the 'greatest translator of all time'.[1] It is a minority viewpoint, but his publications in this area comprise a vital element in Urquhart's output, work that was then, and remains, highly regarded. Whibley's statement gives further fuel to the argument that to assume Highland scholarship in the era before Culloden to be 'peripheral' is based on too simplistic an approach, one which can marginalise places such as Scandinavia and central and eastern Europe, as well as the 'British Isles' beyond England. Such a perspective is certainly of partial relevance at most when applied to the Scottish Highlands prior to the ages of Enlightenment, 'Improvement' and Clearance. A more appropriate approach would represent the combination of the Highlands being treated, at times, by authorities in Edinburgh and London as 'uncivil', liable to 'savagery' and 'barbarism', and yet highlight, paradoxically, its significant level of distinctiveness, in terms of how it engaged with and became entangled in worlds beyond. This has rarely been considered in terms of the scholarly life that is the focus of this book, where, despite the absence of a university, some agency in the face of external pressures is apparent. Kennedy has described the governance of the region in the period as 'semi-colonial', and more 'collaborative' than 'imperialist', although, in understanding Highland scholars of the period, Immanuel Wallerstein's concept of the 'semiperipheral' may offer a more specific framework indicating more internal intellectual dynamism.[2]

Urquhart, an individual well known to Fraser and whose home was less than 20 miles away from his, converted into English, to acclaim, works of the French Renaissance writer Rabelais, and claimed to have scoped a 'universal language' that could, he asserted, provide exact translations 'of any vernaculary tongue, such as Italian, French, Spanish, Slavonian, Dutch, Irish, English, or whatever it be'.[3] Exaggerations aside, in his translations and other literary work, Urquhart was evidently aware of the oral, as well as the written, power of the region's languages, asserting that 'Some languages have copiousness of discourse, which are barren in composition; such is the Latine. Others are compendious in expression, which hardly have any flection [inflection] at all; of this kinde are the Dutch, the English, and Irish.'[4] This suggests a nuanced, flexible approach to domestic and foreign languages and one that relates strongly to his northern Scottish upbringing. Linguistic 'polyglossia' was the norm in the firthlands, it being a region where Gaelic, Scots and English all had their uses for everyday speech.[5] It was also one in which, as the example of Fraser shows, some were accustomed to a relatively high level of education, and, indeed, also to a degree of national and international mobility within a North Sea, Baltic and Atlantic world, for military, socio-economic or cultural reasons, thus to picking up other languages.

Today, we assume that the best way to learn a language is to combine speaking and listening, on one hand, with reading and writing, on the other, although, for many people in modern Scotland, the world can appear monolingual or bilingual at most, in terms of both speaking and writing. But to separate the spoken word from the written word, and to assume the historical Highlands to have had one or, at most, two languages is not always a helpful way of encompassing this everyday experience of linguistic diversity. Urquhart, peculiar though much of his work is, was not simply an oddball operating at the margins in terms of translation. His example provides, instead, an example of how the north Highlands was involved in a seventeenth-century 'Babel of tongues' linking to Europe and empire. Highland polyglossia was real among its scholars and, in part, perhaps a reaction to, even a resistance against, the pressures being put on its majority language of Gaelic. Parts of the region became centres for complex linguistic interplay, a world of code-switching and even 'tricksterism', in both speech and writing, this bearing some similarity to that in Rabelais's *Gargantua and Pantagruel*, regarding which the Black Isle scholar's French–English translation has been viewed, by others besides Whibley, as his 'masterpiece'.[6]

Urquhart conveyed an awareness of the versatility of languages, dialects and registers, both within everyday conversation and within the cosmopolitan 'republic of letters' in which he played a part.[7] As regards the Lovat Fraser lands, too, we would be wrong to assume that Gaelic, and perhaps some Scots, was the limit for all in terms of language skills. The possibility of a significant degree of exposure to other languages is suggested in the case of the ailing Colonel Hugh Fraser, veteran of the Thirty Years' War, who, reputedly, reverted, not to his native Gaelic or Scots, but to 'High Dutch or Slavonick' – what we would call standard High German or an assumed generic 'Slavonic' language – when nearing the end of his life by the Beauly Firth in 1649, presumably drawing on military experiences in Poland or Bohemia (today, roughly, the Czech Republic/Czechia).[8] This chapter will identify the strikingly multilingual aspects of the seventeenth-century north Highlands, by focusing on the local and international networks of both speech and writing within which James Fraser, and the community around him, lived their lives. Fraser read and wrote in many languages, as will be shown in the second part of the chapter. However, his multilingualism began with the oral, so the chapter will turn to that first.

THE SPOKEN WORD: FRASER'S MULTILINGUALISM (I)

Although advances have been made in the 'social history of language', Peter Burke's 1993 assertion that early modern scholars remained a long way from establishing a historical 'ethnography of speaking' continues to be pertinent.[9] It is almost certain that James Fraser uttered his first words in Scots Gaelic, this followed by him acquiring a speaking knowledge of Scots and then English. He had to communicate in Latin, some Greek and some Hebrew as an adolescent pupil and student, while his travel memoirs record his determination, as a young adult, to attain verbal dexterity with French, Spanish, Italian, German, 'Slavonick', Hungarian, 'Bohemian' and Dutch. Certainly, one can gain a sense of him inhabiting a complex oral environment in the way he records language use both at home in Kirkhill and further afield.

One sees an example of this everyday Scots Gaelic, Scots and English 'plurilingual' interchange in Kirkhill in a story Fraser relates about a brother-in-law of his, an individual whose Gaelic name he denotes in partially anglicised form as 'John Mackeanire' (John, son of John?), possibly Mac Iain Uidhir.[10] Fraser records that, in the early 1670s, there occurred an argument between 'Mackeanire' and two other parishioners, a 'John Mᶜkeanvore' (John, son of Big John) and a 'Donald Mackwilliam Chui' (Donald, son of Black William). The latter, a household servant, was stabbed to his death and his body dumped by the firth, but the ebbing tide did not wash it away and the Kirkhill community soon found it and identified him. The community suspected 'Mackeanire' to be the murderer and rumour spread that he had fled inland and southeast, several parishes beyond, to Strathspey. Two years on, Fraser, having travelled eastwards from Kirkhill to attend the Synod of Moray, described the suspect's circumstances and appearance to fellow synod member Sir James Strachan of Thornton, who revealed that he knew 'Mackeanire', claiming him to be living under separate pseudonyms as 'Donald Gailach' or 'Highland Donald' and, in these guises, to be serving a William Fraser of 'Couper hill, near the bridge of Keith'.[11] Consequent to Rev. Fraser revealing this back in The Aird, Lord Lovat 'sent away a country boy that had both languages to Keith, with a line to Couper hil, who presented Hiland Donald openly to his view.' Lovat then travelled to Keith himself with six or seven men to lay a trap for the suspect. On being taken back to Inverness, 'Mackeanire' confessed, and was imprisoned. According to Fraser, the fate of both 'Mackeanire' and 'Mᶜkeanvore' was to be executed and the right arms of each displayed on poles below the church at Kirkhill, in what he deemed to be a righteous application of the principle of 'bloud for bloud'.[12]

Classical and Scots Gaelic

Fraser took enormous interest in the sound and speech of his first language. Evidently, he did not subscribe to the Jacobean policy of subduing the region's majority tongue for local speech that was promulgated by his near neighbours, the Gordons of Sutherland.[13] As a minister, he converted English language texts, as a matter of course, into Gaelic language sermons for his congregation.[14] Moreover, he provides us with compelling evidence that Gaelic was an everyday language of the Lovat household and patrimony, and of the western reaches of the diocese as a whole.

There are two forms of the language which we must consider here: Classical 'Common' Gaelic and vernacular Scots Gaelic. The debate has tended to focus on their written forms rather than their spoken ones, as Aonghas MacCoinnich has shown.[15] Although Classical Gaelic, once a common written language of Scottish and Irish Gaeldom, was in retreat by Fraser's lifetime, the evidence supporting its continued relevance is seen in the Book of Clanranald and several other texts.[16] John Carswell's translation, at the behest of the Synod of Argyll, of the Book of Common Order had occasioned the appearance of the language's first printed publication in 1567, which had been followed, in Fraser's lifetime, by the printing in Edinburgh of a version of Calvin's *Catechismus Ecclesiae Genevensis*.[17] Moreover, the profile of Classical Gaelic would be influenced by Robert Kirk (1644–92), episcopalian minister of Balquhidder, Perthshire, who, in 1684, published the first full metrical psalter in the language, while 1690 saw the publication of the Gaelic text of the Old and New Testaments, using, for the first time, Roman characters. Clashing with these older-fashioned orthographies, scholars have accounted for the simultaneous rise of a vernacular Gaelic in Scotland. The Book of the Dean of Lismore (c.1542) and the Fernaig Manuscript (c.1689), for example, highlight what was becoming a move towards a literary Scots Gaelic, a shift which, gradually, led to the extinguishing of the common form.[18]

In terms of reading and writing, Fraser knew both forms of Gaelic and there is considerable evidence of him negotiating the interplay and tension between the two types, with MacCoinnich arguing that, although Fraser was 'well aware of traditional Gaelic orthographic practices', he was 'much more comfortable' with the Scots form, this including Scots spelling practices.[19] Confusingly for modern readers, although again revealing of Lowland influences on his worldview, Fraser followed the contemporary norms of Scots and English writing by referring to both Irish and Scots Gaelic as 'Irish'. This, in itself, suggests a perception of the two languages as having common elements or, at least, a willingness to describe them as such to an audience who knew no better. But it does not tell us if he could still write in Classical Gaelic as well as vernacular Scots Gaelic.

Certainly, Classical Gaelic remained pivotal for him at certain junctures. Most uniquely, from his travel memoirs, Fraser makes the claim that, as a university-educated seventeenth-century, Highland Gael, he could – even having never met an Irish speaker from Ireland before – communicate verbally with those he met from that background in a mutually intelligible Gaelic form.[20] One sees this oral engagement with Irish émigrés and exiles in a case from a monastery in Lyons, where 'we met w' one father Martin an Irishman, a most discreet man and finding that I could speake Irish he doubled his kindness'.[21] Even more striking is an incident towards the end of his itinerary, in the Spanish Netherlands, between Brussels and Mons, where Fraser had his clothing, bags and papers taken and checked by local officials. Struggling to understand their Spanish speech and guessing at the Gaelic Irish identity of one man within the group, Fraser decided to greet him in a form of Gaelic. The Irishman responded to Fraser in a mutually intelligible tongue, astonishing 'all the rest to see him and me so intimat & speak a language q^h none of them could understand' by employing a phrase he translates as 'Dear Brother Scot, by my Baptism yow shall have your breeches back.'[22]

John Fraser, an early twentieth-century Gaelic scholar, commented on the 'considerable number of Gaelic words and phrases, proverbs, fragments of verse and more written in a "phonetic" spelling in the Wardlaw Manuscript', considering it to provide 'some of the earliest, if not the very earliest, dated evidence for the pronunciation of Gaelic in the Northern Highlands', a point disputed convincingly recently by Martin MacGregor.[23] Despite his aptitude for Classical Gaelic, then, and his favouring of Scots spelling practices, Fraser does suggest frequently, in his surviving writing, that the Lovat Frasers took a particular interest in communicating in the vernacular and local forms of the tongue. For example, he describes how the Gaelic 'MacShimi' title, used for the Lords Lovat, continued to trump all other designations into his own lifetime:

> Of old and yet in our Irish language, the Lord Lovat is called MackHimy [MacShimi] i.e. the sone of Simon, and this for the more quick and expedit delivery in the Vulgar expression of those who, without regard to true Syrnames, are pleased to design men by their Patronymicall titles . . .[24]

Fraser also provides verse inspired by the death of a previous MacShimi in 1576, an event which moved his foster brother to proclaim the following 'in his own vernacular language', provided, in turn, in Fraser's own words, then in Mackay's modernised, 1905 version and, finally, in Mackay's English translation:

> Bheag inih chōse vi bocht,
> Smōre locht rind orm Deā;
> Skin Challig i Tolli Mōre
> McKhimmi seār hanig reave.[25]

> Beag ioghnadh dhòmhsa bhi bochd,
> 'S mòr lochd rinn orm Dia;
> Gu'n chailleadh an Tolli Mor,
> Mac'Shimi's fheàrr a thàinig riamh.

> Little wonder that I am poor,
> Great is the bereavement God has sent me;
> That at Big Tolly has been lost,
> The best Mac-Shimi who ever arose.

Not only that, but Fraser records how Lowland, Scots-speaking women marrying into the Lovat world could experience life differently if they did not possess spoken Gaelic: in 1633, Isobel Wemyss, who was Hugh Fraser, the 7th Lord Lovat's, 'good lady', was 'much in fancy with that country [Stratherrick], and, though she wanted the language, yet gained the love and respect of all that knew her there and else-where'.[26] Some ten years on from that, Fraser records the experiences of 'Dame Katharin Ross, Lady Moynes', widow of Simon, 6th Lord Lovat (d.1633?). While staying in Sutherland, she met a Donald Glasshach [Donald of Strathglass], 'a common servant about the house, who accosted Lady Kathrin, checking her severly for her willfullness, speaking in Irish to her (haveing no other language) *Cathrin, hā tu tōishach*, yow are unwise'.[27] This warning was issued in relation to her proposed marital partner, and involved Donald pleading with Katharin that she marry the laird of Dunbeath instead. One assumes she was either fluent enough to pick up the gist of his warning or had it translated to her.[28]

Fraser's recounting of placenames is equally suggestive of the verbal power of a north Highland form of Gaelic in the Lovat lands, revealing considerable toponymy in that form. In the 'Wardlaw Manuscript', he provides placenames predominantly in a vernacular variety, sometimes favouring these over other linguistic versions that might have been more accessible to an English- or Scots-reading audience. He opts to cite the hilltop spot, 'the watch hill' to which 'Wardlaw' refers, in the Latin 'Mons Mariæ' ('Mary's Hill'), this corresponding with its Gaelic version 'Cnoc Mhuire', a reference to the medieval church there devoted to Mary.[29] Other Scots Gaelic toponyms he references, without translating, are easily recognisable to those today without the language, such as 'Avin ni Mannach' ('The Monks' Water') and 'Port ni Mannach' (The Monks' Ferry), both on the lower River Beauly, and 'Blare Beallach in Broige' ('The Field of the Pass of the Shoe'), a battle site at the place known today as Bealach nam Broig, west of Ben Wyvis, although another Fraser example, 'Spiggadach', has challenged scholars.[30]

Despite his keenness to impress his audience with his cosmopolitan ways, then, and his willingness to disparage elements of north Highland culture when writing for a readership who favoured English, Fraser could be wholly supportive of both written Classical Gaelic and its Scottish form. He conveys a degree of command of, and respect for, the former and yet, more frequently, chooses, or is otherwise reliant, on a vernacular, north Highland type of Scots Gaelic when presenting his immediate physical and natural surroundings to his readers.[31]

Scots

The dark anecdote about 'Mackeanire' and 'Mackeanvore' revealed the tactical, deliberate mixing of Gaelic and Scots naming practices to create pseudonyms and conceal identity across the diocese of Moray, even as far west as Kirkhill. Moreover, the story highlights how the Moravian religious, therefore social and administrative, world in which Fraser worked was a place of linguistic complexity, where neither all Gaelic speakers knew Scots, nor all Scots speakers knew Gaelic, but where frontiers of speech could be negotiated and manipulated, a space that linked Highland and Lowland worlds. Indeed, Fraser's own work reveals how he moved between Gaelic, on one hand, and Scots or English, on the other. Scots was dominant in Elgin, the ecclesiastical headquarters, although even in the most 'Highland' parts of the diocese, the Scots- and English-speaking world impinged regularly, and all of Fraser's surviving manuscripts are written (with local forms sometimes scotticised or anglicised) to appeal to Scottish and other readers who did not share his mother tongue.

Scots is a Germanic language, brought to mainland Britain by Angles, Saxons and Jutes. Along with English, it is part of a linguistic family including what later emerged as Dutch, Frisian, German and the Scandinavian languages. The earliest surviving writings in Scots date from the fourteenth century, at which time it appears to have competed with Latin as an official language. A charter from 1312 exists while, in 1375, John Barbour's narrative poem, *The Brus*, an account of the Scottish Wars of Independence, appeared. The first act of Parliament to be written in the language comes from 1397, while it is often claimed that the first history to be written in the Scots language is Andrew of Wyntoun's *Orygynale Cronykil of Scotland* from 1407.[32] Blind Harry's *The Wallace* is another fifteenth-century example. Moving into the sixteenth century, in 1532, John Bellenden converted Hector Boece's *Scotorum Historia* (1527) into Scots for a wider audience, showing the demand that there was for history in the vernacular.[33] With the Regal Union of 1603, the pressures on it began to increase at national level, although, for example, the Scottish Privy Council survived and continued to function in Scots while Charles I (r.1625–49) had some knowledge of the language too. As a spoken language, it was used throughout Scottish burghal society during Fraser's lifetime, including in Forres or Elgin, two places which he frequented, as well as the entirety of the eastern coastal part of the diocese of Moray.

In his two most substantial works, the 'Wardlaw Manuscript' and the 'Triennial Travels', the approach Fraser takes to translation involving Scots, as well as the Latin still spoken then by some scholars, differs. In the former work, when Fraser translates proverbs, he claims these to be largely taken from Scots or Latin, rather than Gaelic. One example he quotes is 'to tirr the kirk to thack the cure' (to strip the church to thatch the cleric'), another being 'one divil is fittest to ding out another' ('one Devil is fittest to knock out another').[34] Elsewhere, Fraser draws on the phrases '*Non ubi nascor sed ubi pascor*' ('That place be your mother, not which bred you, but which fed you').[35] Fraser may have picked these phrases up orally, as a child, to the extent that Scots or Latin orthography may have come more quickly and easily to him than their Gaelic equivalent. Indeed, in terms of Gaelic words, Roderick Cannon pointed out that Fraser often leaves these in Scots orthography in the 'Wardlaw Manuscript', while in the 'Triennial Travels', when referring to Gaelic sayings, he tends to translate them into English. It suggests a capability in using different registers, depending on which audience he was addressing. It also indicates that, although his mother tongue was Gaelic and his major language of writing English, he also relied on Scots for speech throughout his life.[36]

English

Another key element in Fraser's versatility with spoken languages is his frequent use of them for secrecy, exclusivity and disguise. Strange though it may seem, English was, arguably, of greater relevance than the two forms of Gaelic or of Scots in this regard. While, as a child, Fraser encountered English daily as a written language through the Bible and, almost certainly, other printed texts, it is quite possible that he did not hear it or learn to speak it until his later teens, with the arrival of the Cromwellian soldiers in Inverness.[37] It has been argued that the garrison assisted in Invernessian English growing from the seventeenth century into becoming the dominant linguistic culture there, with perhaps its most prominent visitor of the eighteenth century, Samuel Johnson, claiming that 'The soldiers seem to have incorporated afterwards with the inhabitants, and to have peopled the place with an English race; for the language of this town has been long considered as peculiarly elegant.'[38] Mackay offered a different judgement, in 1905, in concluding that the reason for the relative clarity of Invernessian English, and the decline of the burgh's Scots, was that 'the language was acquired by a

Gaelic-speaking people whose native tongue was remarkably free from brogue or accent'.[39]

Indubitably, during Fraser's lifetime, English grew in significance as a language for speech across all three Stuart kingdoms, with Nicholas Canny claiming that, by the mid-century point, 'the ruling elite in all jurisdictions of the British Crown' understood it. This raises questions for our understanding of Fraser, in that the scholarly network he became a part of relied on its members being able to read, write and converse in it, albeit, ironically, much of his involvement in this circle depended on their interest in what he had to say about Scots Gaelic. Within obvious limits, there may be scope in positing these Stuart period networks as, in some sense, precursors to the idea of the 'English-speaking peoples' outlined by Peter Clarke. While Fraser's 'Britishness' was negotiated and partial, even in a linguistic sense, it would be too simplistic to argue that it was only 'socially privileged, politically conservative and generally establishment-minded circles' who spoke English outside England in the seventeenth century.[40] Across the Stuart kingdoms, its spread was advancing.

English would be key to Fraser's travels beyond Scotland, both in England and on the continent. While Inverness was a bilingual Scots and Gaelic town during his early childhood, his reading knowledge of the English language and its increasing spread meant there were, one assumes, few problems for him in adapting to the startling range of accents and dialects that he must have heard for the first time there with the arrival of the Cromwellian soldiers in the 1650s. Indeed, his broader linguistic aptitude may have helped him ingratiate himself enough with the community there to receive his passport in 1657. Certainly, he makes no comment on any challenges in conversational understanding at that juncture, and use of the language would be paramount in terms of his communication with a growing body of English, Welsh and Protestant Irish contacts while moving through England and, especially, London, in those years. It was through his travels that his social circle began to extend, for the first time, to 'countrymen' from across all three Stuart kingdoms.

While Fraser, again, does not mention facing any linguistic challenges in London, the continent might have been expected to provide greater obstacles in terms of finding a common tongue for communication. The Dutch could be an exception, as Fraser found out in the case of one 'George Rater', with whom, in Padua, he became 'well watered' after sampling 'several sorts of wines' and who spoke 'good English'.[41]

However, generally, English was little known or used across continental Europe and Scandinavia, being, as John Gallagher has shown, the 'little-known and little-regarded language of a small island out on the edge of Europe', this requiring all newcomers to England to become familiar with it, and all those native speakers who relied on it while at home to become language-learners whenever they headed across the North Sea.[42] To a greater extent than Scots or, indeed, the remnants of a mutually intelligible Classical Gaelic which, as has been shown, he is pleased to claim enlivened and deepened his social encounters with Irish travellers, English could provide access to the majority of a Stuart émigré and exile community in continental Europe of many tens of thousands. Among that body from the Stuart kingdoms who by then knew it as a first or second language, it became, once on the continent, a mode of speech allowing for close-knit community, as well as confidentiality.[43]

Continental Languages

This does not take us to the limit of Fraser's language knowledge since, in fact, he did not rely solely on Gaelic, Scots or the English of a nascent British and Irish 'expatriate' community when communicating beyond the archipelago. On the contrary, at every juncture he sought to learn other tongues, an engagement with continental languages which far out-weighed that of the typical grand tourist from the Stuart kingdoms. In 1678, Jean Gailhard published the first two volumes of his aforementioned work, *The Compleat Gentleman*, in which he asserted that language learning should be key:[44]

> Now I must pass to some preparatory dispositions, which a Gentleman must use in order to his Travels [sic]: First, he would do well to get something of the Language of the Country he is next to go to, as an introduction to it, though it were only to understand something of it, and be able to ask for necessary things; this can rid him of the surprizal [sic] others are subject to, who coming into a Foreign Country, and understanding not one word of the Tongue, look as if they were fallen from the Clouds: hereby their Journey is most pleasant to them, and they are sooner disposed to receive the benefit of it: so they ought to have something of the French before they go out of England, of Italian before they leave France, and of the German before they stir out of Italy, and so of the rest.[45]

Twenty years earlier, James Fraser was already taking this positive, pragmatic approach. After boarding the *Roe of Rye*, which took him to Dieppe, he was impressed by the royalist skipper having 'good French'.[46]

Not only that, but, on disembarking in Dieppe harbour, Fraser made clear his wish to 'learn a litle of (the) french language to fit us for our journey'.[47] Indeed, in Dieppe he found 'little difference save in the language'.[48] To an extent that exceeds even that of fellow Scottish adventurers like William Lithgow or Patrick Gordon, Fraser emphasised how linguistic aptitude was key for the traveller in Europe of the time.[49] Indeed, he is at pains to comment on how language learning ensured success while abroad:

> As to your converse you are received but coldly in France without their language which when you begin to express and distribute freely among them you insinuate yourself mightily thereby and by degrees conciliat their favour and in time attain to some kind of confidence, and they grow very communicable and informe you readily of their customes nay they incurrage you so that if you can but call for any thing in intelligible learned they commend your language highly with a *vous parle bon Francais* you speak good French. They do not as Scotch or English scorn your idiom or tone but applaud with a longe to make you fall in love w^t their language.[50]

Moving south, Fraser claims that his brief foray on to the Iberian Peninsula was an unintended consequence of his ship from Marseille to Genoa being attacked by pirates, a setback which saw him disembark temporarily in Catalonia. Once again, though, he was drawn to collect key phrases and comment on the languages he heard around him. His remarks on the Iberian peninsula were no longer reserved to national languages, furthermore, but display a rare openness to regional tongues and dialects too:

> As to the Spanish speech or language it varies more than the tongue of any country that which is common to them all. The vulgar Castilian Spanish which by reason of its affinity and consonancy with the Latin, the Spaniards calle their language Romanie. In Granada and Andalusia the Arabick and Moorish language is much in use still. In Catalonya, Valentia and Portugall it hath a great mixture of the French because of their trade and negotiation. The high countries bordering on the Pyrenees and Cantabrian Ocean have still retained much of the language of the old Spaniard and Goths. But surely it is a very majestic high, lusty swell, my speech as if it were fashioned to command and the Spaniard is so ambitious as to say that qn God forbad Adam eating of the tree of knowledge he spoke in Spanish.[51]

In what would become a typical fashion, Spain gave him an opportunity to draw on his own experience as a native speaker of what we would call today a minority language. Fraser did not visit Biscay. But he was fascinated by Basque ('Biscaian'), believing it to be 'much like our Brittish and Welsh language'.[52]

Moving eastwards, his attitude remained open. For example, conversation with his ailing skipper while heading across a rough sea towards Genoa proved invaluable, he having a 'verie faire plaine smoothe stile of Latin', while a growing knowledge of Italian helped him immediately following that. Further east, the potential obstacles of Hungarian and 'Slavonick' fascinated him more than they troubled him, and the challenges they posed may have been eased by his conversational ease in Latin, still a language that was relatively common parlance in that part of Europe.[53] Certainly, in the section of the memoir on Hungary, his detail is remarkable, comparing favourably with that provided by other English-language visitors to east-central Europe like Moryson, Howell, and also Lewkenor, Ricaut or Brown. Fraser spends a whole paragraph noting key phrases in Hungarian before commenting on 'the high Dutch being generally spoken in the frontier townes, also among the schollars, souldiers and merchants'.[54] He also picks up on more subtle points, such as that there were many Slavic speakers within the Magyar realms and towards the Ottoman frontier, concluding that 'there remains a dialect of the Scythian speech among them still, but among ye better sort and men of sense the Sclavonian language is generally spoken written and printed as in Transilvania, Moledavia and Poleland but keep the Roman character'.[55] On the Ottoman Empire, again, language was to the fore in his claim that 'their Divinity and Law is taught in Sclavonick . . . but the vulgar speak Tartarian which is the common Turkish language', with their 'Law and Divinity' being 'comprehended in a book called the Al-coran [al-Qur'ān]'. Fraser did not actually enter the Ottoman lands, turning north instead through north-eastern Hungary (what is now Slovakia), where he concluded that the everyday language was 'a dialect of the Scythian' but amongst 'the better sort' the 'Sclavonian language is generally spoken written and printed'.

On entering Bohemia, he suggests that 'Sclavonian' was 'universally used as their mother tongue' and the Bohemians 'in their own tongue call themselves Czechi and the high Germans Niemecki'.[56] In Prague, he took an interest in this bilingual 'Sclavonic' and German character again, the city giving him a chance to switch between Latin, Classical Gaelic, English and perhaps other 'speech domains' on visiting, in his estimation, the upwards of fifty fathers then present in the city's Irish Franciscan College. Certainly, it appears from his account that the Irish friars were fluent not only in those three languages, but also in Czech. In particular:

> We had access to their library, to read their manuscripts, diarie, notes, nay all that could be imparted to transient travelers with wonderful freshness, affability and discretion. I heard Father Brian preach in the Sclavonian tongue with as great volability as the natives and had the applause of all his hearers and the emulation of the Dominus's hands . . .[57]

Fraser's effusive description of his communication with the Irish friars and his admiration for their linguistic dexterity are striking and, once again, his interest in the status of Slavic languages reflects, in ways still to be unravelled by linguistic scholars, his Gaelic background too. His route eventually led Fraser 'out of the woods and out of Bohemia withal' into the Upper Palatinate, and, from there, through a section of the Holy Roman Empire, to the United Provinces.

The local language became slightly more familiar to him again from there, with Fraser showing some knowledge of Dutch in Rina [Rhenen?] before Utrecht, where he encountered a woman 'at her *eyn nakt ofen* for so the Dutch call a baking oven'.[58] Once in Utrecht, the reader encounters further evidence of Fraser's curiosity and enthusiasm for languages in his encounter with Anna Maria van Schurman (1607–78), often claimed to be the first female university student in Europe. Fraser noted her then to be 'about 52 yeares of age', a woman 'resolved never to marry and 'never such without papers and books in her hand'.[59] On seeing her worshipping in the English Church there, he commented that she:

> is now at length come to that proficiency and perfection in all the Orientall Originall languages. That she is exactly mistress of ye Hebrew, Chaldaick, Syriack, Greek, Latin, Arabick, high Dutch and Slavonick besids the Common Speaker of Spanish, Italian, French, English, Danish and Swedish tongues every one admires her.[60]

Indicating that it had not taken foreign travel to inspire his interest in Schurman's linguistic skills, Fraser adds that 'her fame had spread as farr as the north of Scotland when I was student in the Kings College of Aberdeen' when a 'Mr Andrew Cant' had dedicated his thesis to her.[61]

Further onwards in the Spanish Netherlands, Fraser experienced a final revealing, multilingual spoken encounter on the 'Sandy Rode' just before Mons. He came across two men on horseback, who asked, in French, what his nationality was, then which part of Scotland he was from, and, eventually, which parish he came from and what his surname was. This eventually produced an emotive response, presumably in Gaelic or Scots, from the interrogator, who turned out to be a John McKenzie, whose Highland home was less than 10 miles away from Fraser's. McKenzie informed him that he had been a 'souldier in Tangiers' but was now a lieutenant in the 'Spanish army going for Brussels'. As well as giving him money, McKenzie arranged for him to meet a 'Ms Lesley', a Scottish nun in the city, presumably a Scots speaker from the Catholic, north-east branch of that family.[62]

From Mons, Fraser headed on into France, with little further comment on language, to London, Gravesend and finally, by sea again, to Scotland, and the firthlands that were his home. While his travels had opened him up to new languages, the experience of being in a multilingual setting, and his curiosity to comprehend the voices he heard, were in no way new. As has been shown, he displayed a remarkable openness to speaking and code-switching in a multiplicity of voices throughout his life, whether these were the everyday Scots Gaelic and Scots of his local parish, presbytery and synod, or the ever more complex linguistic encounters to be experienced at grammar school and university, or while travelling.

THE WRITTEN WORD: FRASER'S MULTILINGUALISM (II)

At the point of embarking on his travels, Fraser was used not only to speaking, but also to reading and writing, in a multitude of languages. As has been shown, he conveyed an unusual level of fascination about national and regional tongues that goes well beyond that of the typical 'grand tourist'. But this openness cannot be explained simply on the basis of him having an 'ear for languages'. The written record that survives under-represents that mixing of and 'interference' between written languages, the 'polyglossia' studied by Bakhtin and summarised by Peter Burke.[63] As a first step towards learning new tongues, Fraser had followed his schoolmasters and university lecturers by reading in preparation, wherever and whatever he could. On the ground, and possibly when writing up his memoirs back at home, he had, almost certainly, also benefitted from the use of a 'conversation manual', what John Gallagher has defined as a 'bi- or multilingual text which usually included some material on pronunciation, orthography, vocabulary, and grammar, and which had at its heart material that mimicked speech and could be employed in conversation by the reader'.[64] Often these manuals were pocket-sized, and, in the case of one of the classics of the type, the *Thesaurus Polyglottus* (1603), provided coverage of all of the languages Fraser cited in his travel memoirs.[65] Certainly, Gailhard would recommend that, when it came to languages, a traveller should be 'capable of improving himself out of all Books written in several Tongues', as well as being able to speak them.[66] Evidently, by the time of his return home, Fraser had collected and written down phrases, and probably also done some reading, in French, Italian, German, 'Slavonick', Hungarian, Czech and Dutch, this foregrounding an adeptness with writing in other languages which went back to his childhood, and perhaps even exceeded his fascination for them in spoken form.

Clearly, Fraser had known since childhood that being able to read and write in several languages could bring prestige and status, what scholars have, since Pierre Bourdieu, called 'social capital'.[67] For example, Bible study, schooling in Inverness and university days in Aberdeen had given him a reading knowledge of Latin, some Greek and possibly Hebrew, his enthusiasm for the latter exemplified later in his stated admiration for a certain Ogilvy, a 'great poet' in London who 'hath set out an English Hebrew grammar, followeing an easier method of learning that language than any yet hath done, a rode which none have ever yet trod'.[68] Sadly, the loss of Fraser's Gaelic manuscripts means that a modern researcher gains little insight into this aspect of his life, while any interest in Scots as a scholarly language is also hard to trace. For much of his career, the evidence suggests that most of Fraser's reading and writing was in a combination of Gaelic, Latin and English.

Embedded within his 'Wardlaw Manuscript' is a 'Catollogue of Manuscripts being bookes bound written & Hilled Be Master James Fraser Pastor Montis Mariæ. In divers volumns *ab anno 1660*'. Compiled towards the end of his life, it lists fifty-three titles, volumes comprising many of his own works along with copies of pieces written by others, and suggests the interconnected nature of his reading and writing in, and translation between, those three key languages.

Gaelic

Starting with Gaelic, one sees on the list 'An Irish Dictionary, in 4°' and 'Hibernilogia a volum of Irish verse'.[69] In these two mentions, we have illuminating evidence that Fraser's interests in vernacular Gaelic went beyond the oral aspects, covered earlier in the chapter, to the linguistic and literary. The extent of his intellectual knowledge becomes abundantly clear again in the fragments of a scholarly exchange from 1699, a letter sent to him by renowned Welsh scholar Edward Lhuyd (1660–1709). While it has not proven possible to ascertain how Lhuyd had come to know of Fraser, the letter, addressed to 'Revd. Mr James Fraser

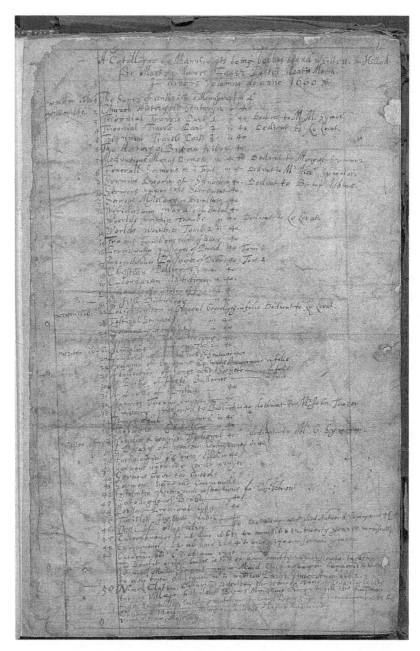

Figure 3.1 'A Catollogue of Manuscripts being bookes bound written & Hilled
Be Master James Fraser Pastor Montis Mariæ. In divers volumns ab anno 1660',
James Fraser, 'Polichronicon seu policratica temporum' or 'The true genealogy of
the Frasers, 916–1674' [the 'Wardlaw Manuscript'], National Library of Scotland,
MS 3658 (photograph)

A Catollogue of Manuscripts being bookes bound written & Hilled Be Master James Fraser Pastor Montis Mariæ. **In divers volumns** *ab anno* **1660.**[1]

Written 1660 1. The Survey of antiquity a manuscript in 4°.
Written 1665 2. Church History to century 12 in 4°.
      3. Triennial Travels, Part 1. in 4° dedicat to Mᵣ. Al. Symur.
      4. Triennial Travels, Part 2. in 4° dedicat to Lo. Lovat.
      5. Triennial Travels, Part 3. in 4°
      6. The History of Britain to 1678, 4°.
      7. Meditations Moral, Divine, &c. in 4 4° dedicat to Margret Symmur.
      8. Funerall Sermons in 3 Tract, in 4°, dedicat to Mᵣ. Alexᵣ Symmur.
      9. Sermons preacht at Synods, in 4°, dedicat to Bishop Atkins.
    10. Sermons uppon the Sacrament, 4°.
    11. Sermons misselany on several texts, 4°.
    12. Wiridarium Wardlaense Herbal., 4°
    13. Woorlds worthies. Tomb, i., in 4°, dedicat to Lo. Lovat.
    14. Worlds worthies. Tomb. 2, in 4°.
    15. Frasers Familiars volum of letters, 4°.
    16. Providentia passages of Provid. 4°, Tom. i.
    17. Providentia passages of Provid. 4°, Tom. 2.
    18. Christian Policy, T. i., in 4°.
    19. Calendarium Catholicum in 4°.
    20. Hibernilogia a volum of Irish verse, 4°.
    21. An Irish Dictionary, in 4°.
Writen 1666 22. Polichronicon, a General Geneology, in folio, dedicat to Lo. Lovat.
    23. Festival Sermons, in 4°.
    24. Sermons of Humiliation, in 4°
    25. A ?? of Sermons for the King, 4°.
Writen 1676 [26.] Ministers Mirrour on Thes. 2, 7, 4°.
    27. Lumbard, a ?? book of Sentences, 4°.
    28. A volumn of Epigrams Epitaphs Anagrams in folio.
    29. A Collection of Songs and Sonets, in folio.
    30. A booke of Jests, Ralleries, in folio.
    31. A booke of Profaces, 4°.
    32. Natures Treasur tryed, 4°.
    33. Privacy preferrd to Publick, in 4*, dedicat to Mᵣ. John Fraser.
    34. Itinerarium Scripturæ, in 4°.
    35. Theologia Cathollica, in 4°.
Written 1670 36. Homolies & exercises Theological, 4*, dedicat to Mᵣ. G. Symmur.
    37. A Dyary of Weather Contingencies, in 4°.
    38. Anthologia his own Life, in 4°.
    39. Sermons upon the Lords Prayer.
    40. Sermons upon the Creed.
    41. Sermons upon the Commands.
    42. Institutio Puerorum, instructions for Children.
    43. Catollogue of Bookes, 4°.
    44. Penitent Prodigal, Luk 15, 4°.
    45. Fruitless Figtree, Luk 18, 4°.
    46. Bill of Mortality, 4°, containing all yᵗ died Natives and Strangers in 46 years.
    47. Catechumenoi, L. i., *ab anno* 1663 to anno 1683, twenty yeares, inclusively.
    48. Catechumenoi, L. 2, *ab anno* 1684 to *anno* 1700, sixteen yeares.
    49. Catechumenoi, L. 3, *ab anno* 1700.
The Benefit of these bookes is this to know exactly what Heretor, tacksman, tenant, Master, servant man or Maid, Child or stranger, happened to live In every town and famely within Wardlaw Parish since *Anno* 1662.
    50. Nomen Clatura; calling and describing the Ancient?? Name of Countries, Cities, townes, villages, hills, dales, Rivers, Mountains, Churches in all the Kingdom.
    Index Universalis; containing a catollogue of Emperors Popes Kings of Europ Commonwalths &c.
    Chirurgo Medicus including experiments of Phisick and Chirurgery
    Vade mecum; Misselany.

---

[1] 'Wardlaw Manuscript'.

Figure 3.2 'A Catollogue of Manuscripts being bookes bound written & Hilled Be Master James Fraser Pastor Montis Mariæ. In divers volumns ab anno 1660' (transcription)

minister of Kirkhill in the Aird near Invernes', shows how Fraser could rival his Gaelic-speaking contemporary Martin Martin in the scholarly circles of Edinburgh and London as an informant on 'Ersh [Gaelic]'. Lhuyd's desire for knowledge from his contact in Kirkhill extended to 'the old Scottish Language & customes, the comparing of which with the Welsh, Cornish, & Armorican is one part of my design'. The letter provides the first of several windows on to Fraser's part in the 'republic of letters', and language is to the fore. On the list of Lhuyd's requests to him were:

> 1. An interpretation of the Nouns in Mr Ray's Dictionariolum Trilingue; with the Addition of the Verbs & Adjectives in the vulgar Nomenclatura into the Northen Ersh would be very acceptable. 2. A catologue of the towns, castles, villages, mountains, vales, Lochs & Rivers, within ten (or twenty) miles; with an interpretation of such of these names as are indubitably intelligible; and Queries or conjectures about some of the others . . .[70]

Bridging the linguistic and the literary, Lhuyd went on to ask Fraser to provide:

> 7. A catologue of the Highland Poets of note, and of all the other writers on what subject soever in the Ersh or [–Irish] Scottish Irish. When they flourish'd: what they writ: How large their works; with the three or four initial & final words; and where their works may be seen at present. 8. A catologue of the Christian names purely Ersh; with a mark of distinction to those still in use.[71]

The focus on Gaelic grammar, toponymy, onomastics and poetry indicates the assumed breadth of Fraser's reading knowledge of the language, an intriguing assumption, given his reliance on twenty-six-letter Scots and English orthography rather than the Gaelic eighteen-letter form.[72] Lhuyd gave Fraser several months to work on his research and, evidently, expected his Highland informant would collaborate with other local experts in collating it. Nevertheless, in referring to English naturalist John Ray's 1675 work, a dictionary in English, Latin and Greek, Lhuyd assumes Fraser's learnedness and ability to be sufficient to understand the current intellectual, especially linguistic, context. Scots Gaelic was included within the 'Babel of Tongues'.

Latin and English

In terms of Latin, while Fraser was not recognised as an expert to the same degree, it is evident that he relied on it as regards his reading of history and his writing of eulogies, homilies and epitaphs.[73] In the 'Wardlaw Manuscript', Fraser quotes directly from the Latin originals of the Scottish histories of Boece and Buchanan and the account of the British past of Mair (Major), rather than use English or, where available, Scots versions.[74] At another point in the text, he provides a Latin eulogy to Montrose without translation.[75] Also in Latin, he supplies an epitaph to the 5th Lord Lovat, who died in 1577, and another to a later seventeenth-century Kirkhill schoolmaster, while presenting ten such tributes on the death of the 8th Lord Lovat, from 1672, in a combination of Latin and English.[76]

CONCLUSION

While reading and writing in Latin allowed him to play a full part in the 'republic of letters', using the fragments that remained from pre-Reformation monastic libraries, learning Scots as a literary language would serve rather a different purpose. Mackay claimed, in 1905, that the reason for Inverness's rejection of the Scots that was so apparent in its sixteenth-century burgh records, in favour of a relatively standard English, was not so much the influence of its waves of monoglot Gaelic-speaking newcomers or of the anglophone, occupying Cromwellian forces. Instead, he argued, it occurred due to the tireless efforts of 'educated school-masters and good English books' introduced following the Reformation. Given Fraser's connections to Elgin and east Moray, and also the fact that Inverness was hardly overflowing with books, lacking a town library until 1706, the relative lack of Scots words in Fraser's writing is perhaps the most striking of all the linguistic puzzles he has left us. The written version of the language began to go into a slow decline in Fraser's lifetime. In its place, Scottish English, as distinct from Scots, slowly came to the fore, with, by the eighteenth century, Scots such as David Hume and Adam Smith desperate to conceal any hint of 'Scotticism' within their writings. Fraser's surviving writings, while they are ripe for harvesting in terms of their references to languages, are in a Scots-influenced English, which, we can conclude, reflects his reading background in the latter language and his wish to reach as wide an audience as possible in his writings. The lack of material in the other language he spoke from early childhood, and which, in the eastern parts of the diocese of Moray, was the lingua franca, is striking.[77] It emphasises that, as with his spoken world, sadly, Fraser has left us only partial, if vital and rare evidence, in terms of the multilingual environment in which he lived. Nevertheless, a plurality of languages, a uniquely Highland polyglossia, remained a feature of his everyday scholarly life after his return home from the continent, as Part Two of this book will show.

NOTES

1. Charles Whibley, *Studies in Frankness* (London, 1898), p. 244.
2. Boatcă, 'Thinking Europe otherwise'; T. C. Smout, 'Scotland and England: is dependency a symptom or a cause of underdevelopment?', *Review (Fernand Braudel Center)*, 3(4) (1980), p. 602; Silke Stroh, *Gaelic Scotland in the Colonial Imagination: Anglophone Writing from 1600 to 1900* (Evanston, IL, 2017); Allan Kennedy, 'Managing the early-modern periphery: Highland policy and the Highland judicial commission, c.1692–c.1705', *Scottish Historical Review*, 96(1) (2017), p. 35. I used Wallerstein's term 'semi-peripheral' in Worthington, 'The settlements of the Beauly-Wick coast'.
3. *The Works of Sir Thomas Urquhart, Reprinted from the Original Editions* (Edinburgh, 1834), p. 202.
4. Ibid., p. 194.
5. David Worthington, 'The multilingual minister: languages and code-switching in the life-writing of Scottish Highland scholar and traveller, Rev. James Fraser (1634–1709)', *Renaissance Studies* (forthcoming).
6. Stephen Ahern, 'Prose fiction: excluding Romance', in Stuart Gillespie and David Hopkins, eds, *The Oxford History of Literary Translation in English, Volume III: 1660–1790* (Oxford, 2005), pp. 328–9.
7. Peter Burke, *Languages and Communities in Early Modern Europe* (Cambridge, 2004), pp. 4, 51; Roger Craik, 'Sir Thomas Urquhart's translation of Rabelais', *Studies in Scottish Literature*, 31(1) (1999), pp. 151–68.
8. 'Wardlaw Manuscript', p. 238.
9. Peter Burke, *The Art of Conversation* (Cambridge, 1993), p. 7; Gallagher, *Learning Languages in Early Modern England*, p. 2.
10. 'Wardlaw Manuscript', pp. 356–7. Thank you also to Iain MacIlleChiar for his assistance on this point.
11. Ibid.
12. Ibid.
13. Fraser, ed., *The Sutherland Book*, II, p. 359.
14. For more on this from the immediate post-Reformation period, see Jane Dawson, *Scotland Re-Formed, 1488–1587* (Edinburgh, 2007), p. 229.
15. Aonghas MacCoinnich, 'Where and how was Gaelic written in late medieval and early modern Scotland? Orthographic practices and cultural identities', *Scottish Gaelic Studies*, 24 (2008), pp. 309–56.
16. Ibid., p. 317.
17. Dawson, *Scotland Re-Formed*, pp. 228–9.
18. MacCoinnich, 'Where and how was Gaelic written', p. 316.
19. Ibid., p. 329.

20. I am grateful to Dr Aonghas MacCoinnich for his advice in this area. I am unaware of other contemporary references to such verbal communication between Irish and Scottish Gaels from the period. However, for code-switching amongst contemporary English travellers in Europe, see Gallagher, *Learning Languages*, pp. 3–5.

21. *Triennial Travels*, I, f. 116r.

22. Ibid., III, f. 133r.

23. John Fraser, 'Notes on Inverness-shire Gaelic in the seventeenth century', *Scottish Gaelic Studies*, 2(1) (1927), p. 92; Martin MacGregor, 'The genealogical histories of Gaelic Scotland', in Adam Fox and Daniel Woolf, eds, *The Spoken Word: Oral Culture in Britain, 1500–1850* (Manchester, 2002), pp. 196–239.

24. Mackay, ed., *Chronicles*, p. 2.

25. Ibid., p. 175.

26. Ibid., p. 268.

27. Ibid., p. 284.

28. Ibid.

29. On Gaelic placenames, see Michael Newton, *Warriors of the Word: The World of the Scottish Highlanders* (Edinburgh, 2009), p. 298.

30. Ronald I. M. Black, 'Scottish fairs and fair-names', *Scottish Studies*, 33 (1999), p. 12.

31. Fraser, 'Notes on Inverness-shire Gaelic', p. 92.

32. David Laing, ed., *The Orygynale Cronykil of Scotland* (Edinburgh, 1879), p. 102.

33. Hector Boece, *The History and Chronicles of Scotland* (trans. John Bellenden), 2 vols (Edinburgh, 1821).

34. Mackay, ed., *Chronicles*, p. 67.

35. Ibid., pp. 9, 241.

36. Cannon, 'Who got a kiss of the King's hand?, pp. 197–226.

37. Kennedy, 'Cromwell's Highland stronghold'.

38. Samuel Johnson, *Journey to the Hebrides: A Journey to the Western Islands of Scotland & the Journal of a Tour to the Hebrides* (Edinburgh, 2010), p. 22. Thomas Kirk, an Englishman who visited Inverness in the Restoration period, wrote: 'All in the town of Inverness do generally use that language' apart from 'some few of the better sort, that can speak Scottish'. See Peter Hume Browne, ed., *Tours in Scotland, 1677 &1681* (Edinburgh, 1892), p. 28.

39. Mackay, ed., *Chronicles*, p. xxvii.

40. Nicholas Canny, 'Irish, Scottish and Welsh responses to centralisation, c.1530–1640: a comparative perspective', in Alexander Grant and Keith J. Stringer, eds, *Uniting the Kingdom? The Making of British History* (London, 1995), p. 157; J. Derrick McClure, 'English in Scotland', in Robert Burchfield, ed., *Cambridge History of the English Language* (Cambridge, 1994), V, pp. 23–38; Peter Clarke, 'The English-speaking peoples before

Churchill', *Britain and the World*, 4 (2011), pp. 201, 213, 224; Peter McLaren, 'White terror and oppositional agency: towards a critical multiculturalism', in D. T. Goldberg, ed., *Multiculturalism: A Critical Reader* (Oxford, 1994), pp. 45–74. For language use amongst the Scots in Europe, see Murdoch, *Network North*, pp. 368–73; Murdoch, 'Children of the diaspora', p. 58. For other works on the use (or lack of use) of English in continental Europe in the same period, see Gallagher, *Learning Languages*; Peter Burke, '*Heu domine, adsunt Turcae*: a sketch for a social history of post-medieval Latin', in Peter Burke and Roy Porter, eds, *Language, Self and Society: A Social History of Language* (Cambridge, 1991), pp. 23–51; David Worthington, 'Introduction', in Worthington, ed., *British and Irish Emigrants*, pp. 18–21.

41. *Triennial Travels*, II, f. 204.
42. Gallagher, *Learning Languages*, p. 1.
43. Ibid., pp. 2, 3–5, 115–25, 171, 190, 200–1; Tobias B. Hug, *Impostures in Early Modern England: Representations and Perceptions of Fraudulent Identities* (Manchester, 2009), Ch. 4; Snyder, *Dissimulation and the Culture of Secrecy*; Groebner, *Who Are You?*; Zemon Davis, *Trickster Travels*; Matt Houlbrook, *Prince of Tricksters: The Incredible True Story of Netley Lucas, Gentleman Crook* (Chicago, 2016); Thomas Kidd, 'Passing as a pastor: clerical imposture in the colonial Atlantic world', *Religion and American Culture: A Journal of Interpretation*, 14(2), 2004, pp. 149–74.
44. Gailhard, *The Compleat Gentleman*.
45. Ibid., p. 23.
46. *Triennial Travels*, I, f. 46r, 49r.
47. Ibid., f. 46v.
48. Ibid., f. 49r.
49. For Lithgow's experiences with Italian, 'Cretan' and 'Slavonian', see Lithgow, *The Totall Discourse*, pp. 42, 80, 483. For Gordon's reliance on Latin while in Poland initially, not knowing any 'Dutch' – i.e. German, see Fedosov, ed., *Diary of Patrick Gordon*, I, pp. 10, 12. For language use among Scots in mid-seventeenth-century continental Europe, see Murdoch, *Network North*, pp. 367–73.
50. *Triennial Travels*, I, f. 49v; Gallagher, *Learning Languages*, pp. 59, 202.
51. *Triennial Travels*, I, ff. 150v–150r.
52. Ibid., I, f. 138.
53. Ibid., II, f. 12; Worthington, *British and Irish Experiences and Impressions*, Ch. 1.
54. Ibid., III, f. 42r.
55. Ibid., III, f. 43r; Worthington, *British and Irish Experiences and Impressions*, Ch. 1. Meanwhile, Lithgow claims that 'their language [Hungarian] hath no affinity with any other kind of speech'. See Lithgow, *The Totall Discourse*, p. 415.
56. Ibid., III, f. 48r.

57. Ibid., f. 50; Pařez and Kuchařová, *Hyberni v Praze*; Worthington, *British and Irish Experiences and Impressions*, pp. 173–4. For use of Czech among the Irish Franciscans in Prague, see Ken Ó Donnchú, 'A Prague poem on purgation? Five languages in a seventeenth century Irish manuscript', *Studia Celto-Slavica*, 12 (2021), pp. 43–62.

58. *Triennial Travels*, III, f. 87.

59. Ibid., III, ff. 87v, 89v.

60. Ibid., III, ff. 89v–90r. For the 'English Church' in Utrecht, see Keith L. Sprunger, *Dutch Puritanism: A History of English and Scottish Churches of the Netherlands in the Sixteenth and Seventeenth Centuries* (Leiden, 1982), p. 212.

61. *Triennial Travels*, III, f. 90r. Cant's name is not revealed in Anderson, ed., *Officers and Graduates of University and King's College*.

62. *Triennial Travels*, III, ff. 133r–134r.

63. Burke, *Languages and Communities*, pp. 4, 113.

64. Gallagher, *Learning Languages*, pp. 5–6, 12, 56, 57–9, 55–6, 60–76, 103, 135–6, 249.

65. Ibid., p. 57; Hieronymus Megiser, *Thesaurus Polyglottus, vel Dictionarium Multilingue* (Frankfurt, 1603).

66. Gailhard, *The Compleat Gentleman*, p. 7.

67. Pierre Bourdieu, 'The forms of capital', in John G. Richardson, ed., *Handbook of Theory and Research for the Sociology of Education* (New York, 1986), pp. 241–58.

68. Mackay, ed., *Chronicles*, p. 427. Presumably, this was the translator John Ogilby (1600–76), for whom, see Charles Withers, 'Ogilby, John (1600–1676), publisher and geographer', *Oxford Dictionary of National Biography*, available at: <https://www.oxforddnb.com/view/10.1093/ref:odnb/9780198614128.001.0001/odnb-9780198614128-e-20583> (last accessed 25 November 2021).

69. '°' is an abbreviation for quarto, or medium-size volume, one quarter the area of a full sheet of writing material, made by 'folding two sheets in half, then in half again'. See <https://www.bl.uk/catalogues/illuminatedmanuscripts/GlossQ.asp> (last accessed 10 December 2021).

70. 18 December 1699, Falkirk, Edward Lhuyd to James Fraser, cited in Hunter, *The Occult Laboratory*, pp. 205–6.

71. Ibid.

72. MacCoinnich, 'Where and how was Gaelic written', p. 326.

73. My thanks to Dave Selkirk, an independent historian of the Lovat Frasers, for his insights regarding this.

74. Mackay, ed., *Chronicles*, pp. 14–15, 17, 38, 50, 54, 70, 79, 172.

75. Ibid., pp. 362–3.

76. Ibid., pp. 175, 497, 504, 510–11.

77. John R. Barrett, ed., *Mr James Allan: The Journey of a Lifetime* (Kinloss, 2004).

PART TWO (1660–1709)

Communicating Knowledge:
Fraser's Adult Life as an Early Modern Scottish Highland Scholar

4

The Scientist:
'Natural Philosophy' in Fraser's
Scholarly Networks and Life-writing

'Queries or conjectures'

INTRODUCTION

> I was imploved in a diversion of another nature, such as optical secrets, mysteries of natural philosophic, reasons for the variety of colours, the finding out of the longitude, the squaring of a circle, and wayes to accomplish all trigonometrical calculations by sines, without tangents . . .[1]

The Highlands produced polymaths as well as polyglots in the age before Culloden. This 1653 quotation, from Sir Thomas Urquhart of Cromarty, hints at the intellectual potential of the region in an era before it had its own scholarly clubs, societies or 'associational culture'. Urquhart was referring not to a metropolitan laboratory or royal court but to his own research space at home in his 'little town' of Cromarty, just 20 miles north-east of Kirkhill, where he hoped to create a dynamic, multidisciplinary research and educational community. However, while Urquhart eventually had to leave, effective cultivation of local and broader scholarly, travelling and ministerial networks allowed James Fraser, even while at home, to be part of that diverse, mercurial but recognisably seventeenth-century body who Laurence Brockliss has referred to as 'the curious'. This was a conglomeration of seventeenth-century virtuosos, scattered across Europe, who sought influence 'irrespective of confessional allegiance' and who communicated to their friends, students and, in some cases, congregations what some modern scholars still refer to as the 'Scientific Revolution'.[2] In the Highlands, its representatives, besides the rather transient Urquhart or Robert Gordon, comprised a somewhat amorphous body of luminaries, one which finds some early expression in the activities of cartographer Timothy Pont (fl.1574–1611), while he was minister in Dunnet, Caithness, or, at the other end of the spectrum, Robert Kirk. Another Highland erudite of the time, Martin Martin, is perhaps closer to Fraser, as a well-connected fellow native speaker of Gaelic, and a scholar with the ability to enthuse his contacts and patrons across the Stuart kingdoms and beyond, as an authority to them on all that seemed unfamiliar, bizarre or intriguing about the region rather than its more prosaic qualities, in which they took much less interest.[3]

Fraser's scholarship was more firmly rooted in the region than all of them: Urquhart was forced into exile and probably died in Zeeland; Gordon's major adult family home was in Salisbury (although his life probably came to an end in Gordonstoun in Moray); while Martin Martin, after a time in Leiden, became a doctor in Middlesex and passed away in London.[4] Unlike the three of them, Fraser spent only six to seven years of his life away from his home parish, and rarely left it at all from the age of twenty-six on. In this sense, Rev. Kirk is his nearest contemporary, although Kirk was not called on for anything like the range of expertise that Fraser was. Perhaps more than that of any other seventeenth-century northern Scottish polymath, then, James Fraser's intellectual contribution highlights the scholarly streams that could filter out from the region, rather than it being isolated or simply a sponge soaking up erudition from outside. While, unlike Urquhart, he did not plan to found a university and could be deferential to centralising polities in both Edinburgh or London, he shows, time and again, the viability, vitality and connected nature of the scholarly activity taking place within the north Highlands of that era, and its ability to produce research, to an extent, on its own terms. Despite a lack of societies, libraries, museums or a seat of higher education in the region to encourage him, Fraser positioned himself skilfully as the key Highland spokesperson of the internationally-known Welsh scholar Edward Lhuyd, and, closer to home, was a correspondent of the Banffshire-born, Orkney-residing minister James Wallace (1642–88), his son, also James Wallace (b. 1684), and, it seems, the Aberdeenshire episcopalians James Garden (1645–1726) and George Garden (1649–1733).[5] While he lacked proximity to a regal court or princely household, Fraser became a cosmopolitan figure who made the most of his regional affiliation in order to engage in the 'republic of letters'. He offers glimpses, through what survives, of a scholarship that captured sufficient local peculiarity, accidental or otherwise, to engage Lowland Scottish, English, Welsh and some Irish audiences, and yet was universal enough to contribute to and influence transnational scholarly spaces.[6]

In categorising those intellectual interests of his that he conveyed and curated in his manuscript collection, it can be easily seen that, as well as a passion for non-metropolitan regional languages and cultures – accounted for already in this book – Fraser wished to impress on his readers his contribution to the mainstream of 'natural philosophy'. This encompassed systematic knowledge of the physical world, including what we could today call 'science', although the latter was not a term Fraser used. 'Natural philosophy' was a sphere of activity which, for Fraser, embraced cosmology, meteorology, geology and natural history, with a 'diversion' also towards human health and medicine. As a possible indication of the depth of his participation and influence in these circles, Dutch scholar Frits Niemeijer has conjectured that Fraser was responsible for first putting on paper (and translating from Latin) a saying about Dutch engineering prowess that is well known in the Netherlands still today (see Chapter Two).[7] More broadly, however, Fraser's engagement in natural philosophy can be seen in numerous other parts of the 'Triennial Travels', also in the 'Wardlaw Manuscript', sections of his other manuscripts and the contents of two surviving letters. Indeed, in looking at Fraser's previously mentioned list of fifty-three (mostly lost) works in his possession, one is struck by how at least four of the lost pieces appear to exemplify the 'natural philosophical' approach: 'A Dyary of Weather Contingencies, in 4°', 'Natures Treasur tried, 4°', 'Wiridarium Wardlaense Herbal., 4°' (to all appearances, a work on a herbal garden at Kirkhill) and 'Chirurgo Medicus including experiments of phisick and chirurgery' (a work, one assumes, dealing with surgery, as well as the broader diagnosis and treatment of injury and disease).[8] One gleans from the titles and, more conclusively, from other specific references in his surviving writings a preoccupation with weather, climate and the natural world, and a clear correlation of these with human wellbeing. It suggests Fraser oscillating between what we might view as irrational beliefs and science when it came to identifying and explaining cosmological and natural phenomena in the north Highlands and his energetic, if sometimes perplexed or even traumatised scholarly response to these provides crucial background to the remainder of this chapter. In the case of Fraser's letter 'concerning the Lake Ness', apparently to the younger James Wallace, a modern reader sees this 'natural philosophical' range in a single document.[9] It is the single most tangible piece of evidence to survive of the scope of Fraser's 'scientific' interests. While it has been shown already that this letter, published in the *Philosophical Transactions of the Royal Society* in 1699, involved Fraser's ruminations on Gaelic language and toponymy, it also contained a potential response to Lhuyd's request for a 'catologue of the towns, castles, villages, mountains, vales, Lochs & Rivers, within ten (or twenty) miles'.[10] Bearing this range of 'curious' interests in mind, the chapter will turn now to examining what Fraser wrote about the world of cosmology, meteorology, geology and physical geography around the Beauly Firth, before moving on towards the animal and plant life which also absorbed him, showing how these latter interests influenced his approach to health and medicine.

COSMOLOGY AND CLIMATE CHANGE IN FRASER'S WORK

Fraser was no Brahan Seer, the legendary early modern prophet from the firthlands, and he does not mention him in his work.[11] Nonetheless, any reader of his manuscripts is struck by his frequent association of what many of us would consider purely natural events with prophecy. Born in the year following the Italian astronomer Galileo's second trial and condemnation for heliocentrism – the belief that the earth revolves around the sun – Fraser fits into that dynamic, inquisitive, yet puzzled scholarly world associated by many English speakers with Sir Isaac Newton. Commitment to astronomical methods and astrology was not mutually exclusive, as would be assumed today. The guiding principles of the Renaissance, in terms of philosophy, politics and biology, for example, but also in areas such as cosmology, were being challenged but not yet entirely overhauled. As a prime example, Fraser possessed a four-part 'booke of Profaces [prophecies]' and it may have been that this tome helped him give meaning to his reading of numerous, otherwise inexplicable, historical and current events. Amongst the explanations that we might today consider most unusual, Fraser supported the argument that the hiding, in 962, of the body of Dub mac Maíl Coluim, King of Alba, under a bridge at Kinloss, caused that 'sun nor moon never sheined for 6 months' in that spot, until he was found.[12] His explanation of certain events from his own lifetime can seem to defy logic too: Fraser's account of the 'Black Moonday' solar eclipse in early 1650s Aberdeen outlines how it had been predicted by contemporary writer William Lilly, albeit he was a 'lying astrollogue [astrologer] and a man infamous for his prognosticks and divinations against the King'.[13] The evidence does not indicate always a reasoned scepticism, on his part, about the connection between cosmic anomalies and political and social breakdown.

Horrific cosmological and meteorological events challenged Fraser and, in terms of explanations, the providence of the Almighty could not be ruled out, being a concept Fraser spent his *Divina Providentia* seeking to explain. The 'Wardlaw Manuscript' provides detail on how he reflected on the association between the celestial and the terrestrial. For example, he reports that around 11pm, on one October night in 1666, he became preoccupied with a 'Critick Constellation whose Influence hangs over our head' and which he thought was the cause of 'clear light' flashing into some local buildings.[14] More traumatically, in 1671, he concluded that a chain of ecological disasters spread out over an entire year in Kirkhill – signalled by multiple lightning strikes, three of them fatal, and other extreme weather events – was a case of divine retribution:

This was a very afflicting yeare in many places; great losse by raines, winds, frosts, the Spring too drye, snow and hard frost, the seed time cold and wett, the summer and fore-harvest constant rain; then ensued tempestuous winds, that all our costs [coasts] south and north had incredible losse by shakeing; and many parts in our Highlands rotting, blasting, and mildew destroyed corns. Lightning did much hurt to Oates on our hights, and many persons thunderstruck. I knew a pretty man who, going in an evening tuixt Boleskin and Mussaty [?] in Stratharick [Stratherrick], found dead in the morning, killed with a thunderbolt. A number of women washing at the river bank of Lossy near Elgin, the thunder rageing about them, two or three cryed out with feare, Lord God be with us, God blisse us. Another wretch replyed Blisse min arse: the word was hardly uttered but she was instantly struck to death in the midest of them, and non hurt but herselfe. One Balife John Dunbarr in Elgin had a labouring two miles above the town; his sone and servants being within a kill barn, tuisting roapes of straw, quhen a blast of lightning Sprung in at a window on the east end of the house and killed the young man, the sone, standing on the floor, and toucht none but himselfe; taken up stark dead. Another servant man on Speyside near Garmach [Garmouth], heareing the Cruell thunder roareing about him, the Atheisticall fellow cryed. Crack on and drown the corn the year as yow did Fornyear [?]. Gods judgement lighted on him deservedly, being instantly chockt w^t lightning, and fell dead uppon the ground. What dreadfull warnings are these, worthy to be regarded and Recorded by all Christians![15]

The sense of divine retribution is powerful and so it would be easy to dismiss these kinds of account as exaggeration. Yet, they are stories based on what was, for contemporaries, increasingly unpredictable and terrifying weather. The seventeenth century – still sometimes viewed as a period of 'general crisis' – sat in the middle of the 'Little Ice Age', an era lasting from the fourteenth to the early nineteenth century, evidenced in Europe by colder and wetter summers, particularly from c.1640 to 1660.[16] This had a particularly debilitating effect on agriculture at various points, with the 1690s the period's coldest recorded decade. Conditions were so bad across much of Scandinavia, the Baltic, France and, indeed, Scotland that populations experienced severe famine and greatly accelerated death rates.[17] The data highlights, for example, the advance of Alpine, Scandinavian and Icelandic glaciers, scarcity of sunspots, and frequency and strength of volcanic eruptions. All of these show reduced solar activity and thus a fall in temperatures in specific years of the century, while tree-ring data highlight fluctuating levels of seasonal precipitation.[18]

As for Fraser, his coverage of the horrors of the 1690s is patchy in terms of direct attribution to meteorology. Nevertheless, throughout the 1637–74 period covered in the 'Wardlaw Manuscript', he provides numerous such references, even if, strangely, the years in which he records extreme weather do not conform with those which modern scientific data associate with the greatest extremes. The reader is given cause to doubt his memory, at times, although, again, these sections of his account should not be dismissed as entirely fanciful. Crucially, excluding the year-long chain of climatic disaster quoted above, he explains them all without reference to prophecy or recourse to any obvious extreme emotion. Indeed, it is intriguing and, again, a suggestion of how we should consider his accounts with some seriousness that Fraser records, fatalistically, the repetition of destructive climatic events through regimes he usually chose to associate with good times (the Restoration) as well as bad times (the civil wars and the Cromwellian period).[19] Perhaps atrocious, life-threatening weather simply occurred too frequently either to be ascribed exclusively to periods he associated with misrule, or to be conveyed always as evidence of Godly retribution for wayward governance or social behaviour? Instead, he was usually persuaded that horrific climatic conditions were something that, while sometimes influenced by the divine, required a deep stoicism and resignation among the communities affected.[20]

Fraser showed a particular preoccupation with the destructive power of wind. Although this kind of destruction is certainly harder to connect to the 'Little Ice Age' than extremes of temperature or precipitation, the lack of analysis in previous scholarship of the impact of wind suggests that historians' assessment of weather in early modern history may require more complex modelling. In their exposure to wind, the Lovat Fraser lands were hardly comparable to the Culbin coast, east of Nairn, where Isobel Gowdie from Auldearn confessed to her coven of accused witches flaying as 'strawes in a whirlwind', perhaps a reference based on personal experience of what would cause the estate to become overwhelmed in a sandstorm in 1694.[21] They were also less changeable or capricious than the machair of the Western Isles or the shifting, sandy ecosystem of parts of Shetland. Nevertheless, Fraser mentions wind-related disruption in his parish and thereabouts between forty to fifty times in his major manuscript. Most strikingly, in 1658 there occurred locally 'a dreadful tempest and violent gusts' leading to a 'whirrycane' [hurricane].[22]

Fraser provides detailed first-hand accounts of ten other extreme weather events around the firthlands from across the middle decades of the century and, unlike with respect to the 'very afflicting yeare' of lightning strikes covered above, he does not suggest divine intervention as regards any of them. For example, in 1666:

> This spring was so wet and rainy that men dispared of Sowing, and frosts in April Impeded the bear [bere] seed. Then Came the Summer in so hot that from the beginning of May to the middle of July I remember not to see one shour [shower] of rain, so that men dispared of reaping. About the 10 of July there came a deludge of rain. This refreshed the corn wonderfully; yet the harvest was so aire and straw so scarce that we feared a generall death of Cattle for want of provender.[23]

More frequent than the suggestion of inexplicable, multifaceted, domino-like, climate-induced destruction spread over six months or more was Fraser's association of particular seasons or shorter periods with phenomenal meteorological harshness. Again, his accounts of these do not map easily to the years associated with the 'Little Ice Age', in northern European or global terms. For example, 1637's harvest at Kirkhill was, he claims, hit by 'inundation', floods which decimated the local grain and cattle yield and destroyed houses, cattle and orchards.[24] In the winter of 1664–5, a 'terrible storm of snow fell' in December and caused disruption 'till the 16 day of March following', involving 'vast loss of cattle', while Fraser recalls especially stormy springs in 1665 and 1667, and an 'unnaturall cold, frosty spring' in or around 1670.[25] The summer of that latter year was windy and wet while the following year a 'sad harvest' took place with 'an incredible shakeing of all cornes'.[26] The early autumn of 1672 was no better, characterised by a repeat of these 'tempestuous winds' and, once more, the 'sadest shakeing'.[27] Fraser's resigned, even stoical allocation of events to years may not always be accurate, then, and it is a long way from matching those years high-lighted as most severe, internationally, in volcanic activity or tree-ring data, for reasons that have yet to be explained.

The 'Wardlaw Manuscript' only goes up to 1674. For any hint of climate in Kirkhill over the next several decades, the historian is dependent on Fraser's aforementioned 'Bill of Mortality', which covers 1661–1709, and his letter to Lhuyd that was published in 1699. The former certainly accounts for increased human suffering in the 1690s, a time associated with the famine of the 'seven ill years', but it is much hazier in terms of relating this back to the local weather that might correlate with the broader patterns suggested in the scientific modelling.[28] Clearly, 1695, 1696 and 1698 brought a devastating series of bad harvests to Kirkhill, which led to pleas for importation of grain and rising prices, with malnutrition, starvation and dysentery replacing smallpox as the major killers in these years in Fraser's parish and across Scotland, according to Karen Cullen.[29] The first two of those devastating harvests led, according to Fraser, to 1697 being 'the year of the greatest mortality that I ever remember in this corner nay all Scotland over a running contagion of a plague, fluxes of all sorts', these including the likes of 'Janet a child of a stranger out of Glenelg died 22 Feb'.[30] Regarding the aforementioned 1699 letter, furthermore, he makes some unusual, possibly traumatised, observations, claiming that there was then a lochan at the top of Meall Fuar-mhonaidh on Loch Ness-side which 'never freezes' and, conversely, that there was a body of water on the mountain called 'Glen-in-tea' in Glen Affric, further north, called 'Lochan Wyn, or Green Lake, 18 foot in diameter, about a Fathom deep', which 'is always covered with Ice, Summer and Winter'.[31] While the climatic factors leading to these two cases appear contradictory, and the date of the letter's writing is unconfirmed, it might be fair to presume that it was the extremely unpredictable and troubling weather associated with the time that led him to comment on the two opposing pieces of evidence in this single letter.

The text's foray away from the lowlands and coast towards his local hilltops is repeated as regards his reflections on the peak of Sgurr na Lapaich, also in Glen Affric, regarding which Fraser comments on the oddity that:

> on the top of it there is a vast heap of white Stones, like Chrystal, each of them bigger than a man can Heave, they will strike fire like Flint, and have the smell of Sea-wrack. How these were brought there, or heap'd together, or what the nature of the Stone is, I do not know, nor is there any Tradition about them. Upon this Mountain is found also Oister-Shells in plenty, Scallop and Limpet shells, yet 20 miles from any Sea. Round about this hill grows the Sea-Pink, in Irish Teartag. It has the Tast and Colour of that [sic] grows upon our Sea Banks.[32]

This is hardly convincing scientific evidence but it does indicate a scholar striving, in trying circumstances, to explain the physical and natural world about him, seeking to balance this with, or indeed separate it from, his faith, and leads the discussion on to his attitudes to animate beings.

NATURAL HISTORY, DIET, HEALTH AND MEDICINE IN FRASER'S ACCOUNTS

As Fraser's search for explanations descends further from the heavens towards the firthlands, a new angle on his 'natural philosophic' interests becomes visible. His writing often occupies a space where cosmological, meteorological and geological preoccupations combine with an interest in natural history, and regarding which his Gaelic learning comes to the fore again. While Fraser affords relatively little evidence of a 'cultural history of animals',[33] he does, in the 'Wardlaw Manuscript', provide mentions of certain upland and lowland species. On one occasion, he reports wistfully, if not specifically, on the 'pretty birds' which 'publish the joifull newes of the springs approach', while, conversely, on 'Black Moonday', in Aberdeen, he recorded 'birds frighted and fluttering' due to the 'starrs being visible' during the daytime.[34] Elsewhere, Fraser mentions wolves (albeit they had died out in Scotland by his time), horses, dolphins, porpoises and whales in or around the Beauly Firth, and, in several cases, appears to reveal a markedly Gaelic worldview of these. Fraser laments species extinction around Abriachan and The Aird, the upland area to the immediate south of his manse, telling his readers about a fifteenth-century Lady Lovat, Meg Lyon of Glamis, a 'stout bold woman' who 'purged Mount Capplach [Caiplich] of the wolves'.[35] One perhaps sees in this an evocation of the *Cailleach*, the divine, female figure connected with nature and usually seen as responsible for the health of deer, in particular.[36] Horses feature especially prominently in Fraser's account, locally bred for both domestic work and for horseracing, while evidence from elsewhere shows that they were exported.[37]

As with dramatic changes in weather, the actions of animals could sometimes symbolise major political events too.[38] In 1644:

> There were also two Purpoises or spout whailes that ran up the River of Ness and under the bridge, and reacht the Isle a mile above the town, where they were killed. Some vented by coniectur [conjecture] that those two bigg whailes were an emblem of the King and Parliament, persueing one the other; but, alas, those things portended no good.[39]

More usually, Fraser offers an analysis of the brutality of marine life in straightforwardly political and social rather than symbolic or religious

Figure 4.1 Horses on a firthland beach, Tain

terms.[40] Again in 1644, 'two prodigious whales came up this firth with a high spring tide, the one persueing the other', and stranded between Tarradale and Spital, just across the firth from Kirkhill. Rory MacKenzie of Redcastle tried, initially, to claim them but, eventually, 'permitted the whole countrys on both sids to make pray of them, and, to my certain knowledge, they were so bigg and high that the people made use of small ladders to reach their top; the like never seen or heard off in the Murray firth'.[41] There was also a memorable and more symbolically significant Inverness case fifteen years later, when Fraser recalled rights being contested to the remains of a 'formidable big whaile' which had:

> stuck upon the lee shoare be-east Inverness, a mile. It was 70 foot long. I was present at the measuring of her. The debate began whither it was Culloden's March or the Townes; butt the Burgers of Inverness ceased the whale under appretiation, John Forbes of Culloden being then at south. The English offered to buy her at a high rate, and they should have got her be right, for all men concluded the whale to be a presage of the garrison's expiration and translation from Inverness, which happened shortly after.[42]

In 1660, three further 'big whales' were caught and landed on the Laird of Cawdor's land at Ardersier, causing the laird's second brother, Alexander Campbell, to load his gun to deal with a 'big sea maw [seagull]' that was tearing flesh from the carcasses. Tragedy occurred when Campbell shot himself dead, by mistake, in the process.[43] In addition, Fraser writes of 'a monstrous sturgeon fish of ten foot long' taken near 'Rindowy [Rhinduie]' on the Kirkhill parish shore, a 'fish, well dressed and pickled' in order to provide both 'meat and medicin' for the Cromwellian garrison.[44] Furthermore, a twelve-foot 'sturgion-fish' was caught in another local fish-trap, the 'Yarr [Yair] of Drumchardeny [Drumchardine]', in 1660, this one again a 'monstrous creatur', which the English members of the Inverness garrison bought and, this time, barrelled and sent to London. Prophecy trumped science on this occasion, in that Fraser thought the outsized beast might be a troubling sign, presaging the imminent death of 'some eminent person'.[45]

Garnering more of Fraser's attention than all other local waterborne creatures, and again reflecting his blend of 'natural philosophical' and religious attitudes, was the Atlantic salmon. Indigenous peoples from as far apart as the Pacific North-West of North America, northern Japan and Siberia have enacted complex rituals to mark the importance of this fish in their respective cultures, and belief in the 'salmon of knowledge' may have run deep for Fraser. Ordinary Highlanders sought, despite legal obstacles, to benefit from the apparent spiritual, commercial and nutritional value of what is often referred to in Scotland as the 'king of fish'. In 1629, the Scottish Privy Council had reported that one of the 'speciall temporall blessings [of] . . . the north pairts of this kingdome consists in the salmound [Atlantic Salmon] fishing'.[46] Several decades later, Daniel Defoe, renowned English trader, writer and spy, claimed that 'the rivers and lakes also in all this country are prodigiously full of salmon; it is hardly credible what the people relate of the quantity of salmon taken in these rivers, especially in the Spey, the Nairn, the Ness, and other rivers thereabout'.[47] For Defoe, salmon was 'in such plenty as is scarce credible, and so cheap, that to those who have any substance to buy with, it is not worth their while to catch it themselves'.[48] A few of Fraser's contemporaries warned against the fish, all the same. When visiting the region in the 1650s, the English traveller Richard Franck was – in contrast to those concerned today about infectious salmon anaemia and other diseases that can spread among and from captive stocks – worried simply that:

> should the inhabitants [of northern Scotland] daily feed upon them, they would inevitably endanger their health, if not their lives, by surfeiting; for the abundance of salmon hereabouts in these parts, is hardly to be credited . . . the danger, in my opinion, lies most in the diet: for as salmon is a fish very apt to surfeit, more especially fresh salmon, when only boiled; which if too frequently fed on, relaxes the belly, and makes the passages so slippery, that the retentive faculties become debilitated; so suffers the body to be hurried into a flux, and sometimes into a fever, as pernicious as death.[49]

The concept of the people of the early modern north Highlands surfeiting on wild salmon – a fish that was already a highly exclusive preserve in the region – seems hard to imagine, although Franck was not alone in claiming its limited role in ensuring a healthy diet. Clearly, despite salmon's high visibility, this 'highly paradoxical fish'[50] occupied a slippery position for the Lovat Frasers too, regarding whom the evidence backs Richard Hoffmann and, more recently, Jane Thomas's assertions that, in contrast to most of Europe, the northern Scottish market was buoyant if highly monopolised, with most profits leaving the region. Fraser reported, in the 1620s, that the 6th Lord Lovat considered salmon fishing should not be overvalued economically, for fear of invoking the wrath of the Almighty.[51] But, as he also makes clear, in his lifetime, the Lovat Frasers regulated fish passages and access, built a corf-house on the River Beauly and cultivated exports, making the most of the Scottish crown's repeatedly imposed public restrictions on salmon fishing, and applying or adapting various other technological, architectural and other innovations to benefit the trade.[52]

It is unclear just how much money the Lovat Frasers made from salmon. However, something of the wide dietary range that was possible in better times and at the higher levels of the household, even earlier in the century, is conveyed in Fraser's account of one occasion when:

> The Spending of this Noble famely extravagant – seven bolls malt, seven boles meale, one bole floure, every weeke; 70 black cowes in the year, besids venison, fish, pullet [chicken], kid, Lamb, veale, moorfoule, partridge, sea-foules, wild goose, Duck and Mallarts [mallards], etc, with all the presents and kists unaccountable; the wines in great [quantities] yearly from France, with Sugar and all manner of Spices, that it is incredible how any house could Spend this store and Provision yearly.[53]

Hospitality remained vital to clanship. In terms of nourishment, Fraser's own favoured drinks, while at home, ranged from ale and beer to wine, with whisky less common, cider an exotic, Cromwellian arrival, and tea or coffee going unmentioned until he went on his travels. Nevertheless, in times of plenty, the range of foodstuffs that the Lovat Frasers consumed widened in Fraser's adult life, combining readily available, locally grown oats, bread, cheese, fish, fowl, beef and venison, seasonal 'field and garden fruits' (apples, pears, cherries, unspecified 'berries' and 'pipens'), along with regular imports like French wine and sugar from the Dutch colonies. On top of this, Fraser notes more occasional products he obtained from visiting vessels like, in 1666, raisins, 'Kinary [Canary] rice', 'oyle, olive and spices' and, in 1670, an unexpected supply of mace, nutmeg, cinnamon, cloves and ginger.[54] These were all products recorded as coming in to the Inverness customs precinct, especially from the 1680s, although Fraser does not mention his local burgesses as a source for them in these years.

As for vegetables, plants and flowers, Fraser's comment in the 'Wardlaw Manuscript' on the joy with which Lord Alexander Fraser looked forward to that 'season which overspreads the gardens with flowers, the fields with grasse, and crownes the trees with blossomes'[55] suggests the attention the Lovat Frasers paid to their local produce. For Fraser, personally, it was an interest that extended to botany, as reflected in his possession of 'Wiridarium Wardlaense Herbal.', a manuscript that related clearly to herbs and plants, and helps us understand his proud mention of 'Allan Fraser My Lord Lovats page', who, 'having skill off plants', had been talent-spotted by the 'chirosurgeon' at the Prince and Princess Palatine's herbal garden in Heidelberg, Germany.[56]

Many of these drinks and foodstuffs had recognised, distinctive health-giving properties. The work of John Bannerman, Mary Beith and Helen Dingwall has emphasised the distinctive aspects of Gaelic Highland medicine in the period, although, conversely, as Wade Cormack has recognised, the connectivity of Highland medics to national and international trends, especially following the founding of the Royal College of Physicians in Edinburgh in 1681, is frequently under-recognised too.[57] A revised assessment of the Highland medical world would surely point to the kind of hybridity that was a feature of the other forms of scholarly life already covered in this book. Vital to understanding this would be to consider the hereditary physicians, the Bethunes or Beatons, once favoured by the Lords of the Isles. The Beatons were translators of Latin works such as the *Regimen Sanitatis*, a fourteenth-century poetic interpretation and set of recommendations regarding preventive medicine, one of twenty-nine surviving Gaelic medical treatises in Scotland. They were also a medical family with scions in Easter Ross, marrying extensively into the dynastic conglomerates presented by the Munros of Foulis and Gordons of Sutherland.[58] The Frasers relied heavily on them too. For example, Tolly Molloch (*an T-Ollamh Muilleach*), the 'Mull Doctor', who treated the Lord Lovat in 1558, was one of the last Beaton healers in Glen Convinth (south of Kiltarlity). James Fraser also records a Gilleandris Beaton, who, in 1612, removed the 'stone in his bladder' of a Thomas Fraser (b.1603), then 'fostered in Abertarfe with the M^ckgrewers' and who, although given a 'grosse milk dyet' to deal with various maladies, died shortly after. The Beatons' physical presence at Culnaskea (near Foulis) and Delny in Easter Ross certainly helped maintain this bond through Fraser's lifetime, paralleling a Neil Beaton on Skye, who used herbal cures 'without the advantage of education', according to Martin Martin's account.[59]

Highland medical knowledge continued to rely on a range of Gaelic, ancient Greek and Arabic theory, then, but the respect for purely local knowledge within that mix does appear to have lessened for the Lovat Frasers over the course of the seventeenth century. For James Fraser, the knowledge of family members, such as that 'Lady Dowager of Lovat' who, in 1564, treated her grandson, Hugh, 5th Lord Lovat, when he 'becam most indisposed, feverish, and somequhat ashmatick', was vital in terms of 'phisick': Fraser described her as the Earl's 'best doctrix' since she 'dyeted him well, and had him at the sea aire'. Chirurgeons (who focused on the diagnosis and treatment of injury, 'deformity' and disease), apothecaries (who prepared and sold medicines to physicians and directly to patients) and 'apothecary-surgeons' were all valued too.[60] The methods they used merged the kinds of medicine that the Beatons sustained with wider practice. Alongside them, and presumably inter-acting with them, was a growing range of local but university-trained medics, from 'Old Doctor Clerk', a 'highland phisitian of singular skill' employed by the Lovat Frasers in 1639–40, to the family's own Dr Alexander Fraser, a London-resident 'phisitian in ordinary' to Charles II. There was also a Dr Andrew Monro, 'phisitian' to the Cromwellian garrison in Inverness and one of the first in a longstanding Munro 'medical dynasty', as well as near-neighbours like Dr William Forbes, 'preferred in Pisa' in the 1650s but a return migrant.[61] The 'Wardlaw Manuscript' also reveals quacks like the Irishman and 'vile varlet' Mr John Sholes ('Dr Sholes'), who, in 1636, caused Lady Lovat's skin to turn 'dim yellow like a jaundice'.[62] Although Gaelic background was no issue when it came to the Lovat Frasers providing employment for medics – inviting comparison with a Gaelic Irish situation charac-terised by 'the endurance of patron-physician relationships at the elite level' – the Beaton dynasty had lost some of its standing among the Lovat Frasers already by Fraser's lifetime and begun moving towards more Lowland practices.[63]

CONCLUSION

In medicine, as in so many other spheres of life, James Fraser's account shows how the Highlands was open to the world, and to other parts of Scotland, and yet still changing and adapting along a distinct tra-jectory regarding which the world of the Beatons remained a striking, if threatened backdrop. Religious explanations were co-existing with, confirming or clashing with ones we would recognise as being scien-tific, for Fraser and his 'natural philosopher' contemporaries. However, there was at least one other supposed agent of good and bad health that one must consider when covering James Fraser: the topic of so-called 'witches' and their persecution is one to which the book's next chapter will turn, connecting this strongly with his life as a minister.

NOTES

1. *The Works of Sir Thomas Urquhart*, p. 331.
2. As Brockliss has asserted, it was the second half of the seventeenth century that would become the 'heyday of the experimental projector, wandering

from court to court'. See Laurence W. B. Brockliss, 'The age of curiosity', in Joseph Bergin, ed., *The Seventeenth Century* (Oxford, 2001), pp. 152, 166.

3. MacGregor, 'The genealogical histories'.

4. Domhnall Uilleam Stiùbhart, 'Martin, Martin (d. 1718), traveller and author', *Oxford Dictionary of National Biography* (Oxford, 2004), available at: <https://www.oxforddnb.com/view/10.1093/ref:odnb/9780198614128.001.0001/odnb-9780198614128-e-18201> (last accessed 23 December 2021).

5. Davidson and Morley, 'James Fraser's Triennial Travels', p. 206; Alex Sutherland, *The Brahan Seer: The Making of a Legend* (Oxford, 2009), p. 98; Kelsey Jackson Williams, 'The network of James Garden of Aberdeen and north-eastern Scottish culture in the seventeenth century', *Northern Studies*, 47 (2015), pp. 102–30.

6. Williams, 'The network of James Garden', p. 108; Roger L. Emerson, 'Sir Robert Sibbald, Kt, the Royal Society of Scotland and the origins of the Scottish Enlightenment', *Annals of Science*, 45 (1988), pp. 41–72; Charles W. J. Withers, 'Geography, science and national identity in early modern Britain: the case of Scotland and the work of Sir Robert Sibbald (1641–1722)', *Annals of Science*, 53 (1996), pp. 29–73.

7. Niemeijer, 'God created the Earth'.

8. Mackay, ed., *Chronicles*, p. xlv.

9. 'Part of a Letter Wrote by Mr. James Fraser, Minister of Kirkhil, near Invernes, to Ja. Wallace at Edinburgh, Concerning the Lake Ness, etc.', pp. 230–2.

10. Ibid.

11. Sutherland, *The Brahan Seer*.

12. Mackay, ed., *Chronicles*, pp. 33, 281–2.

13. Ibid., p. 398.

14. 'Wardlaw Manuscript', p. 318.

15. 'Wardlaw Manuscript', p. 332.

16. Martin Knoll and Reinhold Reith, eds, *An Environmental History of the Early Modern Period* (Berlin, 2014).

17. Geoffrey Parker, *Global Crisis: War, Climate Change & Catastrophe in the Seventeenth Century* (New Haven, CT, 2013), p. 20; Brian M. Fagan, *The Little Ice Age: How Climate Made History, 1300–1850* (New York, 2000); Karen Cullen, *Famine in Scotland – the 'Ill Years' of the 1690s* (Edinburgh, 2012); Robert A. Dodgshon, 'The little ice age in the Scottish Highlands and Islands: documenting its human impact', *Scottish Geographical Journal*, 121(4) (2005), p. 321.

18. Geoffrey Parker and Lesley M. Smith, 'Introduction', in Geoffrey Parker and Lesley M. Smith, eds, *The General Crisis of the Seventeenth Century*, 2nd edn (London, 1997), p. 7. For an Irish comparison, see Francis Ludlow and Arlene Crampsie, 'Climate, debt and conflict: environmental history as a new direction in understanding early modern Ireland',

in Sarah Covington, Vincent P. Carey and Valerie McGowan Doyle, eds, *Early Modern Ireland: New Sources, Methods and Perspectives* (Abingdon, 2019), pp. 269–300.

19. In the 'Epistle Liminarie' to his '*Divina Providentia*', Fraser provides a definition. See '*Divina Providentia*', ff. 1–3.
20. For the Gaelic worldview on cosmology and human ecology that almost certainly influenced Fraser in this regard, see Newton, *Warriors*, pp. 234–5, 284–326.
21. Emma Wilby, *The Visions of Isobel Gowdie: Magic, Witchcraft and Dark Shamanism in Seventeenth-Century Scotland* (Brighton, 2010), pp. 151, 208–9.
22. Dodgshon, *From Chiefs*, pp. 23–4. For contemporary sandstorms in Shetland, see <https://www.bates.edu/history/faculty/gerald-bigelow/shetland-islands-climate-and-settlement-project/> (last accessed 28 July 2022).
23. 'Wardlaw Manuscript', p. 317.
24. Mackay, ed., *Chronicles*, p. 272.
25. Ibid., pp. 455–6.
26. Ibid., pp. 492–4, 498.
27. Ibid., p. 521.
28. It might be useful to compare the climatic evidence he presents with that provided by James Allan, a Moray man who travelled through the firthlands in 1689–90. See Barrett, ed., *Mr James Allan*. For use of early modern Scottish church records to elucidate climate change, see Alan R. MacDonald and John MacCallum, 'The evidence for early seventeenth-century climate from Scottish ecclesiastical records', *Environment and History*, 19(4) (2013), pp. 487–509.
29. Cullen, *Famine in Scotland*.
30. 'Bill of Mortality'.
31. 'Part of a Letter Wrote by Mr. James Fraser'.
32. Ibid., p. 232.
33. Nigel Rothfels, ed., *Representing Animals* (Bloomington, IN, 2002); Dorothee Brantz, ed., *Beastly Natures: Animals, Humans, and the Study of History* (Charlottesville, VI, 2010).
34. Mackay, ed., *Chronicles*, pp. 145, 398.
35. Ibid., p. 110.
36. Newton, *Warriors*, p. 227.
37. See Chapter One; David Eltis, Frank D. Lewis and Kenneth L. Sokoloff, 'Introduction', in David Eltis, Frank D. Lewis and Kenneth L. Sokoloff, eds, *Slavery in the Development of the Americas* (Cambridge, 2004), p. 18.
38. Newton, *Warriors*, p. 291.
39. 'Wardlaw Manuscript', p. 210.
40. The 1650s English visitor Richard Franck described the Inverness to North Kessock route as 'exceeding hazardous' and 'rugged', believing he would be capsized not just due to the 'luxuriant tides, and aggravating winds,

that violently contract the surff of the sea', but because of the 'porposses' [porpoises or dolphins] that he thought were in danger of leaping into the boat. See Richard Franck, *Northern Memoirs, Calculated for the Meridian of Scotland* (London, 1694), pp. 173–5.

41. 'Wardlaw Manuscript', p. 210.

42. Mackay, ed., *Chronicles,* p. 425; John Brand, *A Brief Description of Orkney, Zetland and Caithness* (Edinburgh, 1883), pp. 6–7. Further evidence of a legal dispute in relation to beached whales survives with respect to a case from Findhorn in 1661. See William Macgill, ed., *Old Ross-shire and Scotland, as Seen in the Tain and Balnagown Documents*, 2 vols (Inverness, 1909), I, pp. 228–9.

43. Mackay, ed., *Chronicles*, p. 443.

44. Ibid.

45. Ibid.

46. *Register of the Privy Council of Scotland*, Second Series (Edinburgh, 1901), III, p. 18.

47. Daniel Defoe, *A Tour Thro' the Whole Island of Great Britain: Divided into Circuits or Journeys. Giving a Particular and Entertaining Account of Whatever is Curious, and Worth Observation*, 4 vols (London, 1742), IV, p. 212.

48. Ibid.

49. Franck, *Northern Memoirs*, p. 112.

50. Peter Coates, *Salmon* (London, 2006), p. 10.

51. Mackay, ed., *Chronicles*, p. 250; Richard C. Hoffmann, '*Salmo salar* in late medieval Scotland: competition and conservation for a riverine resource', *Aquatic Sciences*, 77(3) (2015), pp. 355–66; David W. Summers, 'Salmon fishing', in James R. Coull, Alexander Fenton and Kenneth Veitch, eds, *Boats, Fishing and the Sea*, Scottish Life and Society, Vol. 4 (Edinburgh, 2008), pp. 330–52; Jane Thomas, 'From monasteries to monopolisers: the salmon fishing industry of the inner Moray Firth region, 1500–1800', PhD thesis, University of the Highlands and Islands (2021).

52. Mackay, ed., *Chronicles*, pp. 217, 250–1, 345; Thomas, 'From monasteries to monopolisers'.

53. Mackay, ed., *Chronicles*, p. 245.

54. Fraser also relates the story that the family's surname related to 'fraise', the French for 'strawberry'. See ibid., pp. 218, 255, 278, 415, 478, 485.

55. Ibid., p.145.

56. 'Wardlaw Manuscript', p.341.

57. Mary Beith, *Healing Threads: Traditional Medicines of the Highlands and Islands* (London, 1995); John Bannerman, *The Beatons: A Medical Kindred in the Classical Gaelic Tradition* (Edinburgh, 1986); Helen M. Dingwall, *A History of Scottish Medicine* (Edinburgh, 2003), p. 54; Wade Cormack, 'Sport and physical education in the northern mainland burghs of Scotland

c. 1600–1800', PhD thesis, University of the Highlands and Islands (2016), p. 62; Newton, *Warriors*, pp. 24, 92, 93, 98, 192–5.

58. Cormack, 'Sport and physical education', p. 62; Iain Macintyre and Alexander Munro, 'The Monros – three medical dynasties with a common origin', *Journal of the Royal College of Physicians*, 45 (2015), pp. 67–75.

59. Bannerman, *The Beatons*, pp. 73–4, 79–80; Mackay, ed., *Chronicles*, pp. xxxvii, 145, 242, 265, 346–7, 415, 427, 504.

60. Barry Wright, 'Health and wellbeing in Highlands and Islands during the early modern period', MLitt dissertation, University of the Highlands and Islands (2013).

61. Cormack, 'Sport and physical education', p. 62; Mackay, ed., *Chronicles*, pp. 145–6, 242.

62. Ibid., p. 258.

63. John Cunningham, 'The history of medicine in early modern Ireland', in Sarah Covington, Vincent P. Carey and Valerie McGowan Doyle, eds, *Early Modern Ireland: New Sources, Methods and Perspectives* (Abingdon, 2019), p. 201.

5

The Minister:
Fraser's Influence on Kirkhill
Parish and Community

'ample testimony and approbation'

INTRODUCTION

CONTINUITY CAN SOMETIMES BE equated with reactionary attitudes and stasis as much as with elements we perceive more positively, such as stability and loyalty. Given he lived through the religious convulsions associated with the Wars of the Three Kingdoms, the Restoration, the 'Glorious Revolution' and the Treaty of Union, it may seem surprising to highlight it as a feature of Fraser's life as a clergyman. However, from one perspective, this is an appropriate approach to consider in relation to his clerical role. In particular, one enduring, longstanding intolerant element in his attitudes, mirroring that of the early modern Scottish kirk of his time, is its connection to the witch-hunt, the persecution and sentencing to death of many hundred, possibly above a thousand, women across Scotland, for supposed witchcraft. In the burghs of the firthlands, one sees the evidence that Shakespeare drew on, consciously or not, for his inclusion of a local example in his *Macbeth*: there is a stream of witch trials and killings of those accused from 1577 to 1727, in amounts rather similar, proportionately, to those found in many parts of Lowland Scotland, and at levels much higher than in the west Highlands.[1] In Kirkhill, specifically, women died in appalling circumstances as a result of witch persecution during Fraser's ministry and it is vital to consider his possible part in this.

The year of 1662 was particularly agitated in the Moray diocese, and parts further west and north, in terms of oppression of, and violence against, women on these grounds. For Fraser and the parishioners of

Kirkhill, it was a year indelibly altered by the actions of an individual who they initially knew as 'James Paterson'. Paterson was one of eight 'witch prickers' known to have been active in seventeenth-century Scotland. These were individuals who searched for the 'Devil's Mark' on the bodies of those suspected, using a long 'pin' to pierce the flesh of their victims and in order to identify a spot which, they argued, marked where the Devil had intervened. In the later words of Sir George MacKenzie of Rosehaugh, the 'pricker' would pronounce that 'if the place bleed not, or if the person be not sensible, he or she is infallibly a Witch'.[2] Through these brutal means, 'Paterson' became, according to Fraser's own account, responsible that year for the deaths of five women in the Moray diocese: two in Elgin, two in Forres and one in Inverness. The same 'Paterson' is less known, however, for causing women's deaths in Kirkhill, albeit Fraser describes the horror of what took place when this same 'pricker' arrived in his parish, when he:

> came up to the Church of Wardlaw, and w' in the church pricked 14 women and one man brought thither by the Chisholm of Commer [Comar], and 4 brought be Andrew Fraser, chamerlan of Ferrintosh. He first polled all their heads and amassed the heap of haire together, hid in the stone dick [dyke/ wall or ditch], and so proceeded to pricking. Severalls of these dyed in Prison, never brought to Confession.[3]

It is almost certain that Fraser believed that witchcraft was a diabolical act that was based on a pact with Satan, and one that should be punished severely. As Alex Sutherland has stated, Fraser 'does not condemn the accusations nor does he question witchcraft as such'.[4] Indeed, in the passage above, he was not expressing a desire to stop the hunt for witches in Kirkhill entirely, but his revulsion at the 'pricker' and their terrorising methods in removing the women's hair and violating them physically. The fourteen women all appear to have survived the initial assaults, although it is uncertain in which prison several of them died, be that in the parish or, one assumes more probably, Inverness. Furthermore, there is another element to the account that emphasises Fraser's focus as much on the 'pricker' and their unacceptable actions as on what is, to us, the terrible fate of the people accused. An unexpected addition to the story occurs in 'Paterson' turning out, in fact, to be 'a woman disguised in mans cloathes': it is startling to read Fraser express more unease regarding the 'vile, varlet [scoundrel]' nature of this 'imposture' than he does on the subject of the deaths of the assumed witches.[5]

This 1662 case sheds light on what will be, for modern readers, another, less appealing side of Fraser's character. It is certainly vital not to whitewash over his individual responsibility and the apparent misogyny suggested in the incident, recognising too that he was undergoing a drawn-out process of 'trials' connected with the outset of his ministry at the time the first of the incidents occurred. Nevertheless, elements of the 'witch-craze' would seem to have clashed with his scholarly interests in medicine, folklore, Gaelic culture and feminine wisdom.[6] On a superficial level, he conveyed respect for a range of women who sought a greater profile in the world of intellectual, educational and religious debate, this perhaps originating from a worldview in which the *Cailleach* was respected for her learning, albeit more research into this aspect of Fraser's work is necessary before firm conclusions can be drawn.[7] On the debating skills of Margaret Stuart, Lady Duffus (d.1667), Fraser considered her rhetorical abilities to be first-rate, to the extent that she was: '*malleus schismaticorum*, a hammer of phanaticks; they must be musled in her presence; she banterd them out of their persuasions with strong reason'.[8] When travelling through Utrecht he had been highly impressed by the fifty-two-year-old scholar Anna Maria van Schurman, who could 'discourse in the Oriental tongues and Disput of Divines', as well as numerous modern languages.[9] It is striking, and troubling, that none of this respect for the intellectual agency of women prevented him from presiding over the calamitous events that led to the deaths of innocents in Kirkhill in 1662.

From here, this chapter will now look to provide an overview of Fraser's career as a cleric, both before and after the 'Glorious Revolution'. At a superficial level, from being a model minister of the established kirk from 1661, with the arrival in England of William of Orange in 1688, the Scottish Parliament's signing of the Claim of Right in 1689, and the finalising of the 'Revolution settlement' in 1690, he moved to the edges, becoming wrapped up thereafter in a newly subversive, Jacobite-sympathising community. Yet, again, there is continuity to consider, since vital to any consideration of his religious life is that we assess him and his impact on his parish as a lifelong episcopalian. Put simply, episcopalians were (and are) those in Scotland who follow a Protestant church which includes the office of bishop or an equivalent. For them, the episcopate – the bishops as a collective – play a vital role in their respective regions (dioceses or bishoprics). Scottish episcopal bishops are not subordinate to the Pope, as in the Roman Catholic church, but, within the national hierarchy, stand at a level below the archbishops and the crown. At a sub-national level, they preside over dioceses and, in Fraser's time, as was the case for presbyterians, their ministers met in regional synods, in local presbyteries below those (these often in their nearest burgh) and, at the local, parish level, kirk sessions, albeit they were ousted from these during the civil wars and, from many, again upon the 1690 settlement. This chapter will assess whether or not Fraser's almost half-century as a minister exemplifies his part in what Raffe has termed an 'episcopalian confessional culture' across Scotland.[10] Raffe presents this as a worldview that pre- and postdated the Revolution of 1688–90, thus periods in which episcopalians were in the mainstream and on the margins, respectively, albeit which may have paralleled and even, to an extent, overlapped with a corresponding but less explored 'presbyterian culture'. Evidently, however, there is an alternative argument, which would have it that Fraser's fortunes pre- and post-1688 were rather different. As regards the Restoration period, Allan Kennedy presents a picture of a kirk that was, notwithstanding significant evangelical opposition in Argyll and Ross, functioning more effectively at parochial level than is usually considered.[11] John MacInnes went as far as to suggest that the nature of the hierarchy within the episcopalian church of the Restoration period matched well with that of clan society.[12] For those who are positive about the episcopal approach, then, evidence can be presented to the effect that the denomination was strong in the Highlands, a situation which ended abruptly in the decades that followed, although scholarly research is, in fact, not quite as advanced as regards its nature or fate in the period that immediately followed the 'Glorious Revolution'. In terms of histories of Highland religious life at that juncture, we lack the equivalent of Kennedy's work on the preceding decades.[13] Evidently, then, we still need to ask just how effective Fraser was as an episcopalian minister, both from 1661 to 1688 and, even more enigmatically, from 1688/90 until his death in 1709, and this chapter seeks to provide that.

KIRK SESSION, PRESBYTERY AND SYNOD IN KIRKHILL AND THE SCOTTISH HIGHLANDS, 1661–88

During Fraser's lifetime, the Scottish Protestant kirk, in both its major forms, episcopal and presbyterian, had to focus as much on the basic physical and financial challenges of building, populating, maintaining and supplying places of worship as it did on loftier issues of theological reflection and spiritual renewal. It lacked, persistently, and especially in the Highlands, church buildings and furnishings, manses and parish schools, Gaelic-speaking ministers, bibles that the majority could read, and the capital to pay for this from teinds (tithes charged on communities to pay for the clergy).[14] Moreover, it is assumed to have been almost endlessly vexed by how to stem the tide of 'delinquents', adulterers, fugitives and refugees that frequented its parishes. This does not suggest plain sailing. Thankfully, there are primary sources available for presenting how typical or not Fraser's own ministry was in these respects, it, indeed, being only through these materials that we hear any views of others on his character. Expressed another way, church records represent our only major non-autobiographical primary source set for him. Through a combination of the surviving minutes of the three main, concentric bodies of local governance – the Kirkhill kirk session (available for the years from 1707), the Inverness presbytery (available from 1632–44, 1670–88, 1702–8 and 1708–23) and the Moray synod (available from 1623–44, 1646–68, 1668–86 and 1702–13) – it is possible to draw some tentative conclusions about the state of Fraser's ministry and of worship in the parish, both before and after 1690. Given how frequently he attended all three bodies, at least before the Revolution, this will enable us to start to measure Fraser's impact on local and regional church life. Indeed, while the Kirkhill kirk session minutes have not survived for the Restoration period, the Inverness presbytery and, to a lesser extent, Moray synod records are a relative mine of information. They allow for the possibility of providing an outline of his part in the story of Kirkhill parish throughout the period from 1661 to 1709, and something of the nature of church authority and the workings of local politics, albeit, recognising their fragmentary nature, it remains imperative to consider the fault line of 1688–90 and how that altered or disrupted ministry and worship.[15]

Starting with physical geography, the parish of Kirkhill was centred around the southern shores of the Beauly Firth and the River Beauly estuary, stretching out southwards from there to a hillier, upland area ('The Aird'), an expanded area for the local deacons and elders of its kirk session after 1618 due to the union of the parishes of Wardlaw, in the west and south, and Fernua, to the east. In terms of the Inverness presbytery (erected first c.1581), of which the kirk session was a part, its geography was something of an extension of this. In the seventeenth century, Kirkhill's minister joined representatives of the parishes of Inverness and Bona, Kiltarlity, Urquhart and Glenmoriston, Dores, Daviot and Dunlichity, Moy and Dalarossie, and Petty, at these apparently bilingual presbytery meetings, and thus they formed a strongly Gaelic gathering, spread across both east and west sides of Loch Ness, with the burgh of Inverness as its most northerly representation. Completing the picture, in terms of church assemblies, Fraser also attended the Synod of Moray, which usually took place in Elgin, once or twice per year. Like the Kirkhill parish or Inverness presbytery writ large, the diocese of Moray had a northern, coastal hub but, similarly, extended well inland and upland to the south, south-west and west of the current administrative region, this being represented by the presbyteries of Strathbogie, Aberlour, Abernethy, Elgin, Forres, Nairn and Inverness; thus, at this wider level too, there was a Gaelic and Scots mix.[16] Both before and after 1690, parish-level social matters exercised all three of these local church bodies, with cases of male impotence, wife desertion, adultery, fornication, migration and delinquency, all mentioned at the pan-Moravian level, as was a concern about 'Lochaber and Glencoa [Glencoe] robbers'.[17]

Commencing with the kirk session records for Kirkhill, there is little of surprise, although much of colour, in the materials that survive from the last two years of Fraser's life and the first two years of Anglo-Scottish political union. The minutes record, for example, a 1708 distribution of oatmeal for the impoverished within the parish bounds, these including a 'poor south country stranger', as well as several blind parishioners, a cripple, widows, and 'our old mason'. They also deal with cases such as that of Isobel 'Nindowy', 'delinquent and slanderer in Finask [Fingask]', the migration into the parish of 'Kenneth McKay delinquent in Kinmylies', that of another parishioner 'designing for Orkney' and a further individual who was 'transported beyond seas'. Another case is that of 'Donald Mcbeanvickwilliam in Rindow [Rhinduie]', who is 'suspect of incest and fugitive to Strathnaver'. The minutes for February 1709 provide further details on the marginalised, recording an Alex Mcgilliphadrig to be 'an atrocious proflagat habitual whoremonger'. There is also mention of a petition relating to an Angus MacAndrew, a shoemaker in Easter Moniack, requesting a burial place in Kirkhill, and a series of reports regarding the illegitimate offspring of Donald MacAndrew and a Christian MacBride in Rinduy [Rhinduie], a pregnancy that had ensued on the former's return across the firth from 'Redcasttell [Redcastle] mercat'. As with sexual relations, reports of violence from 1709 indicate strongly, once more, the trans-firth nature of community life in Kirkhill, evidenced by the case of Anna Monro, spouse to an Inverness shoemaker, who, coming from the ('Mickel') Market of Beauly, accused a local man (Alexander MacKneel) of assault after 'coming with her from the Ferry in a rude manner'. MacKneel claimed, in his defence, to have 'Crosst the firth with such persons as Donald Dow the Ferrier knew' and to have offered to pay for Monro's ferry ticket.[18]

It is a great loss that we only have these two years of Kirkhill kirk session records from the period of Fraser's ministry and these from a time when he is likely to have been ailing and infirm. Consequently, the

Inverness presbytery records, for which the gaps are slightly fewer, must be considered as the main surviving source for Fraser's ministerial work. In many ways they suggest, accurately or not, Fraser to have been an archetypal, conforming cleric of the 1661–88 period. Without doubt, they convey an impression of him providing intellectual dynamism, as well as experience and stability through the 1670s and 1680s. They also record his enviable linguistic dexterity: in particular, his ability to 'code-switch' between Gaelic, Scots and English, which, as Chapter Three showed, typified church governance in episcopal Moray. Therefore, we should not be surprised that he was actually appointed the lead figure (moderator) in the Inverness presbytery for at least two years, 1677 and 1682, and is, more broadly, mentioned in the minutes frequently between 1661 and 1688. The presbytery was a body that met, weather and communications permitting, once or twice per month. Most crucial for our understanding of Fraser, the records contain information on three presbytery inspections of, or 'visitations' to, Kirkhill (in 1672, 1677 and 1682), each of which reveals something of the perceptions of the parish elders (all of them of the Fraser name), deacons and other church officers, regarding their minister and his character during what was, concurrently, a peak period in his writing. These suggest that Fraser was balancing his solitary, scholarly pursuits with his community responsibilities with some effect. During the July 1672 visit – and on Fraser being requested to leave the room – the moderator

> asked the gentlemen and elders how they were satisfied with their minister in life and conversatione, doctrine and discipline, if he did visit the sick, if he did visit families, if he catechised the people, if he did distribute the sacraments and whatever questions usuall in the like case.

While it was presumably not the place for detailed individual criticism, all present described themselves as 'well pleased' with Fraser before they 'blessed God for him and said that he deserved to be encouraged'.[19] When, in August 1677, the presbytery officers returned to Kirkhill, Fraser was the moderator. It is even less surprising, then, that, once again, the elders and deacons responded positively, pointing to their minister's exemplary use of the Catechism and Sacrament, and also his visiting of the sick, regarding which, they added, 'he was so panefull that they were affrayed that he should thereby shorten his own dayes in all likelihood'.[20] Regarding the May 1682 visit, the tone was similar once more, with the elders and deacons giving Fraser 'ample testimony and approbation [approval]'.[21]

Other references to Fraser in the presbytery records suggest his considerable clerical energy during those productive decades. A striking
example of this is that he was called on to make considerable journeys
to visit and offer guidance to other local ministers on transport links and
other improvements: for instance, to Kilchumin [today Fort Augustus]
(1677), Moy and Dalarossie (1680) and Petty (1682).[22] This advice
seems to have been architectural as much as anything else. Indeed, Fraser
was something of a pioneer in terms of building and furnishing, bearing
in mind what was, increasingly, a well-maintained church in his own
parish. By 1672, Kirkhill parish church had its own communion table
(albeit it had, like all other parishes in the presbytery, to borrow its silver
communion cups, presumably from Inverness).[23] Furthermore, in 1682,
Fraser recorded that John Fraser, 'a great mason, a sharp schollar, and
exact historian', was 'master masson at the building of the wester gavell
of our church', by which time the presbytery too recorded the church
to be 'compleit in thack [thatch], glass windowes, Lofts, dasks [desks,
seats or pews], church bible, pulpit cloath, and an excellent Bell and
bellhouse'.[24] Fraser also had his own manse from the 1670s, ahead of
the curve again in comparison with the other rural parishes in his presbytery. A further Kirkhill construction in Fraser's time was the parish
school, led by schoolmasters Charles Ritchie, in post from 1672, and
Thomas Fraser, who replaced him in 1682.[25] The genesis of these moves
dates back to before the mid-century wars and may have been the brain-
child of Fraser's predecessor, Rev. John Houston (d.1659), albeit he was
a minister who had strained relations with the Lovat Frasers, having
refused to preach at the 6th Lord Lovat's funeral sermon in 1633, and
who had been suspended from his duties by the Bishop of Moray in
Fraser's year of birth.[26] Therefore, this appearance of sustained, committed building work and renovation led by James Fraser as a model minister following the Restoration is almost certainly not an illusion. What
is less clear is whether it terminated with the Revolution of 1688–90,
after which Kirkhill parish was, formally, no longer 'in the pocket' of
the Frasers.[27] In 1707, the presbytery reported working with a glazier
and also an Alexander Clark in Kirkhill, who had been 'called in and
summoned to enter to thatch the Church Roofe and to Clay it firmly the
materialls being now provided'.[28] But there is no mention of Fraser in
this source. It seems either that the renovations of the previous decades
had been less sustainable than Fraser assumed, or else that the church
had fallen into disrepair quickly under the attempted introduction of
Presbyterianism, which coincided with the famines, severe loss of life

and other turmoil of the 1690s. The chapter will now turn to the finer detail of the evidence regarding this final, enigmatic twenty-one-year period of Fraser's ministry to ascertain just how disruptive it was for him and his parishioners.

THE 'GLORIOUS REVOLUTION' TO THE TREATY OF UNION AND BEYOND: FRASER'S ENIGMATIC YEARS AS MINISTER, 1688–1709

If we rely solely on contemporary primary sources, any sense of pre- and post-Revolution continuity in Fraser's life becomes faint. The first signs of a shift in fortune can be found in a reference from 5 September 1688. On that day, the Inverness presbytery was due to convene from within a situation of growing local and national turmoil. The moderator suspected that attendance was likely to be low due to 'the great stirs that were in the Country anent the late rebellion and bloodshed in Lochaber', this referring to the Battle of Mulroy in Lochaber of that August, inter-clan warfare which had pitted a body of MacDonalds of Keppoch against the MacKintoshes.[29] However, the presbytery pointed out another reason for non-attendance: internal dissent. The records outline a disaffected group they defined as 'others necessarily withdrawn as their excuses did carry'.[30] In the end, Fraser, whether loyal or reactionary in his thinking, was one of only two ministers to attend the meeting. Not only that, but this is the last mention of his name in any of the remnant Kirkhill kirk session, Inverness presbytery or Moray synod records.

In November 1688, William of Orange landed in England and the events that would become known to his supporters as the 'Glorious Revolution' began, pitting government forces against Jacobites for more than half a century. All was not calm in the north Highlands that winter. As Tristram Clarke has shown, by early the following year, 1689, reports were rife, at least in Inverness-shire, of ministers appearing 'not only in privat and in publict', where they not only 'doe dayly pray for the late King James but also doe make it their business to ryde and goe up and doun the countrey perswading the people to adhear to their all-edgance to the late King and to ryse in armes for him'.[31] However, there have been too many easy presumptions made by historians about the supposed, initial continuity of northern episcopalian life – at least of the variety which refused to accept William of Orange as king – that need to be assessed and addressed here. The contributor to the Kirkhill section in the *Fasti ecclesiæ scoticanæ* repeated a common assumption by claiming that Fraser 'did not conform at the Revolution, but continued undisturbed'.[32] In 1905, Mackay claimed that 'for many years after the Revolution there was virtually no presbytery either of Inverness or Dingwall, and every man within the bounds did what was right in his own eyes'.[33] The assumption made is that local, 'non-juring' episcopalians were able to continue to minister without the 'rabbling' associated with the south-west of the country, which saw them ejected from their parishes there. Lack of substantial written evidence should not be equated with lack of disturbance or conflict, however. In fact, the scraps of evidence of religious life that remain, when combined with sources covering the disastrous effects of the 1690s famines, suggest significant environmental and social disruption affecting the community at kirk session, presbytery and synod level in places like Kirkhill, an area where, previously, Fraser had received succour and been part of the mainstream.

With the kirk session minutes for Kirkhill only surviving from 1707 and Inverness presbytery records for the period reappearing again only in 1702 (when fears of Jacobitism led to a brief attempt to reorganise it from Forres), Fraser's visibility in these sources would appear to have faded somewhat, even had he conformed. Moreover, whether coincidental or not, the lists of presbytery attendees thereafter no longer separate out parish ministers or elders by name. But there was also some presbytery dynamism in those years. The Forres-run period encouraged renewed discussion around buildings and, more originally, an attempt to establish libraries that would bear fruit, in 1706, with the creation of the Inverness presbyterial library.[34] In 1703, the presbytery also recognised the need, caused by the disruption since 1688–90, to deal with 'several scandals lying over some fourteen years, some twelve, some ten'. Nevertheless, a growing lack of understanding further east in Moray of the largely Gaelic and Highland nature of the territory is highlighted starkly by references to 'desolate places in the Highlands within the bounds of the united presbyteries of Inverness and Forres' where ministers with the vernacular tongue could still not be recruited, and where 'papists' were still viewed as particularly problematic.[35] Certainly, the use of the word 'desolate' does not reflect the language used in the minutes of the bilingual Inverness presbytery or Moray synod as they had been from 1660 to 1688 – that is, more Gaelic gatherings – but is an early indicator of the kind of discourse that would eventually associate the Highlands, simplistically, with being a 'remote' outlier of Episcopalianism or Catholicism, and, from there, ripe for subversive Jacobitism. All of this makes the 1706 presbytery targeting of one 'piskie' minister, Rev. Alexander Denune of Petty, of especial interest as an example. The presbytery's case against, and eventual dismissal of, Denune does not make for easy reading, being focused on his swearing in 'Irish [Gaelic] and English', drunkenness, card-playing at Christmas, and visiting taverns and brewer's houses on the Sabbath for reasons besides 'necessarie busines'. It highlights the new reality, however. The dispute dragged on, with Denune travelling to London in March 1710 'to complain upon the hard usage he has met with from the presbiterians', this showing the stubbornness of formerly conventional, now marginalised, local episcopalian clergy.[36]

Was Fraser in the same boat? We get a fleeting glimpse of his newly subversive status in his involvement in a 1694 trial involving a Rev. Michael Fraser, minister at Daviot.[37] More significantly, by 1697, one sees evidence of a large body of the Lovat Frasers resorting to drastic measures to try to defend what they evidently considered a dramatically threatened inheritance, and, if not James Fraser's clear engagement in this, at least that of his son, Alexander. In 1698, there occurred at the High Court of Justiciary in Edinburgh the 'Proceedings against Thomas Fraser of Beawfort, Captain Simon Fraser, and Others, for Treason and other Crimes'. The Simon Fraser in question was the famous or notorious Simon Fraser, later to become 11th Lord Lovat, the 'Old Fox' who would be executed after Culloden. He and his father had become disaffected from 1696, due to a dispute with John, Lord Murray, following the death of Hugh, 9th Lord Lovat, and regarding the claims of the latter's wife, Amelia Murray. The key question was whether their daughter, also Amelia, should inherit, passing control, and title, to Lord John Murray, Earl of Tullibardine, or else if it should pass to Thomas Fraser of Beaufort. The Beaufort Fraser response had been to force Amelia, the 'lady dowager', to marry Simon. It was this that provoked the government to action. According to the trial, conducted in the absence of the alleged lead conspirators, those involved had then 'unlawfully leagued and combined together for to ryse in armes and prosecute their mischievous practices'.[38] Specifically, they were accused of capturing Tullibardine and another 'redcoat' government agent, Lord Saltoune, sending out the Fiery Cross and gathering over 200 men in arms in 'open and manifest insurrection and rebellione'. The trial sentenced the leaders of the rising to death for the crimes of treason and rape.[39] Simon Fraser fled to Skye, took the title of Lord Lovat from 1699 and then, in 1702, moved on to the Jacobite Court in St Germain, France. He thereafter became a major, if shadowy presence locally, exemplifying the ever-growing drama and complexities surrounding the Lovat Frasers' position, until his death forty-five years later.

Another case of Fraser-led unrest, if also division, locally came in the form of a chain of events leading from a riot in Beauly in August 1702, and ensuing turmoil which led to the quartering of soldiers in Fraser-controlled Stratherrick for part of 1704, this possibly affected also by Lord Lovat's return from France in 1703.[40] But life was going 'underground' not only for those at the top of the Lovat Fraser tree. Evidently, it was far from stable for the septuagenarian Rev. James Fraser too. Aside from one example of scholarly correspondence, published in 1699, historians rely solely on his extraordinary 'Bill of Mortality' as evidence for his actions and attitudes in response to the Revolution. It makes for rather a bleak assessment. If measured in terms of the death rate, 1697 and 1699 appear to be the worst of the 'ill years' of the famine in Kirkhill, with Fraser recording 112 deaths in the former year and 93 in the latter.[41] Mortality occurred within all age groups in these years, and could come to 'infant', 'niece', 'child', 'boy', 'young man', 'spouse', 'goodwife', 'widow', 'old man', 'old woman' or 'stranger'. Finding

Figure 5.1 English and Gaelic language plaque to James Fraser, Wardlaw Mausoleum, Kirkhill

positives in the account is challenging. Slightly more happily, though, one sees Fraser recording the sheer variety of occupations of his parishioners of the time, ranging from ferrier, miller, chapman, cottar, shoemaker, wright, weaver, grieve, shepherd, 'Irish Harper', servant and tenant. Moreover, there does seem to have been some demographic recovery in the parish by 1709, when Fraser reports 'how long people live in our latter age', mentioning no less than seventeen octogenarians who had died in the last several years, also one ninety-year-old and, finally, the impending passing of himself: 'Mr James Fraser Wardlaw 76'.[42]

CONCLUSION

In terms of James Fraser's ministry, those last two decades, the 1690s and 1700s, remain startlingly enigmatic. The 1688 presbytery account and other scraps of evidence suggest that he associated with the nascent Jacobite community, perplexed and galvanised at the turn of events that had led to them moving from being insiders to outsiders. Fraser, the educated and confident traveller, scholar, minister and prophet, lived on the margins in his final years. On his eventual death, in 1709, no new episcopal minister would be appointed to Kirkhill.[43] Eventually, the established church succeeded in appointing a presbyterian incumbent as replacement, but the appearance given is that it took many decades, perhaps longer, before the relative, albeit exaggerated, sense of stability conveyed in records for the 1661–88 period was seen again. Indeed, the unfortunate fate of Fraser's successor at Kirkhill, Robert Thomson, was to have his manse attacked, in 1743. One finds it hard to see evidence of marginalised presbyterians in the parish doing the same to Fraser in the century before. Perhaps those who would have been most justified in protesting to the 'curious cleric' were any still-living representatives of those innocent 'witches' who had survived the 1662 persecution covered at the outset of this chapter. They were a community in early modern Scotland whose testimonies remain much more in the shadows than that of the Highland clergy of the age, whether episcopalian, presbyterian or Catholic.

NOTES

1. Mackay claimed, contentiously, as regards the presbyteries of Inverness and Dingwall, that 'there was little of the nature of religious fanaticism to be found within our bounds during the period of the Records, and the consequence was that when witches and charmers were brought before the

Presbytery they were mercifully spared the cruelties and death which would have been their lot had their lines fallen besouth the Grampians, or in the Lowlands of Moray'. However, this appears to ignore that Inverness presbytery was an intrinsic part of the Synod of Moray. See Mackay, ed., *Records of the Presbyteries of Inverness and Dingwall, 1643–1688* (Edinburgh, 1896), p. xl; Lizanne Henderson, 'Witch-hunting and witch belief in the Gàidhealtachd', in Julian Goodare, Lauren Martin and Joyce Miller, eds, *Witchcraft and Belief in Early Modern Scotland* (London, 2008), pp. 95–118; Michelle Brock, *Satan and the Scots: The Devil in Post-Reformation Scotland, c.1560–1700* (Farnham, 2016).

2. Sir George Mackenzie, *The Laws and Customs of Scotland, in Matters Criminal Wherein is to be Seen how the Civil Law, and the Laws and Customs of Other Nations Do Agree with, and Supply Ours* (Edinburgh, 1678), pp. 91–2.

3. 'Wardlaw Manuscript', p. 297.

4. Sutherland, *The Brahan Seer*, p. 78.

5. Ibid.; S. W. McDonald, 'The Devil's mark and the witch-prickers of Scotland', *Journal of the Royal Society of Medicine*, 90(9) (1997), pp. 507–11; Julian Goodare, 'Men and the witch-hunt in Scotland', in Alison Rowlands, ed., *Witchcraft and Masculinities in Early Modern Europe* (New York, 2009), pp. 149–70; Henderson, 'Witch-hunting and witch belief', pp. 104–5; William Mackay, 'The Strathglass witches of 1662', *Transactions of the Gaelic Society of Inverness*, 9 (1879–80), pp. 113–21. Michael Graham of the University of Akron is currently using Fraser's 'Divina Providentia' to trace his account of the infamous trial of Major Thomas and Jean Weir for witchcraft, in 1670.

6. In a recent article, Brochard has highlighted the significant presence of female teachers in the north Highlands in the period. See Brochard, 'Intellectual and practical education', pp. 177–8.

7. Mackay, ed., *Chronicles*, p. 110.

8. Ibid., pp. 474–5.

9. *Triennial Travels*, III, ff. 89v–90r.

10. Alasdair Raffe, *The Culture of Controversy: Religious Arguments in Scotland, 1660–1714* (Woodbridge, 2012) and the same author's earlier article, 'Presbyterians and episcopalians: the formation of confessional cultures in Scotland, 1660–1715', *English Historical Review*, 125(514) (2010), pp. 570–598.

11. Allan Kennedy, 'The condition of the Restoration Church of Scotland in the Highlands', *The Journal of Ecclesiastical History*, 65(2) (2014), pp. 309–26.

12. Cited in ibid., p. 317.

13. Kennedy, 'Managing the early-modern periphery, pp. 32–60; Paul Hopkins, *Glencoe and the End of the Highland war* (Edinburgh, 1986). For Scotland-wide coverage, see Ann Shukman, *Bishops and Covenanters: The Church*

in Scotland, 1688–1691 (Edinburgh, 2012); Jeffrey Stephen, *Defending the Revolution: The Church of Scotland, 1689–1716* (Aldershot, 2013) and the same author's 'Defending the revolution: The Church of Scotland and the Scottish parliament, 1689–95', *Scottish Historical Review*, 89 (2010), pp. 19–53; and Allan I. Macinnes, Patricia Barton and Kieran German, eds, *Scottish Liturgical Traditions and Religious Politics: From Reformers to Jacobites, 1560–1764* (Edinburgh, 2021).

14. Kennedy, 'The condition'; Kelly, 'The Society in Scotland'; Brochard, 'Intellectual and practical education'. For the roots of these challenges, see Chris R. Langley, Catherine E. McMillan and Russell Newton, eds, *The Clergy in Early Modern Scotland* (London, 2021).

15. These comprise: the Kirkhill kirk session minutes, available for the years from 1707; the Inverness presbytery records, available from 1632–44, 1670–88 (printed), 1702–8 (when Inverness presbytery was united to that of Forres) and 1708–23; the records of the Moray synod, available from 1623–44, 1646–68, 1668–86 and 1702–13. See Highland Archive Centre [hereafter HAC], Kirkhill Kirk Session Minutes, CH2/675/1; HAC, Presbytery of Inverness, CH2/553/1–4; NRS, Synod of Moray, CH2/271/1–4.

16. We see Fraser listed in the synod records for the first time in 1661, as one of seven ministers representing Inverness presbytery, while, between then and 1688, he is a fairly regular attendee, although with intriguing, puzzling gaps in 1662, between 1664 and 1668, and 1676 and 1685, years in which he appears to have been active and influential at presbytery level. See CH2/271/2, p. 363.

17. 19 July 1676, Mackay, ed., *Records of the Presbyteries of Inverness and Dingwall*, p. 72.

18. CH2/675/1.

19. 23 July 1672, Mackay, ed., *Records of the Presbyteries of Inverness and Dingwall*, pp. 29–31.

20. 21 August 1677, ibid., pp. 78–9.

21. 17 May 1682, ibid., pp. 107–9.

22. CH2/675/1; Mackay, ed., *Records of the Presbyteries of Inverness and Dingwall*, pp. 82–3, 97, 107–9, 112, 114.

23. Ibid., pp. xx–xxiv.

24. CH2/675/1; Mackay, ed., *Records of the Presbyteries of Inverness and Dingwall*, p. 109.

25. Kelly, 'The Society in Scotland', pp. 29, 31, 119.

26. Mackay, ed., *Chronicles*, pp. 252, 256–7; Hew Scott, ed., *Fasti Ecclesiæ Scoticanæ: The Succession of Ministers in the Church of Scotland from the Reformation*, 7 vols (Edinburgh, 1926), VI, p. 472.

27. For possible comparison with Kirkhill, see Bill Inglis, 'The impact of Episcopacy and Presbyterianism, before and after 1690, on one parish: a case study of Dunblane kirk session minutes', *Scottish Church History*, 33(1) (2003), pp. 35–61.

28. Scott, ed., *Fasti Ecclesiæ Scoticanæ*, 6, pp. 472–4.
29. 5 September 1688, Mackay, ed., *Records of the Presbyteries of Inverness and Dingwall*, pp. xix, 135.
30. Ibid.
31. Tristram Clarke, 'The Scottish Episcopalians 1688–1720', PhD thesis, University of Edinburgh (1987), pp. 45–6; Macinnes, *Clanship*, Chapters 5 and 6; Hopkins, *Glencoe*, p. 205.
32. Scott, ed., *Fasti Ecclesiæ Scoticanæ*, 6, p. 473.
33. Mackay, ed., *Records of the Presbyteries of Inverness and Dingwall*, p. xix.
34. Manwaring-McKay, 'Charles Fraser-Mackintosh (1828–1901) and his books', p. 133.
35. HAC, CH2/553/3, pp. 1, 15, 39, 41, 49, 88, 101, 114, 179, 253.
36. CH2/553/3, pp. 123–32, 142, 145–7. For the engagement of the Frasers of Petty in India from the early eighteenth century, see Andrew Mackillop, *Human Capital and Empire: Scotland, Ireland, Wales and British Imperialism in Asia, c.1690–c.1820* (Manchester, 2021).
37. Raffe, *The Culture of Controversy*, p. 165.
38. *Proceedings Against Thomas Fraser of Beaufort, Captain Simon Fraser, and Others, for Treason and other Crimes* (Edinburgh?, 1698?), p. 3.
39. Ibid., p. 4.
40. Kennedy, 'Managing the early-modern periphery', p. 48.
41. 'Bill of Mortality'; Cullen, *Famine in Scotland*, pp. 145–8, 165.
42. 'Bill of Mortality'.
43. Clarke, 'The Scottish Episcopalians', pp. 596–7.

6

The Historian:
Fraser's Contribution to Early Modern Highland and Scottish History and Historiography

'that telescope by which we see into distant ages'

INTRODUCTION

L IGHTHEARTED AND IDIOSYNCRATIC ASIDES punctuate James Fraser's work revealing an aspect of what makes his approach to history-writing unique. However, in terms of his weightier reflections on the past, his leading statement of intent is to be found in one specific paragraph in the 'Wardlaw Manuscript', in which he states:

> History being so germin and familiar to men of all Estates, Age, quality, Sex, and Condition, so agreeable to the inclination and suitable to the humor of all, so delightfull in the perusall and profitable in the retention, affording content to the aged, pleasur to the young, and experience to both, comfort to the disconsolat, refreshment to the weary, and ease to discomposed minds; solaceing the tedious houres of pensive watchings, or otherwayes charming anxious thoughtes into a sweet and gentle repose, being never out of season whilst men have life and the world a being, that among the many eulogies it hath received from the learned pieces of ancient and modern writers it may be justly accounted rather the recreation than the application of a Studious man. It is indeed that Telescope by which we see into distant ages, and take up the actiones of our forefathers with as much evidence as the newes of the last Gazette. It is the Mirrour that represents the various transactions of times past, and showes us the dresse of Antiquity according to which we may rectifie or adjust our present fashiones. It is the produce of gentle and easie institutions and laws which ought to oblidge us as much, if not more strickly, than the perceptive Sanctions of Princes, seing the authority of the one dos but inculcat our duty, and the other gives us innumerable instances of the several rewards of vertue, and punishments of vice. It is, in a word,

the Last will and Testament of our deceased Progenitors, which, thoug it dos not expressly leave every one of us a particular Legacie, yet it showes us how we may be possessed of their inheritance, and, according as we follow their Example, live in reputation or Ignominy.[1]

This section of text reveals that, for James Fraser, history had multiple purposes. While it sometimes offered respite, comfort or escape from current woes, it could also provide vital examples of good and bad practice to inform present-day public life. Knowledge of the past was not entirely incontrovertible or immutable but required careful archiving and regular re-presentation by scholars in order to take on its full meaning and purpose. Historians provided consolation or practical guidance for the modern day, not by presenting facts alone, but by applying the best tools, arguments and concepts available in their own time in order to convince contemporary and future readers and audiences. Good history-writing was not a 'naked-eye' view on the past, then, but, using Fraser's own analogy, it was best compared to a 'telescope', a then new, fashionable and rather exclusive instrument, one that could bring into clear view much that had been obscure or invisible previously. In other words, for Fraser, even the most outstanding history did not constitute an infallible or 'irrefutable' presentation of facts and events but relied on interpretation, and it was that which, in the hands of a good, well-equipped historian, brought readers as close as they might get to a 'mirror' view of the features of a given age and place. Indeed, if the historian succeeded in providing such a lens on the past, their work might sometimes, rightly or not, be considered authoritative, even the 'last will and testament' on a given theme, a judgement that might have long-term implications for the relative posterity or infamy of an individual, their family, region or nation.[2] Deploying two of Fraser's metaphors, this chapter will consider how he sought to present his own historical work in the sharpest possible focus and dressed in the best available clothing.

We might reflect critically on Fraser's subjectivities as a historian usefully from the perspective of many other key issues of our own age – gender, ethnicity or race, for example – and these areas are given attention in other chapters.[3] He did not claim to cover these topics in his historical works. However, he was certainly aware of his potential 'biases' on the subjects of politics and religion. As he expressed it, 'judgement and signalised impartiality eternises an historian' so '[t]hat oyl is judged the best that hath no tast, that author should be the most preferred that hath the least tangue [taste] of interested affections'.[4] In this way, Fraser sought, at times, to conceal his opinions on major governmental or confessional issues, making him appear either admirably balanced or else often non-committal and ambiguous, even contradictory, to readers today.

It has been shown already that Fraser had much to comment on when it came to the pasts of all three geo-political spaces he knew best: the Highlands, Scotland and 'Britain'. On the Highlands, his view clashed with one that can be traced via late medieval Lowland writers like Fordun, Bower and Wyntoun, followed by Highland-born Bishop John Leslie, an outlook which considered the region as irredeemably 'wild'. That was a view which had been elaborated on, most recently, in James VI's *Basilikon Doron*, a stark presentation of national history which framed it in terms of Lowland 'civility', on one hand, opposing Highland 'barbarity', on the other.[5] As far as can be told, Fraser's reaction to this should not cause us to regard him as something of a Highland version of the Anglo-Norman-descended, 'Old English' Geoffrey Keating (Seathrún Céitinn) (c.1569–1644): Keating created a new kind of post-Reformation Irish history-writing, written in Irish, that merged Gaelic and 'Anglo-Irish' perspectives there.[6] Yet, while Fraser could be exceptionally critical of his region, even dismissive of some elements of its past, he evinces something other than the 'undiluted rancour' of the Jacobean approach towards the Gaelic or wider Highland world. At a Scottish level, he conformed, in general, to the more recent approach of fellow Gaelic native speaker George Buchanan in seeking a narrative that integrated the Highlands with the Lowlands into a broader Scottish story, rejecting one as unquestionably superior to the other in every aspect.[7] In this way, there was a strong engagement with wider Scottish trends in his work, to the extent that he helped build on what Kidd has called the 'formidable ideology of Scottish nationhood', and is a representative of that 'vigorous tradition of polemical scholarship' that, in David Allan's view, grew up among the country's seventeenth-century intellectuals.[8] On 'Britain' and 'Britishness', furthermore, it will be shown to be difficult, and anachronistic, to pin Fraser down to what we might recognise as an overtly 'nationalist' or 'unionist' stance, albeit the debate was not one that he shied away from.[9] By the sixteenth century, 'British' versions of the Scottish past were appearing, as evident in the work of the Scottish-born John Mair (Major), influenced also, from England, by William Camden, in whose approach Fraser took a keen interest. Important to consider in all of this is that Fraser's surviving works are written in English, confirming their designation for a pan-archipelagic audience. They evince an internal tension between Highland, Scottish and 'multiple kingdoms' approaches to political history in the period of Regal Union in which he lived all but the last two years of his life.[10]

This explains, in part, why Fraser's political affiliations are not always clear-cut. In another sense, though, his apparent ambiguity is a rather unsurprising response to the massive, perplexing scale of political, social and environmental challenges at sub-national, national and supra-national level during the period in which he wrote, this covering the Wars of the Three Kingdoms, Restoration, 'Glorious Revolution' and early years of the Jacobite movement.

On religion and its effects on his history-writing, similarly, and with-out being disengaged, Fraser evades easy categorisation. The last chap-ter positioned him as an episcopalian minister, transplanted from the mainstream to the margins after the 'Glorious Revolution', and we need to consider how this affiliation affected him as a historian. Tremendous scholarship is emerging on the early modern Protestant clergy of Scotland and their attempts to navigate the stormy religious waters of the entire Regal Union period.[11] In light of this, it might be argued that we should view Fraser as part of that 'first Scottish Enlightenment', a group out-lined most recently by Kelsey Jackson Williams as a northern, Aberdeen-oriented, episcopalian or, crucially, Catholic flowering of historians and other scholars that, he argues, commenced in the Restoration period and retained significance until well after Fraser's death.[12] Williams has claimed, rather convincingly, that 'acts of research, interpretation, com-position and correspondence occurred in the privacy of rural manses, island schools and isolated tower houses in highland glens' across late seventeenth-century northern Scotland, interlinking 'a far-flung intellec-tual community, based on a shared education in Aberdeen but stretching north and west to Inverness, to Sutherland, and to Kirkwall'.[13] While Fraser appears to be part of this body of virtuosic polymaths, and the north-east, Aberdeen and, quite possibly, Orkney were a magnet for him, on the whole, he provides evidence of a less partisan, doctrinal or denominational element than Williams's model allows. Living in the firthlands, and as an episcopalian-sympathising minister surrounded by many who were not, Fraser's confessional adaptation, at least before 1688, to a local population that also included a shifting mix of presby-terians (and a wider variety of Protestants in the period of Cromwellian occupation), as well as a smaller proportion of Catholics, is striking. In this way, we might view him as being a rare, episcopalian, Gaelic-supporting representative of that group of largely, but not exclusively, presbyterian writers and bibliophiles already considered in Kelly's 2020 doctoral thesis, who created the basis for what would become, in 1709, the Society in Scotland for the Propagation of Christian Knowledge (SSPCK).[14] This was a body of Protestant divines who sought greater public access to, and engagement with, not only the Bible, but a range of historical and theological books in English, especially across the Highlands and Islands, from the 1690s on.

Although a compelling argument again, this does not fit Fraser perfectly either. When assigning him identities (such as 'royalist' or 'Covenanter' in the civil wars, 'Tory' or 'Whig' in the Restoration period or, after 1688, Jacobite or anti-Jacobite), it is most important to remember that his affiliations took him back to a period even prior to the mid-century wars. Fraser had survived the vicissitudes of the age only by developing an ability to move in several confessional and denominational camps. Indeed, in many ways, we are better to understand the influence of religion on him as a scholar, not in terms of political or theological doctrine or ideology, but by positioning him within a more mercurial clerical grouping which had navigated these tides, an approach supported by the work of Karin Bowie, David Allan and Alasdair Raffe.[15] These historians have emphasised Scottish debate and discussion across denominational lines, both before and after 1689. Away from the south-west, this saw relatively comfortable Restoration supporters of a Protestant church with bishops transform, potentially, into early-Jacobite Protestants in the famine-riven 1690s, and yet continue, against the odds, to occupy part of the political and theological mainstream rather than being consigned, or consigning themselves, to the margins.

Underpinning all of Fraser's writings are further concerns and subjectivities. As has been shown, his admission that, as 'a patriot and homebred historian', he might be 'suspected of partiality' may have been admirable, but it did not extend to any sort of critique of his own kith and kin, whose reputation and standing he did not consider capable of criticism in any significant way.[16] Fraser, a *seanchaidh* – that is, a hereditary genealogist, 'memory-keeper' and storyteller of the Gaelic world – conveys a chauvinism towards his family at many points in his historical writing, and this is another reason why readers should treat his works with caution, when using them as primary sources. Fraser was a representative of what Martin MacGregor has termed a 'transitional era in which the scope of the term seanchaidh(ean) was extended and it becomes debatable whether we should understand it in its original, technical sense of "classical professional historian-cum-genealogist" or as a blend of this and more universal approaches'.[17] To a broader Scottish and English-speaking audience, he was, alongside Martin Martin, the prime Highland 'public historian' of his day. His early passion for his family's genealogy interconnected with a later wish to educate and make available to his community not only religious texts but also the widest range possible of historical accounts relating to the Frasers, the Highlands, Scotland and the wider world. This does not always make him reliable, but it gives him enduring value and significance as a source, offering an extremely detailed and different, if, as yet, poorly known, perspective.

FRASER AND HIS SOURCES FOR HIGHLAND AND SCOTTISH HISTORY

To a modern reader, prejudice is readily apparent as a feature of Fraser's approach to writing history. However, he also brought a strong epistemological bent to his work. As he put it: 'no history admits nor requires a mathematical or legall proofe, but rests satisfied with such moral certanty as is inferred from probable tradition, old manuscripts, credible historians, and persuasive reasone'.[18] He claimed to have little time for mythologising, or those scholars for whom 'so soone as they transgresse the bounds of authentick records and monuments of antiquity, the rest is no more history, but the conjecturs and probabilities of the authors'. In fact, Fraser's history-writing, like much else in his life, mixed approaches, so that he wove together research in physical archives with the oral history, narrative and performative threads expected of the *seanchaidh*.[19] Fraser identified with the *seanchaidh* in the more 'modern' form, then, one in which the written record was taking more prominence. He claimed to be unimpressed by 'compatriot clanes' who asserted their own standing without evidence, instead preferring work that was based, in part, on painstaking use of manuscripts. Fraser argued that good history could not be built on 'feud' or 'traditional fables', it being 'below my spirit and genius, and derogatory to the great subject, to depend upon frivolus vagnes'.[20]

In terms of the range of sources he considered would maximise his objectivity and distinctiveness, he boiled them down to four vital types: 'Manuscripts and charters in our own possession'; 'Church Registers and records in publick offices'; 'Printed history'; and 'Instructions receaved from the Bards, and nearest nighbours and allyes'.[21] His arguments around the first and fourth of these types of source are perhaps most original and of greatest interest here, although his statements regarding all are worthy of reflection. If we take his conceptual, historiographical and personal considerations on each type of source in turn, his contribution to early modern historical research, reading and writing should become evident.

'Manuscripts and charters in our own possession'

Fraser began his manuscript research at home. As has been mentioned in earlier chapters, embedded front and centre in his 'Wardlaw Manuscript' is a 'Catollogue of Manuscripts being bookes bound written & Hilled Be Master James Fraser Pastor Montis Mariæ. In divers volumns *ab anno 1660*'. Compiled towards the end of his life, it lists fifty-three titles, volumes comprising many of his own works along with copies of pieces written by others. Secular works in this collection include his 'Triennial Travels', alongside manuscripts on 'songs and sonets', 'jests and ralleries',[22] and 'epigraphs, epitaphs, anagrams', as well as pieces on geography, local demography, natural history, pedagogy, herbalism, medicine and meteorology. The bulk of the works are on theology and scripture, only some of which informed his history-writing directly. However, others are on religious history ('Church History to century 12 in 4°', finished in 1665) and a handful also on the secular past, as exemplified by 'The Survy of antiquity a manuscript in 4°',[23] completed in 1660, and 'The History of Britain to 1678, 4°'.

Evidently, Fraser considered it was his duty as Fraser *seanchaidh* not just to acquire and tell stories but to write as much as possible down from manuscript, book and oral historical research. That could involve, for example, transcribing his conversations with Hugh Fraser, 8th Lord Lovat, and his servant, relating to his travels: 'In the long Nights I wrot the History of his own travels in the Netherlands and low Germany from his own and servants mouth, which I set down in Mundo in this volumne . . .'[24] It is unclear if he deposited these writings in the Frasers' precious 'charter chest' or 'kist' at the Lovat Frasers' Beaufort Castle, a collection he valued highly, reporting the family to have been immensely relieved to have saved it from a fire in the early sixteenth century.[25] But he reported his own use of the manuscripts there for researching his 'Polichronicon', '*Divina Providentia*', 'Short Chronologie and Genealogie of the Bissets and Frasers of Lovat' and 'A True Genealogie of the Frasers'.[26] At times, he also ventured elsewhere to research in the records held by Fraser scions in Struy, Strathfarrar and Strichen. In addition, Fraser borrowed, and took notes from, other local family histories. Key here was Sir Robert Gordon's 'Genealogical History of the Earldom of Sutherland', a work that circulated in manuscript in the later seventeenth century but that was not published in print until 1813. Less certain is Fraser's degree of indebtedness to written genealogies by fellow Gaelic scholars and from beyond the Highlands, manuscript accounts such as that by David Hume of Godscroft, who, as secretary to the Douglas earls of Arran, compiled a history of the House of Douglas that has similarities with Fraser's work.

'Church Registers and records in publick offices'

Regarding Fraser's second class of sources, 'Church Registers and records in publick offices', he provides more detail. By these, he was not referring to his local kirk session, presbytery or synod records from the immediate past – some of which survive today and were considered in the previous chapter – but pre-Reformation ecclesiastical materials. As Fraser put it:

> All our Historians rely most upon Churchmens information, these being the greatest Secretaries and most Carefull searchers into and Recorders of antiquity. Nay, our monks being reputed men of best learning and most leasur, our Kings alwayes Choose one of their order to writ the remarkable passages of their time, passing by the name of *Historicus Regius*, the Kings Historian.[27]

It was a convenient argument for him to claim that clerics were the most reliable compilers, guardians and interpreters of manuscripts and to criticise secular researchers, even some of the mightiest of Scottish chroniclers and historians, on the basis of them being much less respectful of archival material.[28] Nevertheless, Fraser obtained access to surviving records from two major, local, pre-Reformation ecclesiastical repositories, the 'manuscripts of Fern and Beuly'. These were, respectively, the 'Abbacy book of Fern' – collated and deposited by Premonstratensian monks at Fearn Abbey, across two firths to the north – as well as those 'annals, actings and genealogies' and 'bills of mortality' formerly guarded by the Valliscaulian order at Beauly priory, just a few miles from his home.[29] Evidently, he was appalled by the destruction 'our confused Reformation' had visited on both collections, and the process by which he used the scattered fragments of these manuscript collections, or even their location at the time he worked with them, is not clear. Yet, his research using these materials led him to detailed theories such as that of the former existence of a cell of hermits at Bunchrew, adjacent to Phopachy.[30] Moreover, these were not the only local church histories in manuscript to which he found access. He also engaged with material of considerable local relevance in the *Liber pluscardenisis* (Book of Pluscarden), a chronicle from c.1461 created when the Valliscaulian abbey of Pluscarden, further east in the diocese of Moray, became a cell of the Benedictine abbey of Dunfermline. In addition, there were the 'Records of Moray', sections of which he claimed to have 'had a long time by me': that is, one assumes, that he borrowed on an extended basis. Moreover, this material on the diocese of Moray was supplemented by short periods of access to wider Scottish manuscripts such as the 'Black Booke of Paisley', part of the fifteenth-century *Scotichronicon* chronicle, the 'Book of Melrose' or *Chronicle of Melrose*, and a copy, apparently for personal use only, made from Peter Lombard's twelfth-century 'Book of Sentences'.[31]

'Printed Books'

When it came to Fraser's third category, 'Printed Books', the chief problem for him was their paucity. Not all substantial publications, even religious ones, proved to be entirely welcome in his locality. In the Chanonry of Ross, according to John Gordon of Rothiemay's contemporary account, the Bishop of Ross, John Maxwell (d. 1647), fled in early 1638 due to his faltering efforts to impose Charles I's 1637 Scottish Prayer Book ('Laud's Liturgy') on his 'enflamed' congregation. Locals

> tore in peeces such copyes of the Service Booke as he had established for publicke use in the Chanonrie church of Rosse, and threw the leaves thereof into the sea, which, by the wynde, flotted after the passage boat (where the Bishop was) upon the top of the water.[32]

Fraser also commented on the introduction in Kirkhill of the Prayer Book, books that he reported became known locally as 'Leurichin Dearg' (*Na Leabhraichean Dearg*), or the 'Reed [Red] Books'.[33] In general, his own appetite for books, religious or secular, was voracious, but was suppressed due to their minimal availability locally. Fraser was deeply troubled by the lack of access in the firthlands to printed works – in particular, the major histories – to the extent that:

> Raphael Hollinshad, Hec. Boetius [Boece], John Major, Bishop Lessly And Dempster, are all rare, truly, to be found, and no hopes of ever reprinting them again, and in all the north I never saw but one torn volume of Boetius, another of John Major, a 3d. of Dempster, so that we expect not to see new editions, and how shall we have recourse to such bookes as are not to be found?[34]

In terms of his immediate locality, his wish for greater access would be met only in his very final years through his enigmatic connections to the founders of what would be named, in 1709, as the SSPCK, under the leadership of an exiled episcopalian minister working from Bedfordshire, James Kirkwood.[35] As the last chapter suggested, the genesis of this desire for a public library in the Highlands lay in the episcopalian atmosphere of the Restoration period, albeit the foundations were put firmly in place only in the much more presbyterian climate of the 1690s and early years of the 1700s.[36] In any case, Fraser was, it seems, proactive in the developments which inspired the creation of the Highlands' first burgh library, Inverness Presbyterial Library, in 1706. It was hosted initially in a room in Dunbar's Hospital on Church Street (an institution built in 1668, and which would serve subsequently as the grammar school too). The Inverness library was a foundation that, in some ways, stood in the shadow of Edinburgh's Advocates Library (inaugurated in 1689) and in which fellow royalist episcopalian George MacKenzie was a major player. But its founding should also be seen in the context of the north of Scotland's other famous contemporary library, the 'Kirkwall Bibliothek' in Orkney, established in 1683, although often argued to have been in existence before that.[37]

Although Fraser is not mentioned as an initial benefactor, local donations (made by local lairds, ministers, merchants, 'a periwig maker', an apprentice surgeon, students and ministers) to the Inverness institution included histories of the Ottoman Empire and French civil wars, a 'Low Dutch' grammar, an English–Italian dictionary and thirty Irish bibles.[38] However, his own input into the Inverness venture is evident in a gift: his inscribed copy of the Church of Ireland Bishop William Bedel's first translation into Classical Gaelic of the Old Testament. This work had been completed originally in c.1635–6 and published, following financial assistance from Robert Boyle, Earl of Cork, in 1685.[39] Fraser's copy was one of many sent to Scotland in the years before 1700, and a text which, since unintelligible to most Scottish Gaels due to its Irish font, Robert Kirk of Aberfoyle had set about converting into more accessible Roman characters, in a version published in 1690.[40] Intriguingly, Fraser seems to have remained quiet about Kirk's part in encouraging the updated Gaelic text. As has been seen, though, his own interests in the comparisons and contrasts between Irish and Scottish Gaelic were of long standing and reflected in his copy of the Bedel version. While any further evidence of Fraser's part in the founding of the Inverness library remains enigmatic, then, his connection to the populating of it with books reflected his life-long, tangible endeavours to connect his family, congregation and local community with the great historical texts, via his contacts with fellow bibliophiles of the firthlands, and with religious and secular scholars of the past at Scottish and British levels. Inverness Library still holds that copy of Bedel's Old Testament gifted by 'the Famous Mr. Boyle sone to the Earl of Cork in Ireland To Mr James Fraser to be kept for he use of

Figure 6.1 'Dunbar's Hospital', the first location for Inverness Presbyterial Library, Church Street, Inverness

his church, Kirkhill'.[41] Moreover, suggestive of Fraser's further connections with the origins of the library is its modern-day possession of early editions of the very books by Dempster, Boece and Buchanan which Fraser referred to in his historical writing.[42] The full story of these early bequests has yet to be told. Undeniably, though, Fraser's desire for better access to historical and religious texts allowed him to become an outspoken campaigner for, and supplier to, what is today – due to the input of other, more recent benefactors such as Charles Fraser-Mackintosh – the library's impressive 'Rare Books' collection.[43]

In another sense, the 1706 founding of the library in Inverness was not a revolutionary moment for Fraser and his Highland bibliophile friends. Fraser had managed to consult, borrow, buy or receive donations of several history books, earlier in life, even without the aid of such an institution. In terms of ancient and foreign texts, school, university and his travels gave him access to many, with Livy, Seneca, Cicero and Diogenes being among the writers he cites most frequently. Furthermore, whether an instance of karma or not, in 1670, Fraser received a special reward for saving the life of London timber speculator, Phineas Pett, whose vessel ran aground in the Beauly Firth. On Fraser extending to him a fire, a roof and hospitality for the night, Pett gave him a copy of Camden's 'great work', possibly his anglocentric 'British' history, *Britannia* (first published in 1586 and, in English, in 1610), and another 'booke or two'.[44]

It is possible also to posit a book-lending network in the north involving Fraser by comparing the authors he cites in his major history with those referenced by three fellow contemporary historians from the firthlands: as has been shown, Sir Robert Gordon and Sir Thomas Urquhart of Cromarty were two such figures with whom Fraser was familiar, while also well known to Fraser, albeit less rooted in the firthlands, was Sir George MacKenzie of Rosehaugh.[45] In addition, Fraser considered the late 1660s household of George Sinclair, 6th Earl of Caithness (d.1676), to host 'all manner of recreation and divertisment without and within, Gameing and Play, and one of the finest Libraries in the Nation'.[46] A reading of Fraser's surviving works reveals that he was acquainted with many of the major histories of Scotland cited in the last indented quotation, while elsewhere he refers to recent books by Spotiswood, William Drummond of Hawthornden, Wishart's memoirs of the marquis of Montrose and the Marquis of Argyll's *Instructions to a Son*. In these later cases, it is not clear if he copied from, possessed or borrowed these in printed form, while at university or later.[47] Therefore, it is worth an initial comparison of Fraser's list of consulted historical books with

Gordon's, Urquhart's and MacKenzie's references in their equivalent works. All reference ancient authors, but also cite a range of Scottish and British histories too, albeit in a slightly different complexion to Fraser. At the start of his family history, Gordon provides a 'catalogue' of the principal authors (printed books and manuscripts) he had used, this including Camden, Holinshed, Dempster, Boece (Bellenden's translation), Buchanan, Major and Leslie, all works which he hoped might furnish his 'bibliotheck in Dornoch' with 'sufficient store of books, boith for your credit and the weell of this countrey, to amend ther ignorance which increases through laik of bookes'.[48] Urquhart's more expansive but less-focused references are to Boece, Dempster, Spotiswood and Holinshead.[49] In turn, MacKenzie's citations in his *A Defence of the Antiquity* are rather closer to Gordon's and Fraser's.[50] Evidently, in the range of his reading and knowledge, James Fraser ranks among a circle of north Highland historians who were active in their own region and beyond in the period, although the degree of informal circulation, lending and borrowing between them remain enigmatic.

'Instructions receaved from the Bards, and nearest nighbours and allyes'

While, in much of his reading, Fraser is fairly orthodox, in his attitude towards non-written evidence, his fourth type of source, he is unique, this being revealing again of his *seanchaidh* position. Consider Robert Gordon's stark expression of the range of primary sources he considered acceptable:

> I will onlie set doun such things as I find in old records, charters, manuscripts, registers, histories, and monuments, grounded vpon evident probabilities, and such things as are yit recent in our memories that live in this aige; leaving all forged auntient traditions and whatsoever els bairds and rymers (delyting in decayed antiquitie) doe religiouslie father vpon tymes out of mynd.[51]

Fraser's tone towards orality was utterly different. Unlike Gordon, he was completely open to learning from the 'bairds and rymers', the 'druids' who were the historians of a pre-literate age, the term 'druid' having a wider, more Scottish connotation in terms of pre-Christian scholar than it does today. As Fraser wrote, those

> who were unacquainted w^t letters, and Consequently ignorant of refined Sciences, thought Hystory, next to their Religion, the onely usefull and proper study of mankind; and judging the forming of the manners and Regulating

the actions of man to be the chiefe duty and care of societies, they thought Documents, precepts, and lawes too weake a meanes to work so great effect without they were Confirmed and Strengthened by the Examples of their Predecessors, to which prone nature, even amongst the most Barbarous, dos willingly render an implicit veneration; and therefore, seing their liberaries were their Memories, and word their Characters, so Songs and Rud Rimes were the onely bookes, whereby their Bards and Druids instructed their Children in the Historys of former ages.[52]

For these 'heathenish' scholars, 'songs and rud [simple] rimes' had formed the equivalent of books, and thus the 'druids' had once had the responsibility of researching and teaching history. In stark contrast to what Gordon considered 'forged auntient [ancient] traditions', then, for Fraser, the oral record deserved respect. In other words, it was not a question of dismissing what we would call 'intangible cultural heritage' but interpreting spoken or sung evidence for an age where it could be compared and contrasted with written accounts. While Gordon would have baulked at this, Urquhart and, to an even greater extent, MacKenzie drew on similar wells of knowledge in terms of their respect for the 'druids', while it is possible that a further influence came via Fraser's Royal Society connection with English scholar John Aubrey.[53] But the most vital factor is, without doubt, Fraser's emergence from a Gaelic tradition, one which continued to prize oral testimony and helped pass it down the generations.

For Fraser, the oral record stood alongside manuscripts and books as a key source for historians. Further evidence for this comes in Fraser witnessing the 8th Lord Lovat's final illness, when he wrote:

> All January and February my Lord Lovat kept close at home, not able to goe out of doores; and that was a well spent time in reading and discoursing of divinity and history. He had his uncle, Beufort, and John Eraser of Clunwaky [Clunvackie] an old experienced gentleman, still with him. The later entertained him with history and genealogy: and, for my part, I never left him but on Fridayes nights or Satturdayes morning, to attend my charge . . .[54]

CONCLUSION

It seems fair to conclude by agreeing with Sally Mapstone that, from the earliest record, 'storytelling has formed a dynamic part of the imagining of Scottish identity'.[55] Nowhere has this been truer than in the Highlands, where the position of oral history, particularly that of the Gàidhealtachd, is to the fore in today's debates about the nature of the sources that should be interrogated in order to convey the region's past. For Fraser, the application of the best technology and narrative skills was as vital to enhancing historical understanding as the less capricious process of training in historiography and how to move from transcription and translation through to editing of what we would now call primary sources. Ultimately, Fraser trusted his own 'ocular inspection', whether or not filtered through a telescope, the human voice, or the manuscripts and books he deemed essential in a historian's set of instruments and gadgets. In this way, Fraser problematises any assumed decline of Gaelic history-writing in the seventeenth century and supports the argument of Martin MacGregor in showing that, even when writing in English, Highland historians could make a vital contribution, one that, assaulted and challenged by alternative approaches, was, nonetheless, still open, engaged and self-critical.[56] Fraser does not represent an eviscerated, moribund type of history-writing, then, but positions himself as blending older and newer approaches, many of which were decidedly, perhaps even defiantly, Highland in flavour, some impressively cosmopolitan and one or two simply confused. His history-writing reflects who he presented himself as in other spheres of life. While it provides far from the last word on the pre-Culloden age, the copious evidence he leaves us presents a uniquely detailed and focused view on an energetic, Highland-rooted historian of the time.

NOTES

1. 'Wardlaw Manuscript', p. 6.
2. Ibid., p. 18.
3. MacGregor, 'The genealogical histories', pp. 200–8.
4. Ibid., p. 7.
5. MacGregor, 'Gaelic barbarity and Scottish identity', pp. 23–6, 30, 32, 33, 40, 47. For perspectives on broader Scottish history-writing from the seventeenth century, see David Allan, *Philosophy and Politics in Later Stuart Scotland* (East Linton, 2000) and the same author's *Virtue, Learning and the Scottish Enlightenment: Ideas of Scholarship and Society in Early Modern Scotland* (Edinburgh, 1993), Part One; Colin Kidd, *Subverting Scotland's Past: Scottish Whig Historians and the Creation of an Anglo-British Identity, 1689–1830* (Cambridge, 1993), pp. 16, 18, 23, 29; Roger A. Mason, 'Debating Britain in seventeenth-century Scotland: multiple monarchy and Scottish sovereignty', *Journal of Scottish Historical Studies*, 35(1) (2015), pp. 1–24.
6. For Fraser's engagement with Irish history, nonetheless, see Mackay, ed., *Chronicles*, pp. 192–4, 404, 411; Bernadette Cunningham, *The World*

of Geoffrey Keating: History, Myth and Religion in Seventeenth-Century Ireland (Dublin, 2000).

7. MacGregor, 'Gaelic barbarity and Scottish identity'.
8. Allan, *Virtue, Learning and the Scottish Enlightenment*, p. 30.
9. Kidd, *Subverting Scotland's Past*, p. 29.
10. Although Fraser died in 1709, his only surviving writing from after the incorporating Anglo-Scottish Union of 1707 was his 'Bill of Mortality' for Kirkhill parish, and so it would be better to view him as working across at least four to five decades, and within an always volatile, fluctuating, uncertain but also dynamic political setting. The vast bulk of his surviving historical work was written within the context of two major regime changes: the Restoration of 1660–88 and, to a lesser extent, the period of the 'Glorious Revolution' of 1688–90. Evidence suggests that Fraser identified more with the former settlement, unsurprising given the limitations put on episcopacy via the Claim of Right of 1689. As well as the 'Wardlaw Manuscript', see Fraser's '*Divina Providentia*'.
11. Margo Todd, *The Culture of Protestantism in Early Modern Scotland* (Cambridge, 2002); Langley, McMillan and Newton, eds, *The Clergy in Early Modern Scotland*.
12. Kelsey Jackson Williams, *The First Scottish Enlightenment: Rebels, Priests, and History* (Oxford, 2020).
13. Williams, 'The network of James Garden of Aberdeen', pp. 111, 113, 114. The need for the inclusion of Kirkwall and Orkney in this nexus, albeit on less denominational lines, is echoed in Brochard, 'Intellectual and practical education'.
14. Kelly, 'The Society in Scotland'.
15. Raffe, *The Culture of Controversy*, pp. 257, 260, 265–6; Karin Bowie, 'New perspectives on pre-Union Scotland', in T. M. Devine and Jenny Wormald, eds, *The Oxford Handbook of Modern Scottish History* (Oxford, 2014), pp. 303–19; Allan, *Virtue, Learning and the Scottish Enlightenment*, Part One.
16. Mackay, ed., *Chronicles*, p. 15.
17. Martin MacGregor, 'Writing the history of Gaelic Scotland: a provisional checklist of "Gaelic" genealogical histories', in Nancy R. McGuire, Donald E. Meek and Colm Ó Baoill, eds, *Caindel Alban: Fèillsgrìobhainn do Dhòmhnall E. Meek* (Aberdeen, 2008), pp. 358–60.
18. Ibid., p. 1.
19. Ibid.
20. 'Wardlaw Manuscript', p. 2.
21. Mackay, ed., *Chronicles*, pp. 10–11.
22. These were something akin to satires.
23. '°' is an abbreviation for quarto, or medium-size volume, one quarter the area of a full sheet of writing material, made by 'folding two sheets in half,

then in half again'. See <https://www.bl.uk/catalogues/illuminatedmanu-scripts/GlossQ.asp> (last accessed 10 December 2021).

24. 'Wardlaw Manuscript', p. 349.

25. Mackay, ed., *Chronicles*, p. 125.

26. James Fraser, 'Short chronologie and genealogie of the Bissets and Frasers of Lovat' and 'A true genealogie of the Frasers', in A. Mitchell, ed., *Geographical Collections Relating to Scotland Made by Walter Macfarlane*, 3 vols (Edinburgh, 1900), II, pp. 85–96.

27. 'Wardlaw Manuscript', p. 4.

28. Mackay, ed., *Chronicles*, p. 15.

29. Ibid., pp. 3, 120.

30. Ibid., p. 3.

31. Ibid., p. 15; Cosmo Innes, ed., *Registrum Episcopatus Moraviensis, e Pluribus Codicibus Consarcinatum circa A.D.MCCCC. Cum Continuatione Diplomatum Recentiorum usque ad A.D.MDCXXIII* (Edinburgh, 1837).

32. Worthington, 'A northern Scottish maritime region', pp. 208–9.

33. Mackay, ed., *Chronicles*, p. 272.

34. 'Wardlaw Manuscript', pp. 5–6.

35. Kelly, 'The Society in Scotland'.

36. Donald Maclean, 'Highland libraries in the eighteenth century', *Transactions of the Gaelic Society of Inverness*, 31 (1922–4), pp. 91–119; CH2/553/3, Inverness presbytery, minutes (1702–8), pp. 88, 114, 179.

37. Jackson Williams, *The First Scottish Enlightenment*, pp. 26–8; Myrtle Anderson-Smith, 'The Bibliotheck of Kirkwall', *Northern Scotland*, 15(1) (1995), pp. 127–34.

38. University of Aberdeen Special Collections, MS 1066, 'Inverness Presbyterial Library catalogue and borrowers' register, 1706–1743', pp. 1–17.

39. Kelly, 'The Society in Scotland', pp. 44, 47, 54.

40. Ibid., pp. 42–3.

41. Inverness Reference Library, Special Collections, Charles Fraser-Mackintosh Collection, FM 22148, *Leabhuir na Seintiomna ar na ttarrving go Gaidlig tre Cúram & Dútraś an Doctúir Uilliam Bedel* (London [s.n.], 1685) 'Inscribed from Mr. Boyle to James Fraser of Kirkhill'. See <https://www.highlifehighland.com/libraries/wp-content/uploads/sites/128/2015/03/Pages_from_1700_FM_card_catalogue.pdf> (last accessed 10 December 2021); Alexander Mitchell, *The Library of Inverness* (Inverness, 1901); Brian Moffat, 'Fraser, James (1645–1731), book dealer', *Oxford Dictionary of National Biography* (Oxford, 2004), available at: <https://www.oxforddnb.com/view/10.1093/ref:odnb/9780198614128.001.0001/odnb-9780198614128-e-73233> (last accessed 10 December 2021).

42. 'Inverness Presbyterial Library catalogue and borrowers' register, 1706–1743'; Mitchell, *The Library of Inverness*; Colin A. McLaren and Margaret A. Stephen, 'Reports and surveys of archives in Northern Scotland', *Northern Scotland*, 2 (1977), pp. 187–8.

43. Manwaring-McKay, 'Charles Fraser-Mackintosh (1828–1901) and his books', p. 133.
44. Mackay, ed., *Chronicles*, p. 485.
45. Clare Jackson, 'Mackenzie, Sir George, of Rosehaugh (1636/1638–1691), lawyer and politician', *Oxford Dictionary of National Biography* (Oxford, 2004), available at: <https://www.oxforddnb.com/view/10.1093/ref:odnb/9780198614128.001.0001/odnb-9780198614128-e-17579> (last accessed 10 December 2021).
46. 'Wardlaw Manuscript', p. 324.
47. Mackay, ed., *Chronicles*, pp. 107, 438, 363.
48. Sir Robert Gordon, *Genealogical History of the Earldom of Sutherland from its Origin to the Year 1630. With a Continuation to the year 1651* (Edinburgh, 1813), pp. viii–x; Fraser, ed., *The Sutherland Book*, II, p. 365.
49. *The Works of Sir Thomas Urquhart of Cromarty, Knight* (Edinburgh, 1834), pp. 167, 213, 258, 269.
50. Sir George MacKenzie, *A Defence of the Antiquity of the Royal Line of Scotland with a True Account when the Scots Were Govern'd by Kings in the Isle of Britain* (London, 1685), pp. 5, 8, 10, 11, 16, 28–30, 40–1, 49, 58.
51. Gordon, *Genealogical History of the Earldom of Sutherland*, pp. 21–2.
52. Mackay, ed., *Chronicles*, p. 18.
53. Alston, *My Little Town of Cromarty*, p. 36.
54. Ibid., p. 503.
55. Sally Mapstone, 'Scotland's stories', in Jenny Wormald, ed., *Scotland: A History* (Oxford, 2005), p. 304.
56. Jackson Williams, *The First Scottish Enlightenment*, pp. 76–80; MacGregor, 'Gaelic barbarity and Scottish identity'; MacGregor, 'Writing the history of Gaelic Scotland'.

Conclusion:
Memory, Biography and
Scottish Highland History before Culloden

STUDYING JAMES FRASER LEADS to some troubling reflections. This book has suggested aspects of his character that will be unpalatable to many twenty-first-century readers, in terms of his attitudes to race and ethnicity, sex and gender, for example. If we view Fraser's surviving written work as an expression of the social position he held, or wished to hold, the evidence can seem to confirm a male, clerical hegemony we might associate with the Restoration period.[1] However, one of the notable features of the Highlands and Scotland that the book has sought to highlight is how the civil wars of 1638–60, the 1688–90 period, the beginnings of Jacobitism and the Treaty of Union of 1707 made rigidity and complacency extremely poor survival strategies, and placed Fraser towards the social, political or religious edge at several points in his life. If we consider his seventy-five years as a whole, the 'curious cleric' was a subversive as much as he was a conformist.[2] In general, one hopes that his life-writing has been shown to be more idiosyncratic, and harder to pigeonhole, than any convenient identification of him using modern terms like 'reactionary' or 'conservative' might suggest. History involves us seeking to comprehend periods and situations with features that, at times, appear strikingly recognisable and, at other points, alien to the times and places in which we live today. Key to understanding this, as regards Fraser, has been to position him within the dynamic, distinct social and cultural context of the Highlands of his time. Fraser's part of Scotland was being deeply affected by metropoles further south in his lifetime, certainly, but not exclusively by them. It took influences from peoples to its east, north and west too. Due to this, its people were making striking, distinctive contributions to the world of their own, and, to some extent, continuing to determine their trajectory while within the Scottish state and Stuart multiple kingdom, a situation in which clanship remained dynamic and the Gaelic language vital. Fraser represents that situation, both when in the mainstream and, to a lesser extent, when on the margins.

In writing this book, I have become keenly aware of the dangers of what Leon Edel called 'transference', whereby the biographer can move towards 'excessive idealisation of a subject', although also, in other cases, towards the opposite of that, what Barbara Caine has referred to as an 'unbalanced form of vilification'.[3] In the dramatic terms that Caine employs, biographers need to be willing either to 'fall out of love' with their subjects, or else to present reasons and explanations for personalities and behaviours which seem odd, perplexing, alienating or even disturbing.[4] Readers will be the judge of whether this book has found the correct balance between being curious about, even finding empathy with, Fraser, while not glossing over the less attractive aspects of his life that the available records present. It is a tightrope that many historians who tackle biography topple from, and perhaps a factor in why it remains, in David Nasaw's view, an 'unloved' part of the discipline of history.[5]

However, there is cause for hope among historians in the biographical approach. The recent 'biographical turn' indicates that the area is no longer dominated by works on prominent (whether 'great' or appalling) men, albeit these can be hugely revealing, but characterised by more inclusive and exciting methodologies.[6] In her 2006 book, *Trickster travels: A Sixteenth-Century Muslim Between Worlds*, Natalie Zemon Davis considered an ambiguous and, to most of her readers, lesser-known figure, a scholar (a 'trickster bird') who flitted between Christian and Islamic circles. The subject of her work, Leo Africanus, or al-Hasan al-Wazzan as he remained known within the Islamic world, came up with 'strategies for maintaining distance' in order to retain individual agency, so he could work and communicate in both of those spheres during the course of his intellectual life.[7] Davis's approach has resonance when considering James Fraser's positioning of himself between two worlds: Highland and Lowland, Gaelic and Scots, Protestant and Catholic, even Covenanter and Royalist. An equally insightful case to Davis's consideration of Leo Africanus, and similarly controversial, is recent writing on Olaudah Equiano, whose story is known to many history students: that of an eighteenth-century, African-born freed slave who wrote up his horrific experiences of this as evidence. Any who doubt the historiographical value of integrating travel accounts along with broader life-writing as a primary source set, or the ability of biography to interpret this, to spur vital debate and disagreement, might consider the historiographical turmoil around Vincent Carretta's work on Equiano. In a 2005 book, Carretta sought to challenge previous assumptions about Equiano's African birth and journey on a slave ship, claiming, instead, that he was more probably born in South Carolina. Thereby, Carretta ignited a controversy that has, in effect, not diminished Equiano's significance since, but emphasised it: Equiano's account remains a crucial, respected and much-cited one for understanding the Atlantic slave trade of the time.[8]

As the cases above show, there is a rapidly 'changing relationship between biography and history'. This is one in which the potential for human beings to 'curate' elements of their experience when describing themselves, and for personal identities to shift and change considerably over a lifetime, is being reckoned with more and more, and placing great onus on historians. The results of that reflection and subsequent critical consideration have, in due course, sometimes amplified, not weakened, the narrative value life-writing provides to readers and future researchers.[9] Certainly, one is unlikely ever to come to an abrupt endpoint when researching the life of James Fraser. One hopes this book has shown his accounts to be of value not only in terms of the veracity of their factual detail, crucial consideration though that is, but also in the way they often exaggerate or misunderstand situations and events. Fraser does this in a manner which is thoroughly human and indicative both of the complexity of his character and of broader social and cultural features. This book has made the case that the extent and detail of Fraser's life-writing that survives, both the accurate and the less plausible parts, is so striking and unique that the biographical approach offers a crucial, alternative route, not just towards understanding him, but towards comprehending the scholarly world of the Scottish Highlands in the century before Culloden.

The book sought to bring this to the fore via six thematic chapters, each of which emphasised Fraser as a polymath, polyglot and 'polychronicler',[10] a scholar who represents a little recognised, outward-looking, multicultural element to seventeenth-century Highland life. The first chapter presented the blend of Highland and Lowland educational practices that influenced his scholarly thought, highlighting him as a Moray Firth and North Sea-facing thinker, whose childhood and teenage experiences in Phopachy, Kirkhill, Inverness and Aberdeen connected him with a cosmopolitan world. This intellectual training also formed the foundation for his energetic approach, later in life, and as a minister, towards providing school buildings and recruiting qualified Gaelic-speaking teachers for them in Kirkhill and across Inverness presbytery. The second chapter emphasised how Fraser's education, his ability to adapt to a fluctuating, unpredictable social and political situation at home, and his early exposure to, and curiosity about, a European and inter-imperial world prepared him for what he would encounter on the continent, this allowing us to place him in context alongside other early modern, north-west European, Protestant 'grand tourists'. It also made the point that these experiences of England and continental Europe did, nonetheless, transform him. Fraser's travel influenced his move towards both autobiography and life-writing and encouraged a growing knowledge of and aptitude with languages, as covered in the third chapter. This chapter explored Fraser as a linguist, considering his approach to both the spoken and the written word and, most strikingly, his fascination with minority or regional languages, and his taking for granted that there was what we would call a 'Gaelosphere' with representatives across Europe and beyond. For Fraser, his first language was a valuable part of the 'Babel of Tongues'. Moving to Part Two of the text, the first of the three remaining chapters introduced the later Fraser as a 'scientist' or, less anachronistically, a 'natural philosopher', who – respected in Kirkwall, Aberdeen, Edinburgh, London and beyond for his command not only of Gaelic, English and Latin but of much broader areas of knowledge – played a significant part among the literati at national and international levels, without leaving his region for any lengthy period after 1660. The next chapter, the fifth, began by foregrounding Fraser's connection with a major case of witch persecution in his parish in 1662, assigning him a degree of culpability, as an emerging parish minister, for failing to prevent multiple fatalities among those accused. As a 'man of the cloth', it became possible, for the first time, to bring in local, contemporary evidence relating to his character in this chapter, this also providing a glimpse of local politics and of Fraser's challenges on being faced with the convulsive regime change of 1688–90. It is perhaps as a historian that Fraser's Highland upbringing was shown to be most obvious and influential on him, however. The sixth and final chapter sought to illuminate how his standing as a *seanchaidh*, as this position entered a transitional period in Gaelic society, was one in which Fraser viewed his responsibilities as being multiple. The seventeenth-century *seanchaidh* was obliged, on one hand, to present the most complete and satisfying results as regards their clan or family, and, on the other, to use the best tools available so as to ensure their interpretation provided the combination of sharp focus and wide range that a professional historian was expected to impart.

Ultimately, Fraser provides a scholar's perspective on the mix of conflict, co-existence, resilience and confidence that characterised the

Highlands in the century before Culloden. One hopes that the book has shown how the autobiographical evidence of a scholar can evince broader social and cultural features, in his case, derailing assumptions about the region's intellectual remoteness or lack of potential for broader collective agency in that period. But it does not claim to be exhaustive. There are numerous areas of James Fraser's life which could and should be scrutinised further. The key one must be for a team project to be established and funded that will allow for the 'Triennial Travels' to be transcribed in full and a critical scholarly edition of it to be published. It is an extraordinary text that provides a vital counterpoint to the 'Wardlaw Manuscript' and would, if made available in full, cement Fraser's standing and relevance internationally. At the other end of the spectrum, a new and full edition of the 'Wardlaw Manuscript', inclusive of its more outward-facing elements, would strengthen the case further. I am also very much aware that a fuller understanding of Kirkhill in that period could be reached than I have been able to provide. This might consider wider Lovat Fraser family history and the social history of the parish, using a broader primary source base than I have in order to identify the 'weapons of the weak'. A coastal history perspective on Fraser and the firthlands could prove fruitful, in addition. As has been highlighted, knowledge of Fraser would benefit from greater consideration from within a Gaelic linguistic context, an assessment of his work from this angle being one which could build significantly on what this work has been able to.[11] His theological reflections, captured in the ten 'homilies' and ten 'exercises' from 1661 to 1688 that he has left (a manuscript that provides his thoughts on themes such as adultery, charity, children, divorce, eunuchs, fasting, idleness and sloth, love and transubstantiation), constitute another area of his writing that could reveal much if interrogated in more detail.[12] The '*Divina Providentia*' is, similarly, worthy of greater attention in telling us more about how he combined the 'foreign and domestick' in his approach to the past, and in the manuscript's typically complex history.[13]

The book has emphasised that James Fraser was a complex, multi-faceted figure. Indeed, there are 'other James Frasers' who might have been presented, not just different interpretations of his own character, but scholarly namesakes. It is striking that the *Oxford Dictionary of National Biography* has entries for eight people with the name James Fraser. Two of these eight are northern Highland intellectuals and contemporaries of the subject of my book. A brief biographical sketch of both of them conveys parallels with 'our' minister in terms of their itinerant trajectories, although showing, crucially, a move towards London not just as a place visited but as a transplanted home and as a stepping-stone towards empire, a feature that would become such a huge factor for Highland families in the eighteenth century. The first of these two other James Frasers was born eleven years later than 'our' subject, in Petty, just a few miles to the eastern side of Inverness. This James Fraser studied at Inverness Grammar and King's College in Aberdeen, then, at some point in the late 1660s, left northern Scotland for London. To this point, the similarities with 'our' Phopachy teenager's itinerary of just a few years earlier are notable, although, in contrast, James Fraser from Petty struck down roots in the English capital, becoming a tutor and secretary of the Royal Chelsea Hospital as well as a book trader, a vocation which would allow him to assist, in later life, in endeavours which reconnected him with his home country, as mentioned in an earlier chapter, as he became both one of the founders of the SSPCK and a scholarly benefactor. He not only donated books to King's College but also, along with funds for a schoolmaster/librarian and twelve bursaries, helped establish the Inverness Library in 1706, a foundation to which, as has been shown, 'our' James Fraser also made a contribution.[14] The second Highland contemporary and third point in this triangle of scholarly, seventeenth-century James Frasers from the firthlands was James Fraser of Brae. He came from Resolis (Kirkmichael) on the Black Isle, was a presbyterian man of the cloth and a scholar of Hebrew, Greek and, in his case, Oriental languages. Like the Petty-born James Fraser, he set up home in London as an adult, in the 1680s, before returning as far as Culross in 1689 and then, in 1695, the Highland capital, where he was elected to the presbytery for a short time before returning southwards.[15] Evidently, these two James Frasers show both comparisons and contrasts with the man that I have presented. What unites them, and also figures like Sir Robert Gordon, Sir Thomas Urquhart and George Mackenzie of Rosehaugh, is the northern Highland background to their Scots and English-language scholarship.[16] Where the James Fraser I have covered in my book is most obviously radically different from all of them is that, in contrast, he did not have to leave his home in order for his scholarship to be recognised and flourish. He could hold his own as a cosmopolitan erudite while working in Kirkhill or Phopachy.

There were Frasers who followed this array of intellectuals who are even better known, while some may also point to the fictional 'Jamie Fraser' of *Outlander* as a further re-presentation of this world. As Chapter Five showed, there is also the very real Simon Fraser, the 'Old Fox' of the Jacobite period and the subject of a biography by Sarah Fraser. She has revealed the 'swashbuckling' story around him, 'one of Scotland's most notorious and romantic heroes' and a 'man whose loyalty had no home, whose sword had a price'.[17] The subject of my biography was less swashbuckling, although, nonetheless, a kenspeckle, scholarly Fraser from just a few miles away. One hopes that this study of him marks a significant, accessible addition to historical understanding of a person, their place, their time and their community. As we look, in the 2020s, to see the University of the Highlands and Islands play its part in brightening the region's prospects again, the 'curious cleric' I have presented may, one hopes, offer insights, good and bad, into what an earlier scholarly Highlands and Islands, one that was relatively populated and intellectually dynamic, looked like.[18] James Fraser's Highlands was a place which maverick, exceptional scholars, those with curious minds, were not always forced to abandon in order to make their mark on the world. The evidence that he has bequeathed to us provides testimony of the energetic, impressive scholarly life that it is possible to cultivate from within the region.

NOTES

1. Barbara Caine, *Biography and History* (Basingstoke, 2010), p. 100.
2. The term is a reference to my Twitter profile, on which I have used the hashtag #CuriousCleric frequently, when tweeting about Fraser in recent years.
3. Caine, *Biography*, p. 72.
4. Ibid.
5. David Nasaw, 'Introduction: AHR roundtable on historians and biography', *American Historical Review*, 114(3) (2009), pp. 573–8.
6. Hans Renders, Binne de Haan and Jonne Harmsma, eds, *The Biographical Turn: Lives in History* (London, 2016).
7. Zemon Davis, *Trickster Travels*. See also the same author's *Women on the Margins: Three Seventeenth-Century Lives* (New York, 1997) and *The Return of Martin Guerre* (New York, 1984).
8. Bryan Wagner and Parker Kjellin-Elder, 'Olaudah Equiano', available at: <https://www.oxfordbibliographies.com/view/document/obo-9780190280024/obo-9780190280024–0084.xml> (last accessed 10 January 2022); Vincent Carretta, *Equiano, the African: Biography of a Self-Made Man* (Atlanta, 2005); Paul E. Lovejoy, 'Autobiography and memory: Gustavus Vassa, alias Olaudah Equiano, the African', *Slavery & Abolition*, 27(3) (2006), pp. 317–47; Vincent Carretta, 'Response to Paul Lovejoy's "Autobiography and memory"', *Slavery & Abolition*, 28(1) (2007), pp. 115–19.
9. Caine, *Biography*, p. vii.

10. In the 'Wardlaw Manuscript', Fraser employed the term 'polichronicon' in its title, which implies a chronicle of numerous events and ages. The word 'polychronicler' is less elegant and does not appear in the *Oxford English Dictionary* in reference to the author and compiler of such a work, but has been employed very occasionally: for example, in James Storer, *History and Antiquities of the Cathedral Churches of Great Britain*, 4 vols (London, 1819), IV.

11. James C. Scott, *Weapons of the Weak: Everyday Forms of Peasant Resistance* (New York, 1985).

12. University of Aberdeen Special Collections, James Fraser, 'Homilies and exercises theological and moral, 1661–88', MS 630.

13. The manuscript was later in the hands of the Bairds of Auchmedden via a family connection with the Frasers of Findrack, Aberdeenshire. See '*Divina Providentia*'.

14. Brian Moffat, 'Fraser, James (1645–1731), book dealer', *Oxford Dictionary of National Biography* (Oxford, 2004), available at: <https://www.oxforddnb.com/view/10.1093/ref:odnb/9780198614128.001.0001/odnb-9780198614128-e-73233> (last accessed 20 January 2022). His papers can be found in the University of Aberdeen, Special Collections, as GB 0231, MS 3191.

15. John Callow, 'Fraser, James, of Brae (1639–1699), Church of Scotland minister', *Oxford Dictionary of National Biography* (Oxford, 2004), available at: <https://www.oxforddnb.com/view/10.1093/ref:odnb/9780198614128.001.0001/odnb-9780198614128-e-10106> (last accessed 20 January 2022).

16. Perhaps even closer to the minister of Kirkhill in terms of social and cultural background was John Fraser (d.1702), Minister of Coll and Tiree and Dean of the Isles, who was, like his northern Highland contemporary, a keen enthusiast for local custom and folklore to the extent that, in his case, he was, similarly, a correspondent of Robert Sibbald. See Hunter, *The Occult Laboratory*, pp. 26, 248.

17. Sarah Fraser, *The Last Highlander* (London, 2012). See also the publisher's blurb, available at: <https://harpercollins.co.uk/products/the-last-highlander-scotlands-most-notorious-clan-chief-rebel-double-agent-sarah-fraser?variant=32798414012494> (last accessed 20 January 2022).

18. James Hunter, 'History: its key place in the future of the Highlands and Islands', *Northern Scotland*, 27(1) (2007), pp. 1–14.

Bibliography

MANUSCRIPT SOURCES

Highland Archive Centre, Inverness
'Bill of Mortality – Containing All y^t Died Natives and Strangers in 48 Years', Old Parish Register, 52.
Kirkhill Kirk Session Minutes, CH2/675/1.
Presbytery of Inverness, CH2/553/1–4.

Inverness Library, Special Collections, Charles Fraser-Mackintosh Collection
Leabhuir na Seintiomna ar na Ttarrving go Gaidlig tre Ćúram & Dútraś an Doctúir Uilliam Bedel (London [s.n.], 1685) FM 22148.

National Library of Scotland
Extima Scotiae septentrionalis ora, ubi Provinciae sunt Rossia, Sutherlandia, Cathenesia, Strath-Naverniae, cum Vicinis Regiunculis quae eis Subsunt, etiamque Moravia, EMW.X.015.
James Fraser, *Divina Providentia* ('A Collection of Providential Passages Ancient and Modern, Foreign and Domestick'), Adv.MS.32.4.7.
James Fraser, '*Polichronicon seu Policratica Temporum*' or 'The True Genealogy of the Frasers, 916–1674' [the 'Wardlaw Manuscript'], MS 3658.

National Records of Scotland
Exchequer Records: Customs Books, Second Series, E72/11/7.
Records of the Synod of Moray, CH2/271/1–4.
Russell Papers, RH15/106.

University of Aberdeen Special Libraries and Archives
'Inverness Presbyterial Library catalogue and borrowers' register, 1706–1743', MS 1066.

James Fraser, 'Homilies and exercises theological and moral, 1661–88', MS 630.

Triennial Travels, containing a succinct and briefe narration of the journay and voyage of Master James Fraser through Scotland, England, all France, part of Spain, and over the Savoyan Alps to Italy [also in the Tyrol, Bavaria, Austria, Bohemia, Germany, Holland, Picardy etc. and back to France, England and Scotland], 3 vols, MS 2538.

PRINTED PRIMARY SOURCES

Anderson, P. J., ed., *Officers and Graduates of University and King's College, Aberdeen, 1495–1860* (Aberdeen, 1926).

Anderson, P. J., ed., *Roll of Alumni in Arts of the University and King's College of Aberdeen 1596–1860* (Aberdeen, 1900).

Bishop Burnet's Travels through France, Italy, Germany and Switzerland (London, 1750).

Boece, Hector, *The History and Chronicles of Scotland* (trans. John Bellenden), 2 vols (Edinburgh, 1821).

Brand, John, *A Brief Description of Orkney, Zetland and Caithness* (Edinburgh, 1883).

Burnet, Gilbert, *Some Letters Containing an Account of What Seemed Most Remarkable in Switzerland, Italy etc.* (Rotterdam, 1686).

Butler, Charles, ed., *Basilikon Doron; or, His Majestys Instructions to his Dearest sonne, Henry the Prince* (London, 1887).

Carruthers, Robert, *The Highland Note-Book* (Edinburgh, 1843).

Crawford, Donald, ed., *Journals of Sir John Lauder* (Edinburgh, 1900).

Defoe, Daniel, *A Tour Thro' the Whole Island of Great Britain: Divided into Circuits or Journeys. Giving a Particular and Entertaining Account of Whatever Is Curious, and Worth Observation*, 4 vols (London, 1742).

Fedosov, Dmitry, ed., *Diary of Patrick Gordon of Auchleuchries*, 6 vols (Aberdeen, 2009–16).

Franck, Richard, *Northern Memoirs, Calculated for the Meridian of Scotland* (London, 1694).

Fraser, James, 'Short chronologie and genealogie of the Bissets and Frasers of Lovat' and 'A true genealogie of the Frasers', in A. Mitchell, ed., *Geographical Collections Relating to Scotland Made by Walter Macfarlane*, 3 vols (Edinburgh, 1900), II, pp. 85–96.

Fraser, William, ed., *The Sutherland Book*, 3 vols (Edinburgh, 1892).

Gailhard, Jean, *The Compleat Gentleman, or, Directions for the Education of Youth as to Their Breeding at Home and Travelling Abroad in Two Treatises* (London, 1678).

Gordon, Sir Robert, *Genealogical History of the Earldom of Sutherland from its Origin to the Year 1630. With a Continuation to the Year 1651* (Edinburgh, 1813).

Howell, James, *Epistolae Ho-elianae Familiar Letters Domestic and Forren Divided into Sundry Sections, Partly Historicall, Politicall, Philosophicall, vpon Emergent Occasions* (London, 1650).

Howell, James, *A New English Grammar Prescribing as Certain Rules as the Languages Will Bear, for Forreners to Learn English: Ther Is also Another Grammar of the Spanish or Castilian Toung, with Some Special Remarks upon the Portugues Dialect, &c.* (London, 1662).

Hume Browne, Peter, ed., *Tours in Scotland, 1677 &1681* (Edinburgh, 1892).

Innes, Cosmo, ed., *Fasti Aberdonenses: Selections from the Records of the University and King's College of Aberdeen, 1494–1854* (Aberdeen, 1854).

Innes, Cosmo, ed., *Registrum Episcopatus Moraviensis, e Pluribus Codicibus Consarcinatum circa A.D.MCCCC. Cum Continuatione Diplomatum Recentiorum usque ad A.D.MDCXXIII* (Edinburgh, 1837).

Johnson, Samuel, *Journey to the Hebrides: A Journey to the Western Islands of Scotland & the Journal of a Tour to the Hebrides* (Edinburgh, 2010).

Laing, David, ed., *The Orygynale Cronykil of Scotland* (Edinburgh, 1879).

Lithgow, William, *The Totall Discourse, of the Rare Aduentures, and Painefull Peregrinations of Long Nineteene Yeares Trauayles, from Scotland, to the Most Famous Kingdomes in Europe* (London, 1632).

Macgill, William, ed., *Old Ross-shire and Scotland, as Seen in the Tain and Balnagown Documents*, 2 vols (Inverness, 1909).

Mackay, William, ed., *Chronicles of the Frasers: The Wardlaw Manuscript Entitled 'Polichronicon seu Policratica Temporum' or 'The True Genealogy of the Frasers', 916–1674* (Edinburgh, 1905).

Mackay, William, ed., *Records of the Presbyteries of Inverness and Dingwall, 1643–1688* (Edinburgh, 1896).

Mackay, William, and Boyd, Herbert Cameron, eds, *Records of Inverness*, 2 vols (Aberdeen, 1911).

MacKenzie, Sir George, *A Defence of the Antiquity of the Royal Line of Scotland with a True Account when the Scots Were Govern'd by Kings in the Isle of Britain* (London, 1685).

MacKenzie, Sir George, *The Laws and Customes of Scotland, in Matters Criminal Wherein is to be Seen How the Civil Law, and the Laws and Customs of Other Nations Do Agree with, and Supply Ours* (Edinburgh, 1678).

Megiser, Hieronymus, *Thesaurus Polyglottus, vel Dictionarium Multilingue* (Frankfurt, 1603).

'Part of a Letter Wrote by Mr. James Fraser, Minister of Kirkhil, near Invernes, to Ja. Wallace at Edinburgh, Concerning the Lake Ness, etc.', *Philosophical Transactions of the Royal Society*, 21 (1699), pp. 230–2.

Proceedings against Thomas Fraser of Beaufort, Captain Simon Fraser, and Others, for Treason and other Crimes (Edinburgh?, 1698?).

Register of the Privy Council of Scotland, Second Series (Edinburgh, 1901).

Report by Thomas Tucker upon the Settlement of the Revenues of Excise and Customs in Scotland [1655–56] (Edinburgh, 1824).

Spreull, John, *An Accompt Current Betwixt Scotland and England* (Glasgow, 1705).

The Works of Sir Thomas Urquhart, Reprinted from the Original Editions (Edinburgh, 1834), several editors (Edinburgh, 1834).

Withington, Lothrop, ed., *Elizabethan England: from 'A Description of England,' by William Harrison* (London, 1876).

SECONDARY SOURCES

Ahern, Stephen, 'Prose fiction: excluding Romance', in Stuart Gillespie and David Hopkins, eds, *The Oxford History of Literary Translation in English, Volume III: 1660–1790* (Oxford, 2005).

Allan, David, *Philosophy and Politics in Later Stuart Scotland* (East Linton, 2000).

Allan, David, *Virtue, Learning and the Scottish Enlightenment: Ideas of Scholarship and Society in Early Modern Scotland* (Edinburgh, 1993).

Alston, David, *My Little Town of Cromarty* (Edinburgh, 2006).

Anderson-Smith, Myrtle, 'The Bibliotheck of Kirkwall', *Northern Scotland*, 15(1) (1995), pp. 127–34.

Arcangeli, Alessandro, *Recreation in the Renaissance: Attitudes Towards Leisure and Pastimes in European Culture, 1350–1700* (Basingstoke, 2003).

Ash, Marinell, *This Noble Harbour: A History of the Cromarty Firth* (Bristol, 1991).

Bajer, Peter Paul, *Scots in the Polish-Lithuanian Commonwealth, XVIth to XVIIIth Centuries: The Formation and Disappearance of an Ethnic Group* (Leiden, 2012).

Baldwin, John R., ed., *Firthlands of Ross and Sutherland* (Edinburgh, 1991).

Bannerman, John, *The Beatons: A Medical Kindred in the Classical Gaelic Tradition* (Edinburgh, 1986).

Bardgett, Frank D., 'The Reformation in Moray and Mr Robert Pont', *Journal of Scottish Historical Studies*, 39(1) (2019), pp. 1–39.

Barrett, John R., ed., *Mr James Allan: The Journey of a Lifetime* (Kinloss, 2004).

Barrow, Geoffrey W. S., *The Kingdom of the Scots: Government, Church and Society from the Eleventh to the Fourteenth Century*, 2nd edn (Edinburgh, 2003).

Behringer, Wolfgang, 'Arena and pall mall: sport in the early modern period', *German History*, 27(3) (2009), pp. 331–57.

Beith, Mary, *Healing Threads: Traditional Medicines of the Highlands and Islands* (London, 1995).

Bergin, Joseph, ed., *The Seventeenth Century* (Oxford, 2001).

Bibby, Miriam, 'How northern was Pistol? The Galloway nag as self-identity and satire in an age of supra-national horse trading', in Kristen Guest and Monica Mattfeld, eds, *Horse Breeds and Human Society: Purity, Identity and the Making of the Modern Horse* (London, 2019).

Black, Ronald, 'Scottish fairs and fair-names', *Scottish Studies*, 33 (1999), pp. 1–75.

Boatcă, Manuela, 'Thinking Europe otherwise: lessons from the Caribbean', *Current Sociology*, 69(3) (2021), pp. 389–414.

Bosworth, Clifford Edmund, *An Intrepid Scot: William Lithgow of Lanark's Travels in the Ottoman Lands, North Africa, and Central Europe, 1609–21* (London, 2006).

Bourdieu, Pierre, 'The forms of capital', in John G. Richardson, ed., *Handbook of Theory and Research for the Sociology of Education* (New York, 1986), pp. 241–58.

Bowie, Karin, 'New perspectives on pre-Union Scotland', in T. M. Devine and Jenny Wormald, eds, *The Oxford Handbook of Modern Scottish History* (Oxford, 2014), pp. 303–19.

Brantz, Dorothee, ed., *Beastly Natures: Animals, Humans, and the Study of History* (Charlottesville, VI, 2010).

Brochard, Thomas, 'Intellectual and practical education and its patronage in the northern Highlands in the century after the Reformation', *Northern Scotland*, 12(2) (2021), pp. 174–95.

Brochard, Thomas, 'The integration of the elite and wider communities of the northern Highlands, 1500–1700: evidence from visual culture', *Northern Scotland*, 6(1) (2015), pp. 1–23.

Brochard, Thomas, 'The socio-economic relations between Scotland's northern territories and Scandinavia and the Baltic in the sixteenth and seventeenth centuries', *International Journal of Maritime History*, 26(2) (2014), pp. 210–34.

Brock, Michelle, *Satan and the Scots: The Devil in Post-Reformation Scotland, c.1560–1700* (Farnham, 2016).

Brockliss, Laurence W. B., 'The age of curiosity', in Joseph Bergin, ed., *The Seventeenth Century* (Oxford, 2001).

Broun, Dauvit, and MacGregor, Martin, eds, *Mìorun mòr nan Gall, 'The Great Ill-Will of the Lowlander'? Lowland Perceptions of the Highlands, Medieval and Modern* (Glasgow, 2009).

Burke, Peter, *The Art of Conversation* (Cambridge, 1993).

Burke, Peter, '*Heu domine, adsunt Turcae*: a sketch for a social history of post-medieval Latin', in Peter Burke and Roy Porter, eds, *Language, Self and Society: A Social History of Language* (Cambridge, 1991), pp. 23–51.

Burke, Peter, *Languages and Communities in Early Modern Europe* (Cambridge, 2004).

Burnett, John, *Riot, Revelry and Rout: Sport in Lowland Scotland Before 1860* (East Linton, 2000).

Burnett, John, 'The sites and landscapes of horse racing in Scotland before 1860', *The Sports Historian*, 17(2) (1998), pp. 55–75.

Burns, James Robert, 'William Lithgow's Totall Discourse (1632) and his science of the world', PhD thesis, University of Oxford (1997).

Caine, Barbara, *Biography and History* (Basingstoke, 2010).

Cameron, Ewen A., *The Life and Times of Fraser-Mackintosh Crofter MP* (Aberdeen, 2000).

Cannon, Roderick D., 'Who got a kiss of the King's hand? The growth of a tradition', in James Porter, ed., *Defining Strains: The Musical Life of Scots in the Seventeenth Century* (Bern, 2007).

Canny, Nicholas, 'Irish, Scottish and Welsh responses to centralisation, c.1530–1640: a comparative perspective', in Alexander Grant and Keith J. Stringer, eds, *Uniting the Kingdom? The Making of British History* (London, 1995).

Carretta, Vincent, *Equiano, the African: Biography of a Self-Made Man* (Atlanta, 2005).

Carretta, Vincent, 'Response to Paul Lovejoy's "Autobiography and memory"', *Slavery & Abolition*, 28(1) (2007), pp. 115–19.

Carrington-Farmer, Charlotte, 'Trading horses in the eighteenth century: Rhode Island and the Atlantic world', in Kristen Guest and Monica Mattfeld, eds, *Equestrian Cultures: Horses, Human Society, and the Discourse of Modernity* (Chicago, 2019).

Carter, Jennifer J., and MacLaren, Colin A., *Crown and Gown - 1495–1995: An Illustrated History of the University of Aberdeen* (Aberdeen, 1994).

Cathcart, Alison, *Kinship and Clientage: Highland Clanship, 1451–1609* (Leiden, 2006).

Cérino, Christophe, Geistdoerfer, Aliette, Le Bouëdec, Gérard, and Ploux, François, eds, *Entre terre et mer: sociétés littorales et pluriactivités (XVe–XXe siècle)* (Rennes, 2004).

Cipriano, Salvatore, '"Students who have the Irish tongue": the Gaidhealtachd, education, and state formation in Covenanted Scotland, 1638–1651', *Journal of British Studies*, 60(1) (2021), pp. 66–87.

Clarke, Peter, 'The English-speaking peoples before Churchill', *Britain and the World*, 4 (2011), pp. 201, 213, 224.

Clarke, Tristram, 'The Scottish Episcopalians 1688–1720', PhD thesis, University of Edinburgh (1987).

Coates, Peter, *Salmon* (London, 2006).

Colley, Linda, *The Ordeal of Elizabeth Marsh: A Woman in World History* (London, 2008).

Cormack, Wade, 'Playing by the rules? Early modern sport and control in the northern mainland royal burghs of Scotland', *Sport in History*, 36(3), pp. 305–27.

Cormack, Wade, 'Sport and physical education in the northern mainland burghs of Scotland c. 1600–1800', PhD thesis, University of the Highlands and Islands (2016).

Craik, Roger, 'Sir Thomas Urquhart's translation of Rabelais', *Studies in Scottish Literature*, 31(1) (1999), pp. 151–68.

Cullen, Karen, *Famine in Scotland - the 'Ill Years' of the 1690s* (Edinburgh, 2012).

Cullen, Louis M., 'The Irish diaspora of the seventeenth and eighteenth centuries', in Nicholas Canny, ed., *Europeans on the Move: Studies in European Migration, 1500–1800* (Oxford, 1994).

Cunningham, Bernadette, *The World of Geoffrey Keating: History, Myth and Religion in Seventeenth-Century Ireland* (Dublin, 2000).

Cunningham, John, 'The history of medicine in early modern Ireland', in Sarah Covington, Vincent P. Carey and Valerie McGowan Doyle, eds, *Early Modern Ireland: New Sources, Methods and Perspectives* (Abingdon, 2019).

Davidson, Peter, and Morley, Carol, 'James Fraser's Triennial Travels', in Iain Beavan, Peter Davidson and Jane Stevenson, eds, *The Library and Archive Collections of the University of Aberdeen: An Introduction and Description* (Manchester, 2011), pp. 206–11.

Dawson, Jane, *Scotland Re-Formed, 1488–1587* (Edinburgh, 2007).

Demuth, Bathsheba, *Floating Coast: An Environmental History of the Bering Strait* (New York, 2019).

Devienne, Elsa, *La Ruée vers le sable: une histoire environnementale des plages de Los Angeles au XXe siècle* (Paris, 2020).

Dilworth, Mark, O.S.B., *The Scots in Franconia: A Century of Monastic Life* (Edinburgh, 1974).

Dingwall, Helen M., *A History of Scottish Medicine* (Edinburgh, 2003).

Ditchburn, David, 'Educating the elite: Aberdeen and its universities', in E. Patricia Dennison, David Ditchburn and Michael Lynch, eds, *Aberdeen Before 1800: A New History* (East Linton, 2002), pp. 327–46.

Dodgshon, Robert A., *From Chiefs to Landlords: Social and Economic Change in the Western Highlands and Islands, c.1493–1820* (Edinburgh, 1998).

Dodgshon, Robert A., 'The little ice age in the Scottish Highlands and Islands: documenting its human impact', *Scottish Geographical Journal*, 121(4) (2005), pp. 321–37.

Edwards, Peter, *Horse and Man in Early Modern England* (London, 2007).

Eliav-Feldon, Miriam, and Herzig, Tamar, eds, *Dissimulation and Deceit in Early Modern Europe* (London, 2015).

Eltis, David, Lewis, Frank D., and Sokoloff, Kenneth L., eds, *Slavery in the Development of the Americas* (Cambridge, 2004).

Emerson, Roger L., 'Sir Robert Sibbald, Kt, the Royal Society of Scotland and the origins of the Scottish Enlightenment', *Annals of Science*, 45 (1988), pp. 41–72.

Fagan, Brian M., *The Little Ice Age: How Climate Made History, 1300–1850* (New York, 2000).

Fradkin, Jeremy, 'Protestant unity and anti-Catholicism: the irenicism and philo-semitism of John Dury in context', *Journal of British Studies*, 56(2) (2017), pp. 273–94.

Fraser, John, 'Notes on Inverness-shire Gaelic in the seventeenth century', *Scottish Gaelic Studies*, 2(1) (1927), pp. 92–9.

Fraser, Sarah, *The Last Highlander* (London, 2012).

Furgol, Edward M., *A Regimental History of the Covenanting Armies* (Edinburgh, 1990).

Gallagher, John, *Learning Languages in Early Modern England* (Oxford, 2019).

Games, Alison, *Migration and the Origins of the English Atlantic World* (Cambridge, 1999).

Gange, David, *The Frayed Atlantic Edge: A Historian's Journey from Shetland to the Channel* (London, 2019).

Gillis, John, *The Human Shore: Seacoasts in History* (Chicago, 2012).

Glassman, Bernard, *Anti-Semitic Stereotypes Without Jews: Images of the Jews in England 1290–1700* (Detroit, 1975).

Glozier, Matthew, 'Scottish travellers abroad 1660–1688', *Journal of the Sydney Society for Scottish History*, 8 (2000), pp. 25–39.

Goeing, A., Parry, G., and Feingold, M., eds, *Early Modern Universities* (Leiden, 2020).

Goodare, Julian, 'Men and the witch-hunt in Scotland', in Alison Rowlands, ed., *Witchcraft and Masculinities in Early Modern Europe* (New York, 2009), pp. 149–70.

Grant, I. F. and Cheape, Hugh, *Periods in Highland History* (London, 1987).

Green, Adrian, and Pollard, A. J. 'Introduction', in Adrian Green and A .J. Pollard, eds, *Regional Identities in North-East England, 1300–2000* (London, 2007).

Gregory, Donald, *The History of the Western Highlands and Isles of Scotland, 1493–1625* (Edinburgh, 1836).

Groebner, Valentin, *Who Are You? Identification, Deception, and Surveillance in Early Modern Europe* (New York, 2007).

Grosjean, Alexia, and Murdoch, Steve, eds, *Scottish Communities Abroad in the Early Modern Period* (Leiden, 2005).

Hale, Alex, 'Phopachy (Kirkhill parish): intertidal crannog', in Colleen E. Batey and Muriel King, eds, *Discovery and Excavation in Scotland* (Edinburgh, 1994), pp. 35–6.

Hale, Alex, 'Phopachy (Kirkhill parish), intertidal crannog', in Colleen E. Batey, ed., *Discovery and Excavation in Scotland* (Edinburgh, 1995), p. 40.

Henderson, Lizanne, 'Witch-hunting and witch belief in the Gàidhealtachd', in Julian Goodare, Lauren Martin and Joyce Miller, eds, *Witchcraft and Belief in Early Modern Scotland* (London, 2008), pp. 95–118.

Hill, Jeffrey, *Sport in History: An Introduction* (Basingstoke, 2010).

Hoffmann, Richard C., '*Salmo salar* in late medieval Scotland: competition and conservation for a riverine resource', *Aquatic Sciences*, 77(3) (2015), pp. 355–66.

Holmberg, Eva Johanna, 'Writing the travelling self: travel and life-writing in Peter Mundy's (1597–1667) *Itinerarium Mundii*', *Renaissance Studies*, 31(4) (2017), pp. 608–25.

Hopkins, Paul, *Glencoe and the End of the Highland War* (Edinburgh, 1986).

Houlbrook, Matt, *Prince of Tricksters: The Incredible True Story of Netley Lucas, Gentleman Crook* (Chicago, 2016).

Houston, Rab A., *Scottish Literacy and the Scottish Identity: Illiteracy and Society in Scotland and Northern England, 1600–1800* (Cambridge, 2002).

Hug, Tobias B., *Impostures in Early Modern England: Representations and Perceptions of Fraudulent Identities* (Manchester, 2009).

Hunter, James, 'History: its key place in the future of the Highlands and Islands', *Northern Scotland*, 27(1) (2007), pp. 1–14.

Hunter, James, *The Making of the Crofting Community*, 3rd edn (Edinburgh, 2010).

Hunter, Michael, *The Occult Laboratory: Magic, Science and Second-Sight in Late Seventeenth-Century Scotland* (Woodbridge, 2001).

Inglis, Bill, 'The impact of Episcopacy and Presbyterianism, before and after 1690, on one parish: a case study of Dunblane kirk session minutes', *Scottish Church History*, 33(1) (2003), pp. 35–61.

Jütte, Daniel, 'Interfaith encounters between Jews and Christians in the early modern period and beyond: toward a framework', *The American Historical Review*, 118(2) (2013), pp. 378–400.

Kelly, Jamie, 'The Society in Scotland for Propagating Christian Knowledge: education, language & governance in the British state and empire, c.1690–c.1735', PhD thesis, University of Glasgow (2020).

Kennedy, Allan, 'Civility, order and the Highlands in Cromwellian Britain', *The Innes Review* (2018), 69(1), pp. 49–69.

Kennedy, Allan, 'The condition of the Restoration Church of Scotland in the Highlands', *The Journal of Ecclesiastical History*, 65(2) (2014), pp. 309–26.

Kennedy, Allan, 'Cromwell's Highland stronghold: the Sconce of Inverness', *Scottish Local History*, 106 (2020), pp. 3–7.

Kennedy, Allan, *Governing Gaeldom: The Scottish Highlands and the Restoration State, 1660–1688* (Leiden, 2014).

Kennedy, Allan, '"A heavy yock uppon their necks": Covenanting government in the northern Highlands, 1638–1651', *Journal of Scottish Historical Studies*, 30(2) (2010), pp. 93–122.

Kennedy, Allan, 'Highlanders and the city: migration, segmentation, and the image of the Highlander in early modern London, 1603–c.1750', *Northern Scotland*, 12(2) (2021), pp. 111–31.

Kennedy, Allan, 'Managing the early-modern periphery: Highland policy and the Highland judicial commission, c.1692–c.1705', *Scottish Historical Review*, 96(1) (2017), pp. 32–60.

Kennedy, Allan, 'Military rule, protectoral government and the Scottish Highlands, c.1654–1660', *Scottish Archives*, 23 (2017–19), pp. 80–102.

Kennedy, Allan, 'Reducing that barbarous country: centre, periphery and Highland policy in Restoration Britain', *Journal of British Studies*, 52(3) (2013), pp. 597–614.

Kennedy, Allan, 'The urban community in Restoration Scotland: government, society and economy in Inverness, 1660–c.1688', *Northern Scotland*, 5 (2014), pp. 26–49.

Kidd, Colin, *Subverting Scotland's Past: Scottish Whig Historians and the Creation of an Anglo-British Identity, 1689–1830* (Cambridge, 1993).

Kidd, Thomas, 'Passing as a pastor: clerical imposture in the colonial Atlantic world', *Religion and American Culture: A Journal of Interpretation*, 14(2) (2004), pp. 149–74.

Knoll, Martin, and Reith, Reinhold, eds, *An Environmental History of the Early Modern Period* (Berlin, 2014).

Land, Isaac, 'Tidal waves: the new coastal history', *Journal of Social History*, 40(3) (2007), pp. 731–43.

Langley, Chris R., McMillan, Catherine E., and Newton, Russell, eds, *The Clergy in Early Modern Scotland* (London, 2021).

Le Bouëdec, Gérard, 'Small ports from the sixteenth to the early twentieth century and the local economy of the French Atlantic coast', *International Journal of Maritime History*, 21(2) (2009), pp. 103–26.

Lovejoy, Paul E., 'Autobiography and memory: Gustavus Vassa, alias Olaudah Equiano, the African', *Slavery & Abolition*, 27(3) (2006), pp. 317–47.

Ludlow, Francis, and Crampsie, Arlene, 'Climate, debt and conflict: environmental history as a new direction in understanding early modern Ireland', in Sarah Covington, Vincent P. Carey and Valerie McGowan Doyle, eds, *Early Modern Ireland: New Sources, Methods and Perspectives* (Abingdon, 2019), pp. 269–300.

McCallum, John, '"Nurseries of the poore": hospitals and almshouses in early modern Scotland', *Journal of Social History*, 48(2) (2014), pp. 427–49.

McClure, J. Derrick, 'English in Scotland', in Robert Burchfield, ed., *Cambridge History of the English Language* (Cambridge, 1994), V, pp. 23–38.

MacCoinnich, Aonghas, *Plantation and Civility in the North Atlantic World: The Case of the Northern Hebrides, 1570–1639* (Leiden, 2015).

MacCoinnich, Aonghas, 'Where and how was Gaelic written in late medieval and early modern Scotland? Orthographic practices and cultural identities', *Scottish Gaelic Studies*, 24 (2008), pp. 309–56.

MacDonald, Alan R. and MacCallum, John, 'The evidence for early seventeenth-century climate from Scottish ecclesiastical records', *Environment and History*, 19(4) (2013), pp. 487–509.

McDonald, S. W., 'The Devil's mark and the witch-prickers of Scotland', *Journal of the Royal Society of Medicine*, 90(9) (1997), pp. 507–11.

MacGregor, Martin, 'Gaelic barbarity and Scottish identity in the later Middle Ages', in Dauvit Broun and Martin MacGregor, eds, *Mìorun mòr nan Gall, 'The great ill-will of the Lowlander'? Lowland Perceptions of the Highlands, Medieval and Modern* (Glasgow, 2009), pp. 7–48.

MacGregor, Martin, 'The genealogical histories of Gaelic Scotland', in Adam Fox and Daniel Woolf, eds, *The Spoken Word: Oral Culture in Britain, 1500–1850* (Manchester, 2002), pp. 196–239.

MacGregor, Martin, 'Writing the history of Gaelic Scotland: a provisional checklist of "Gaelic" genealogical histories', in Nancy R. McGuire, Donald

E. Meek and Colm Ó Baoill, eds, *Caindel Alban: Fèillsgrìobhainn do Dhòmhnall E. Meek* (Aberdeen, 2008).

Macinnes, Allan I., *Clanship, Commerce, and the House of Stuart, 1603–1788* (East Linton, 1996).

Macinnes, Allan I., Barton, Patricia, and German, Kieran, eds, *Scottish Liturgical Traditions and Religious Politics: From Reformers to Jacobites, 1560–1764* (Edinburgh, 2021).

Macintyre, Iain, and Alexander Munro, 'The Monros – three medical dynasties with a common origin', *Journal of the Royal College of Physicians*, 45 (2015), pp. 67–75.

Mackay, William, 'The Strathglass witches of 1662', *Transactions of the Gaelic Society of Inverness*, 9 (1879–80), pp. 113–21.

MacKenzie, Graeme M., 'The life and work as a historian of Dr William Mackay - a founder of the Gaelic Society of Inverness', available at: <https://soundcloud.com/user806452300/graeme-m-mackenzie-2013–09–27>.

Mackillop, Andrew, *Human Capital and Empire: Scotland, Ireland, Wales and British Imperialism in Asia, c.1690–c.1820* (Manchester, 2021).

McLaren, Colin A., and Stephen, Margaret A., 'Reports and surveys of archives in northern Scotland', *Northern Scotland*, 2 (1977) pp. 187–8.

McLaren, Peter, 'White terror and oppositional agency: towards a critical multiculturalism', in D. T. Goldberg, ed., *Multiculturalism: A Critical Reader* (Oxford, 1994), pp. 45–74.

Maclean, Donald, 'Highland libraries in the eighteenth century', *Transactions of the Gaelic Society of Inverness*, 31 (1922–4), pp. 91–119.

MacLean, Loraine, ed., *The Seventeenth Century in the Highlands* (Inverness, 1986).

Manwaring-McKay, Melanie, 'Charles Fraser-Mackintosh (1828–1901) and his books: book collecting, bibliomania and antiquarianism in the Victorian Scottish Highlands', Masters dissertation, University of the Highlands and Islands (2019).

Mapstone, Sally, 'Scotland's stories', in Jenny Wormald, ed., *Scotland: A History* (Oxford, 2005).

Mason, Roger A., 'Debating Britain in seventeenth-century Scotland: multiple monarchy and Scottish sovereignty', *Journal of Scottish Historical Studies*, 35(1) (2015), pp. 1–24.

Miller, James, *The Gathering Stream: The Story of the Moray Firth* (Edinburgh, 2012).

Miller, James, *Inverness: A History* (Edinburgh, 2004).

Mitchell, Alexander, *The Library of Inverness* (Inverness, 1901).

Mowat, Ian R. M., *Easter Ross, 1750–1850* (Edinburgh, 2006).

Murdoch, Steve, 'Children of the diaspora: the "homecoming" of the second-generation Scot in the seventeenth century', in Marjory Harper, ed., *Emigrant Homecomings: The Return Movement of Emigrants, 1600–2000* (Manchester, 2005), pp. 55–76.

Murdoch, Steve, *Network North: Scottish Kin, Commercial and Covert Associations in Northern Europe 1603–1746* (Leiden, 2006).

Murdoch, Steve, ed., *Scotland and the Thirty Years' War* (Leiden, 2001).

Murdoch, Steve, and Mijers, Esther, 'Migrant destinations, 1500–1700', in T. M. Devine and Jenny Wormald, eds, *Oxford Handbook of Scottish History* (Oxford, 2012), pp. 320–7.

Nasaw, David, 'Introduction: AHR roundtable on historians and biography', *American Historical Review*, 114(3) (2009), pp. 573–8.

Newton, Michael, *Warriors of the Word: The World of the Scottish Highlanders* (Edinburgh, 2009).

Niemeijer, Frits, 'God created the Earth, but the Dutch made their own country', published on the Internet and available at: <http://vakbladvitruvius.nl/images/essay/TheDutchMade_F.Niemeijer_May2021_DEF-dd27mei.pdf> (last accessed 21 November 2021).

Nugent, Janay, and Ewan, Elizabeth eds, *Children and Youth in Premodern Scotland* (Woodbridge, 2015).

Nutkiewicz, Michael, 'A rapporteur of the English civil war: the courtly politics of James Howell (1594?–1666)', *Canadian Journal of History*, 25 (1990), pp. 21–40.

O'Connor, Thomas, 'Ireland and Europe, 1580–1815: some historiographical remarks', in Thomas O'Connor, ed., *The Irish in Europe, 1580–1815* (Dublin, 2001).

O'Connor, Thomas, and Lyons, Mary Ann, eds, *Irish Communities in Early Modern Europe* (Dublin, 2006).

Ó Donnchú, Ken, 'A Prague poem on purgation? Five languages in a seventeenth century Irish manuscript', *Studia Celto-Slavica*, 12 (2021), pp. 43–62.

O'Donnell, Paris, 'Pilgrimage or "'anti-pilgrimage'"? Uses of mementoes and relics in English and Scottish narratives of travel to Jerusalem, 1596–1632', *Studies in Travel Writing*, 13(2) (2009), pp. 125–39.

Oram, Richard D., Martin, Paula F., McKean, Charles A., Neighbour, Tim, and Cathcart, Alison, *Historic Tain: Archaeology and Development* (York, 2009).

O'Reilly, William, 'Ireland in the Atlantic world: migration and cultural transfer', in Jane Ohlmeyer, ed., *The Cambridge History of Ireland, Volume II: 1550–1730* (Cambridge, 2018).

Pařez, Jan, and Kuchařová, Hedvika, *Hyberni v Praze - Éireannaigh i Prág: Dějiny Františkánské Koleje Neposkvrněného Početí Panny Marie v Praze (1629–1786)* (Prague, 2001).

Parker, Geoffrey, *Global Crisis: War, Climate Change & Catastrophe in the Seventeenth Century* (New Haven, CT, 2013).

Parker, Geoffrey, and Smith, Lesley M., eds, *The General Crisis of the Seventeenth Century*, 2nd edn (London, 1997).

Pearson, Michael, 'Littoral society: the concept and the problems', *Journal of World History*, 17(4) (2006), pp. 353–73.

Pierce, Helen, '"The bold adventure of all": reconstructing the place of portraits in Interregnum England', *British Art Studies*, 16 (2020), available at: <https://doi.org/10.17658/issn.2058–5462/issue-16/hpierce>.

Raffe, Alasdair, *The Culture of Controversy: Religious Arguments in Scotland, 1660–1714* (Woodbridge, 2012).

Raffe, Alasdair, 'Presbyterians and episcopalians: the formation of confessional cultures in Scotland, 1660–1715', *English Historical Review*, 125(514) (2010), pp. 570–98.

Raymond, Joad, 'A Scotsman in Cromwellian London: the diary of James Fraser of Phopachy', *History Today*, 47(7) (1997), pp. 35–41.

Renders, Hans, de Haan, Binne, and Harmsma, Jonne, eds, *The Biographical Turn: Lives in History* (London, 2016).

Robertson, Barry, *Lordship and Power in the North of Scotland, 1603–1690* (Edinburgh, 2011).

Rothfels, Nigel, ed., *Representing Animals* (Bloomington, IN, 2002).

Sandrock, Kirsten, *Scottish Colonial Literature: Writing the Atlantic, 1603–1707* (Edinburgh, 2021).

Saville, Richard, 'Intellectual capital in pre-1707 Scotland', in S. J. Brown and Christopher Whatley, eds, *The Union of 1707: New Dimensions (Scottish Historical Review Supplementary Issue)* (Edinburgh, 2008), pp. 45–60.

Schlichting, Kara, *New York Recentered: Building the Metropolis from the Shore* (Chicago, 2019).

Scott, Hew, ed., *Fasti Ecclesiæ Scoticanæ: The Succession of Ministers in the Church of Scotland from the Reformation*, 7 vols (Edinburgh, 1926), VI.

Scott, James C., *Weapons of the Weak: Everyday Forms of Peasant Resistance* (New York, 1985).

Shukman, Ann, *Bishops and Covenanters: The Church in Scotland, 1688–1691* (Edinburgh, 2012).

Smout, T. C., 'Scotland and England: is dependency a symptom or a cause of underdevelopment?', *Review (Fernand Braudel Center)*, 3(4) (1980), p. 602.

Smout, T. C., *Scottish Trade on the Eve of Union, 1660–1707* (Edinburgh, 1963).

Snyder, Jon R., *Dissimulation and the Culture of Secrecy in Early Modern Europe* (Berkeley, 2009).

Sprunger, Keith L., *Dutch Puritanism: A History of English and Scottish Churches of the Netherlands in the Sixteenth and Seventeenth Centuries* (Leiden, 1982).

Stephen, Jeffrey, *Defending the Revolution: The Church of Scotland, 1689–1716* (Aldershot, 2013).

Stephen, Jeffrey, 'Defending the Revolution: The Church of Scotland and the Scottish Parliament, 1689–95', *Scottish Historical Review*, 89 (2010), pp. 19–53.

Stevenson, Jane, and Davidson, Peter, *The Lost City: Old Aberdeen* (Edinburgh, 2008).

Stewart, Alan, *The Oxford History of Life-Writing, Volume 2: Early Modern* (Oxford, 2018).

Stewart, Laura A. M., *Rethinking the Scottish Revolution: Covenanted Scotland 1637–1651* (Oxford, 2016).

Stiùbhart, Domhnall Uilleam, 'Women and gender in the early modern western Gàidhealtachd', in Elizabeth Ewan and Maureen Meikle, eds, *Women in Scotland c.1100–c.1750* (East Linton, 1999), pp. 233–49.

Storer, James, *History and Antiquities of the Cathedral Churches of Great Britain*, 4 vols (London, 1819).

Stroh, Silke, *Gaelic Scotland in the Colonial Imagination: Anglophone Writing from 1600 to 1900* (Evanston, IL, 2017).

Summers, David W., 'Salmon fishing', in James R. Coull, Alexander Fenton and Kenneth Veitch, eds, *Boats, Fishing and the Sea*, Scottish Life and Society, Vol. 4 (Edinburgh, 2008), pp. 330–52.

Sutherland, Alex, *The Brahan Seer: The Making of a Legend* (Oxford, 2009).

Sweet, Rosemary, Verhoeven, Gerrit, and Goldsmith, Sarah, eds, *Beyond the Grand Tour: Northern Metropolises and Early Modern Travel Behaviour* (London, 2017).

Thayer, Johnathan, 'Merchant seamen, sailortowns, and the philanthropic encounter in New York, 1843–1945', in David Worthington, ed., *The New Coastal History: Cultural and Environmental Perspectives from Scotland and Beyond* (London, 2017), p. 73.

Thomas, Jane, 'From monasteries to monopolisers: the salmon fishing industry of the inner Moray Firth region, 1500–1800', PhD thesis, University of the Highlands and Islands (2021).

Todd, Margo, *The Culture of Protestantism in Early Modern Scotland* (Cambridge, 2002).

Todorova, Maria, 'Spacing Europe: what is a historical region?', *East Central Europe*, 32(1–2) (2005), pp. 59–78.

Tomalin, Claire, *Samuel Pepys: The Unequalled Self* (London, 2002).

Van Strien, C. D., *British Travellers in Holland during the Stuart Period: Edward Browne and John Locke as Tourists in the United Provinces* (Leiden, 1993).

Whibley, Charles, *Studies in Frankness* (London, 1898).

Wilby, Emma, *The Visions of Isobel Gowdie: Magic, Witchcraft and Dark Shamanism in Seventeenth-Century Scotland* (Brighton, 2010).

Williams, Gwyn A., *The Search for Beulah Land: The Welsh and the Atlantic Revolution* (London, 1980).

Williams, Kelsey Jackson, *The First Scottish Enlightenment: Rebels, Priests, and History* (Oxford, 2020).

Williams, Kelsey Jackson, 'The network of James Garden of Aberdeen and north-eastern Scottish culture in the seventeenth century', *Northern Studies*, 47 (2015), pp. 102–30.

Williams, Mark R. F., 'The inner lives of early modern travel', *The Historical Journal*, 62(2) (2019), pp. 349–73.

Williamson, Eila, 'Horse-racing in Scotland in the sixteenth and early seventeenth centuries', *Review of Scottish Culture*, 14 (2001–2), pp. 31–42.

Withers, Charles W. J., 'Geography, science and national identity in early modern Britain: the case of Scotland and the work of Sir Robert Sibbald (1641–1722)', *Annals of Science*, 53 (1996), pp. 29–73.

Withrington, Donald, 'Education in the seventeenth century Highlands', in Loraine MacLean, ed., *The Seventeenth Century in the Highlands* (Inverness, 1986), pp. 60–9.

Worthington, David, ed., *British and Irish Emigrants and Exiles in Europe, 1603–88* (Leiden, 2010).

Worthington, David, *British and Irish Experiences and Impressions of Central Europe* (Aldershot, 2012).

Worthington, David, 'Ferries in the firthlands: communications, society and culture along a northern Scottish rural coast (c.1600–1809)', *Rural History*, 27(2) (2016), pp. 129–48.

Worthington, David, ed., *The New Coastal History: Cultural and Environmental Perspectives from Scotland and Beyond* (London, 2017).

Worthington, David, 'A northern Scottish maritime region: the Moray Firth in the seventeenth century', *International Journal of Maritime History*, 23(2) (2011), pp. 181–210.

Worthington, David, 'The settlements of the Beauly-Wick coast and the historiography of the Moray Firth', *The Scottish Historical Review*, 95(2) (2016), pp. 139–63.

Worthington, David, 'Sugar, slave-owning, Suriname and the Dutch imperial entanglement of the Scottish Highlands before 1707', *Dutch Crossing: Journal of Low Countries Studies*, 44(1) (2019), pp. 3–20.

Wright, Barry, 'Health and wellbeing in Highlands and Islands during the early modern period', MLitt dissertation, University of the Highlands and Islands (2013).

Zagorin, Perez, *Ways of Lying: Dissimulation, Persecution and Conformity in Early Modern Europe* (Cambridge, MA, 1990).

Zemon Davis, Natalie, *The Return of Martin Guerre* (New York, 1984).

Zemon Davis, Natalie, *Trickster Travels: A Sixteenth-Century Muslim Between Worlds* (New York, 2006).

Zemon Davis, Natalie, *Women on the Margins: Three Seventeenth-Century Lives* (New York, 1997).

Zickermann, Kathrin, *Across the German Sea: Early Modern Scottish Connections with the Wider Elbe-Weser Region* (Leiden, 2013).

Index

Note: *italic* indicates a figure, n indicates a note